The Ethical and Legal Implications of Commercial Surrogacy for Healthcare

In this groundbreaking work, the authors explore the intricate interplay between commercial surrogacy and the global healthcare system, challenging conventional views with fresh insights into ethical, legal, and medical dimensions.

Delving into a rapidly evolving landscape, this book reveals how commercial surrogacy transcends economic transactions to question the very core of healthcare ethics. It scrutinises international legal frameworks and exposes the delicate balance between a surrogate's autonomy and the financial pressures that can undermine it. At the heart of the discussion is the pivotal role of healthcare providers, who navigate complex ethical dilemmas while upholding the rights and well-being of surrogates, intended parents, and children. Through incisive analysis and compelling case studies, this book argues for the urgent need for robust safeguards, comprehensive guidelines, and specialised training to equip professionals for the challenges of modern surrogacy practices.

This engaging narrative not only maps the evolving dynamics of commercial surrogacy but also calls for a sustainable, ethical future where healthcare remains a cornerstone of the surrogacy journey. Essential reading for researchers, advanced students, healthcare professionals, and policymakers alike, this book offers a holistic and provocative examination of an issue at the crossroads of ethics, law, and medicine.

Dr Jutharat Attawet is a senior lecturer at the Swinburne University of Technology, specialising in surrogacy research.

Dr Mark Brady is a senior lecturer in law and examines how technology impacts society, viewed through ontological, social, and critical legal discourse.

Kabir Sattarshetty is a nursing lecturer at Charles Darwin University and has a background in medical-surgical, ICU, and emergency nursing.

Sarah Jefford is a family creation lawyer and practises in surrogacy and donor conception across Australia.

Routledge Studies in the Sociology of Health and Illness

Techniques of Hearing
History, Theory and Practices
Edited by Michael Schillmeier, Robert Stock and Beate Ochsner

Becoming with Care in Drug Treatment Services
The Recovery Assemblage
Lena Theodoropoulou

Health and Care in Neoliberal Times
Neil Small

Gender and Welfare Service Work in Biocapitalism
Lean in Action
Eeva Jokinen, Helena Hirvonen, Laura Mankki, Timo Aho and Iiris Lehto

Social Crisis and Mental Health
Signs of Sanity
Peter Morrall

Sex, Intimacy and Living with Life-Shortening Conditions
Edited by Sarah Earle and Maddie Blackburn

The Ethical and Legal Implications of Commercial Surrogacy for Healthcare
A Global Perspective
Jutharat Attawet, Mark Brady, Kabir Sattarshetty and Sarah Jefford

For more information about this series, please visit: https://www.routledge.com/Routledge-Studies-in-the-Sociology-of-Health-and-Illness/book-series/RSSHI

The Ethical and Legal Implications of Commercial Surrogacy for Healthcare

A Global Perspective

Jutharat Attawet, Mark Brady, Kabir Sattarshetty and Sarah Jefford

Routledge
Taylor & Francis Group
LONDON AND NEW YORK

First published 2026
by Routledge
4 Park Square, Milton Park, Abingdon, Oxon OX14 4RN

and by Routledge
605 Third Avenue, New York, NY 10158

Routledge is an imprint of the Taylor & Francis Group, an informa business

British Library Cataloguing-in-Publication Data
A catalogue record for this book is available from the British Library

ISBN: 978-1-032-84257-8 (hbk)
ISBN: 978-1-041-08010-7 (pbk)
ISBN: 978-1-003-51193-9 (ebk)

DOI: 10.4324/9781003511939

Typeset in Times New Roman
by codeMantra

Contents

Acknowledgements

The authors would like to thank Nantaporn Santagna, IVF Registered Nurse, Thailand, for advising with tests.

Abbreviations

ACART	Advisory Committee on Assisted Reproductive Technology
ACOG	The American College of Obstetricians and Gynecologists
ANZICA	The Australian and New Zealand Infertility Counsellors Association
ART	Assisted Reproductive Technology
ASRM	American Society for Reproductive Medicine
CRsC	The United Nations Convention on the Rights of the Child
ESHRE	The European Society of Human Reproduction and Embryology
eSET	Elective Single Embryo Transfer
hCG	Human Chorionic Gonadotropin
HCCH	The Hague Conference on Private International Law
HCCW	Hague Convention on the Civil Aspects of International Child Abduction
HCIA	The Hague Convention on Protection of Children and Co-operation in Respect of Intercountry Adoption
HFEA	Human Fertilisation and Embryology Authority
ICSI	Intracytoplasmic Sperm Injection
ISS	The International Social Services
IVF	In Vitro Fertilisation
MET	Multiple Embryo Transfer
NHMRC	National Health and Medical Research Council
PGT	Preimplantation Genetic Testing
RCOG	Royal College of Obstetricians and Gynaecologists
SASREG	Southern African Society of Reproductive Medicine and Gynaecological Endoscopy
SEEDS	The Society for Ethics in Egg Donation and Surrogacy
SET	Single Embryo Transfer
UN	The United Nations

About the Authors

Dr Jutharat Attawet is a senior lecturer at the Swinburne University of Technology, specialising in surrogacy research. Her work, which has been published internationally, focuses on improving the health of all parties involved in surrogacy and enhancing surrogacy arrangement policies. She is widely recognised for her expertise in commercial surrogacy, particularly in Southeast Asia. With a background in healthcare, she has worked in both public and private sectors, striving to improve health outcomes.

Dr Mark Brady is a senior lecturer in Law. Mark examines how technology impacts society, viewed through ontological, social, and critical legal discourse. Mark's research aims to understand society's legal and technological futures, drawing on law and technology theory to consider the legal, social, and ontological issues raised by increasingly sophisticated technologies, and to explore how law and technology shape each other. Ultimately, this research aims to chart the future trajectory of human society in an increasingly technological reality.

Kabir Sattarshetty is a nursing lecturer at Charles Darwin University, with a background in medical-surgical, ICU, and emergency nursing. His research focuses on mental health, meditation, and nursing education. He has contributed to textbooks, developed a meditation app for youth, and published on international nursing education. He also examines internationally qualified nurses for Australian Health Practitioner Regulation Agency (AHPRA). His work bridges clinical practice, education, and research to improve healthcare outcomes.

Sarah Jefford is a family creation lawyer, practising in surrogacy and donor conception across Australia. Sarah was an IVF parent, later became an egg donor, and then delivered a baby as a surrogate for two dads, in 2018. Sarah produced the *Australian Surrogacy Podcast* and published a book, *More Than Just a Baby*, a guide to surrogacy for intended parents and surrogates.

1 Introduction to Commercial Surrogacy

Section 1: Understanding Surrogacy

Family represents a fundamental human necessity, fulfilling the innate need for connection and belonging. The desire to have children is driven by the wish to create a family unit. However, infertile couples, same-sex couples, or individuals facing reproductive challenges often find it difficult to fulfil this desire. Modern fertility advancements provide hope for these groups to have biological children. Consequently, surrogacy has gained popularity among infertile or childless couples, same-sex couples, individuals, and even celebrities opting for later parenthood (Malhotra et al., 2023). Surrogacy involves a woman who agrees to carry a pregnancy to term for another person or couple. In the context of surrogacy, the woman who carries the baby is known as a "surrogate mother", "surrogate", or "carrier" and the people intending to be the legal parents are known as "intended parents" or "commissioning parents" (Armour, 2012). Research recommends "surrogate" and "intended parents" as the appropriate terms for parties in a surrogacy agreement (Hobzová, 2018).

However, this path is littered with complexities and ethical dilemmas. The terminology itself—"surrogate" for the gestational carrier and "intended parents" for those anticipating the arrival of a child—illustrates the evolving discourse surrounding surrogacy. It is an ongoing negotiation, continually evolving at the intersection of medical practices, ethical considerations, and deeply personal aspirations (Ellenbogen et al., 2021).

The reasons driving individuals towards surrogacy are varied, ranging from the medical to the social. Some face barriers insurmountable by nature: uterine issues, the scars of illness, or the heartbreak of repeated miscarriages (Patel et al., 2018). For these people, surrogacy stands as a testament to human ingenuity and compassion, a chance to hold in their arms a child of their own.

Surrogacy itself unfolds in two primary narratives: traditional and gestational. Each story, unique in its unfolding, reflects the diversity of human experience and the boundless capacity for love. It's a journey, not just of the surrogate and the intended parents but of humanity itself, as we redefine the boundaries of family, kinship, and love in an ever-evolving world.

DOI: 10.4324/9781003511939-1

History of Surrogacy: From Traditional Surrogacy to Gestational Surrogacy Arrangements

Traditional Surrogacy: The Original Tale

In the annals of human history, traditional surrogacy stands as the earliest form of this profound journey towards parenthood. Traditional surrogacy is defined as "straight," "partial," "natural," or "genetic" surrogacy, in which the surrogate is inseminated with the sperm of the intended father or a donor, using her own egg to conceive the child.

The concept of traditional surrogacy is illustrated in the Bible's Book of Genesis, where Sarah, unable to conceive, arranges for her servant Hagar to bear a son, Ishmael, for her husband Abraham (Berndt, 2018). Perhaps the earliest reference to surrogacy is found in the ancient Hindu epic, the Mahabharata. Written over 2,000 years ago is an intriguing story that resonates with modern concepts of surrogacy. In the Mahabharata, Gandhari, the wife of King Dhritarashtra, faced an unusual situation—her pregnancy lasted far longer than normal. When she eventually gave birth, it wasn't a baby but rather a lifeless lump of flesh. She sought the help of the sage Vyasa who divided the flesh into 101 pieces and placed each one into a pot filled with ghee. Through sacred rituals and careful nurturing, these pots eventually produced 100 sons and one daughter. This ancient story mirrors modern concepts of nurturing life outside the womb, surrogacy and assisted reproductive technology (ART) (Buck, 2019).

Nowadays, traditional surrogacy typically involves the artificial insemination of the surrogate with sperm from the intended father or a donor (Armour et al., 2019). The surrogate, as the biological mother, generally holds parental rights over the child but is expected to relinquish these rights upon the child's birth. This method avoids medical procedures for the intended mother, which can be seen as advantageous. However, it denies her a biological connection to the child, potentially leading to legal and emotional challenges if the surrogate decides to retain custody.

The complexities of traditional surrogacy were highlighted in the landmark "Baby M" case in the 1980s, where the surrogate, Mrs. Whitehead, chose to keep the baby, leading to significant legal battles and highlighting the risks inherent in traditional surrogacy arrangements (duBeth, 1988; Margalit, 2015). This case prompted a shift towards gestational surrogacy to minimise these legal and psychological complexities (Trowse, 2011).

Despite perceptions that traditional surrogacy poses higher risks due to the biological connection between the surrogate and the child, recent research by Dickinson (2023) indicates no significant differences in the support, mental health, or conflict levels experienced by surrogates in traditional versus gestational surrogacy. Over 80% of participants reported no conflict, challenging the assumption that traditional surrogacy inherently involves greater relational strains (Dickinson, 2023). It suggests that the risks associated with traditional surrogacy may not be as pronounced as previously thought. However, the overall complexity of surrogacy arrangements persists, emphasising the need for thorough consultation and clear agreements among all parties involved before proceeding with any surrogacy process.

Gestational Surrogacy: A New Chapter

With the dawn of ART and the birth of Louise Brown, the world's first in vitro fertilisation (IVF) baby, a new chapter in surrogacy began. Louise Brown was reported in July 1978 in Manchester, England (Steptoe & Edwards, 1978), and in 1984 the world's first birth from donated oocytes was reported in Australia (Buster, 1998).

The combination of these two innovative ART treatments resulted in the emergence of gestational surrogacy, with the first successful gestational surrogacy reported in 1985 by Utian and colleagues in the United Kingdom (Utian et al., 1985). The intended parents were a couple that strongly wished to have children, but the female partner had undergone a hysterectomy. The surrogate, a married 22-year-old mother with proven fertility, including two uncomplicated pregnancies, was a friend of the couple. A baby girl was born following the gestational surrogacy pregnancy, using the oocytes and sperm of the intended parents, allowing the couple to have their own genetic offspring (Utian et al., 1985).

The emerging practice of gestational surrogacy, also called "IVF surrogacy", "full surrogacy", or "host surrogacy", involves an ART procedure (Brinsden, 2003). Gestational surrogacy, a marvel of medical science, allows for a baby to be born without a genetic link to the surrogate. Instead, embryos created via IVF, using the gametes of the intended parents or donors, are implanted in the surrogate's womb. The baby born from a gestational surrogacy arrangement, therefore, could be either genetically related or not related to the intended parents (Brinsden, 2003).

Nevertheless, as with all significant narratives, the story of gestational surrogacy is not without its challenges. The complexities of IVF procedures, the legal nuances surrounding parental rights, and associated ethical considerations create a multifaceted situation, prompting continuous navigation, debate, and reflection.

Within the realms of traditional and gestational surrogacy, there exist two distinct forms to organising these surrogacy relationships: altruistic and commercial surrogacy arrangements.

Altruistic Surrogacy

Altruistic surrogacy is first recognised in the Surrogacy Arrangement Act 1985 in the United Kingdom, which was the first country to regulate surrogacy worldwide (duBeth, 1988; Hibino, 2022; Utian et al., 1985). In altruistic surrogacy, the surrogate agrees to carry a child for the intended parents without financial compensation. Typically, the surrogate is someone familiar to the intended parents, such as a family member or friend, enhancing comfort and trust in their relationship (Söderström-Anttila et al., 2002). For altruistic surrogacy to work a rare set of circumstances need to align. These agreements, along with issues of accessibility, mean altruistic surrogacy is infrequently chosen by intended parents. For example, in the 2021–2022 financial year, the Australian Department of Home Affairs reported 213 Australian babies born through international surrogacy arrangements (Australian Government, 2022), compared to only 100 surrogacy births recorded domestically in the Australia and New Zealand Assisted Reproduction Database (ANZARD) annual report (Newman et al., 2023). Consequently, even in a country where altruistic surrogacy is promoted, most intended parents opt for commercial surrogacy arrangements abroad.

Commercial Surrogacy

On the other side of the spectrum lies commercial surrogacy, a pragmatic alliance where the miracle of life meets the realities of financial compensation. Here, the surrogate enters into an agreement to carry and care for the intended parents' child, receiving monetary payment beyond the mere coverage of medical bills (Brandão & Garrido, 2023). This type of surrogacy, permitted in many places, offers a more accessible yet equally complex pathway for many to achieve their dream of becoming parents (Table 1.1).

Commercial surrogacy arrangements provide a structured and reassuring path to parenthood, offering intended parents peace of mind as they begin their surrogacy journey. However, this clarity also introduces ethical considerations and debates, reflecting varied opinions on the value of surrogacy as a service and the implications of financial transactions in the creation of lives.

Hybrid Surrogacy Form: The Case of Israel

However, not all countries adhere strictly to either altruistic or commercial models. For instance, Israel adopts a unique hybrid approach. Surrogacy in Israel is regulated under the Embryo Carrying Agreements Law (1996), which permits gestational surrogacy for heterosexual couples—recently expanded to include same-sex couples and single individuals (Bashiri et. al., 2024). While the arrangement is not considered fully commercial, the law allows payment to compensate the surrogate for her time and suffering (Schuz, 2003). This includes not only the reimbursement of medical and related expenses but also financial recognition of the physical and emotional toll of pregnancy and childbirth. All agreements must be approved

Table 1.1 Countries supporting commercial surrogacy

Continents	*Countries*
North America	The United States: states permitting commercial surrogacy: California, Illinois, Arkansas, New Jersey, New York, Washington State, New Hampshire Mexico
Europe	Georgia, Ukraine, Russia, Armenia, Greece
Asia	Kazakhstan, Kyrgyzstan
South America	Colombia

Note: This is updated in 2024.

by a state-appointed committee, ensuring ethical oversight and compliance with national standards (Bashiri, Cherlow, & Kresch-Jaffe, 2024).

This framework blends altruistic intentions with regulated financial support, positioning Israel's model between purely altruistic and commercial approaches. It offers a state-controlled pathway that balances reproductive access with the protection of surrogates and intended parents.

Party Involvement in Surrogacy Arrangements

In this complex and multifaceted field of surrogacy, a diverse array of individuals and professionals collaborate to construct a framework that usually ensures the creation of new life within ethical, legal, and emotionally supportive parameters. Each stakeholder contributes critically to the intricate network of relationships and responsibilities that define surrogacy arrangements. The main parties involved in surrogacy arrangements include:

Intended Parent

At the core of every surrogacy journey are the intended parents, previously the term was used as commissioning parents, whose profound desire to become parents propels the entire process forwards. These individuals, or couples, often face considerable challenges such as infertility, genetic risks, age-related concerns, or health conditions that make natural conception and pregnancy untenable. For same-sex couples, surrogacy opens a vital pathway to parenthood, offering a biological connection to their child—a link that might be unattainable through other means. Additionally, the role of intended parents is not confined to couples alone; it can also encompass single individuals who wish to embark on the journey of parenthood independently.

Surrogates

In surrogacy arrangements, the surrogate—often referred to traditionally as the surrogate mother—stands as the pivotal figure in the equation. In traditional surrogacy, the surrogate carries a pregnancy where the child is genetically her own. Conversely, in gestational surrogacy, the surrogate carries an embryo to which she has no genetic connection. This distinction highlights the varying roles a surrogate may assume within these different types of surrogacy.

Egg Donor and/or Sperm Donor

When intended parents are unable to contribute their own genetic gametes (sperm or egg), the incorporation of egg and/or sperm donors becomes necessary. These donors, whether known or anonymous, provide the essential genetic material, introducing additional layers of complexity related to heritage and genetic lineage. Their involvement prompts significant questions regarding the nature of biological connection and identity, both personal and cultural, adding depth to the ethical and psychological considerations surrounding surrogacy.

Medical Professionals

Medical professionals play a non-negotiable role, acting as the technical custodians of the surrogacy. Fertility specialists manage the delicate process of IVF, ensuring the embryo's viability, while obstetricians focus on the health of the surrogate throughout the pregnancy. Their expertise ensures the medical journey adheres to the strictest standards of care and ethical practice, with the medical mandate of safeguarding all involved.

Legal Professionals

Lawyers play an essential role in surrogacy arrangements by ensuring that all legal aspects are meticulously managed. They are responsible for making sure that the legal documentation accurately reflects the agreed-upon terms and protects the rights of all parties involved and in navigating the postnatal legal landscape. Surrogacy agreements are complex documents that cover a wide range of details, from parental rights to financial arrangements, and must be carefully drafted to prevent any future legal conflicts.

A critical aspect of these agreements is the necessity of finalising them "pre-conception". Establishing a legal framework before conception provides several important benefits. First, it offers legal clarity by clearly defining the intentions and responsibilities of all parties before the pregnancy begins, ensuring that the arrangement is recognised as surrogacy rather than adoption. This is particularly important because, unlike adoption where legal proceedings typically start after the child's birth, surrogacy agreements are set in advance to clearly outline the surrogate's role and the intended parents' rights from the beginning.

This pre-emptive approach not only differentiates surrogacy from adoption but also safeguards the rights of all parties, helping to avoid misunderstandings and potential post-birth legal disputes. Furthermore, many jurisdictions require these agreements to be established pre-conception to legally acknowledge the intended parents as the child's legal parents from birth, thereby simplifying the legal process and avoiding the complexities involved in transferring parental rights after the birth.

Accordingly, the role of lawyers in crafting pre-conception agreements is crucial in ensuring that the surrogacy arrangement is both legally sound and clear in its intent, effectively protecting everyone involved.

Surrogacy Agency

Many international surrogacy arrangements are facilitated by a surrogacy agency. These agencies play a crucial role in matching surrogates with intended parents, for profit, but their responsibilities extend far beyond matchmaking. They coordinate between medical and legal professionals, offer counselling, and provide ongoing support to ensure that the process is smooth and stress-free for everyone involved. However, surrogacy agencies are restricted and even prohibited in some countries such as Australia.

Counsellors and Support Staff

Lastly, the counsellors and support staff provide the emotional and psychological support crucial to navigating the surrogacy journey. They address the complex emotions that surface, ensuring that each person involved is heard, supported, and emotionally prepared for the challenges and changes inherent in such a deeply personal endeavour. While counselling is not legally compulsory in all surrogacy arrangements, it is highly recommended for the involved parties to consult to ensure the emotional well-being of all those involved.

Section 2: The Advent of Commercial Surrogacy

First Commercial Surrogacy Case

The first legally documented case of commercial surrogacy occurred in 1985 with the Baby M case in the United States. This case involved Mary Beth Whitehead, who was contracted by William and Elizabeth Stern to carry and give birth to a child. Elizabeth, diagnosed with multiple sclerosis, and her husband William opted for surrogacy out of concern for her health and the health of a potential biological child. The contract specified that Mary Beth would serve as both an egg donor and a surrogate, to be artificially inseminated with William Stern's sperm. The terms were explicit: Whitehead would carry the pregnancy to term and relinquish all parental rights to the Sterns for a fee of $10,000. Additionally, Whitehead requested occasional updates on the child through photos and letters. However, the legal clarity could not encapsulate the emotional complexities of human bonds. Upon the birth of a baby girl, named Melissa by the Sterns but publicly known as Baby M, Mary Beth Whitehead decided to keep the baby, despite the initial agreement.

The ensuing legal battle was both bitter and public, igniting debates over the legitimacy of surrogacy contracts, the commodification of women's bodies, and the very nature of parenthood. The New Jersey court ultimately sided with the Sterns, influenced in part by a harrowing recorded conversation in which Whitehead threatened harm to the baby if her demands were not met. This led to the complete denial of parental rights for Whitehead. Yet, upon appeal, the New Jersey Supreme Court took a more nuanced approach. While awarding custody to the Sterns, recognising the stability and parental commitment they offered, they also voided the surrogacy contract and restored Whitehead's parental rights, criticising paid surrogacy as potentially degrading and illegal.

This landmark decision reshaped surrogacy laws across the United States, with many states opting to outlaw or tightly regulate paid surrogacy arrangements. However, despite the legal controversies, the Baby M case highlighted surrogacy as a viable means of family creation, leading to a rise in its acceptance and practice, particularly among those who might otherwise be unable to conceive.

The ripple effects of Baby M have been felt in subsequent legal challenges and have guided the practices of surrogacy clinics, which now implement rigorous screening processes to ensure that all parties understand the emotional and legal implications of their agreements.

Melissa Stern, once Baby M, has moved past the case that defined her early life. In a significant act in 2004, she severed her legal ties with Mary Beth Whitehead and underwent a formal adoption process to affirm Elizabeth Stern as her mother, thus closing a chapter on one of the most contentious surrogacy cases in American history. This case remains a touchstone in discussions on reproductive technologies, parental rights, and the ethical dimensions of surrogacy.

High-Profile Cases of Commercial Surrogacy

High-profile cases of commercial surrogacy involve scenarios where surrogates are paid to carry and give birth to children for individuals or couples who are unable to conceive or carry a pregnancy themselves. These cases often gain significant attention due to the involvement of celebrities, complex legal issues, or ethical debates surrounding the practice. Notable cases include Baby M in the United States during the 1980s, Baby Manji in India in 2007, Baby Gammy in Thailand in 2014, and the "Baby Factory" case involving Japanese father Mitsutoki Shigeta (Points, 2009; Whittaker, 2016, 2019). These cases have spotlighted the legal and ethical complexities of surrogacy agreements. More recently, celebrities like Kim Kardashian, Kanye West, and Cristiano Ronaldo have used surrogates to expand their families, further bringing visibility and public discussion to the practice of commercial surrogacy. These instances highlight the varying legal, ethical, and social dimensions of surrogacy in different jurisdictions and cultures. Here are the example stories of high-profile commercial surrogacy cases:

Baby Manji

In 2008, the Baby Manji case unfolded when a Japanese couple, Ikufumi and Yuki Yamada, engaged Pritiben Mehta, an Indian surrogate, to bear their child under an arrangement facilitated by Dr. Nayna Patel of the Akanksha Clinic (Points, 2009). Mehta was compensated with a house worth 325,000 rupees (US $6,825), a lump sum of 50,000 rupees (US $1,050), and a monthly stipend of 5,000 rupees (US $105) during her pregnancy. The embryo, combining Ikufumi's sperm with an egg from an anonymous donor, was implanted in Mehta.

The Yamadas' divorce prior to the birth complicated the situation. Born on July 25, 2008, Baby Manji found herself entangled in a web of legal and ethical dilemmas, with Yuki refusing involvement and Ikufumi struggling to establish parental rights. This left Manji with three maternal figures—the intended mother, the egg donor, and the surrogate—yet legally, she had none.

When Ikufumi tried to take Manji back to Japan, he faced significant hurdles. The Japanese Embassy denied Manji a passport because Japanese law only recognised the birth mother's citizenship rights for the child, disqualifying Manji from receiving citizenship through her biological father. Concurrently, Indian officials would not issue a birth certificate for Manji, as their laws required at least one Indian parent for citizenship at birth. However, the legal recognition of Mehta as Manji's mother was ambiguous in India since her responsibilities as a surrogate ended at birth. This left Manji effectively stateless, complicating her legal status further.

This lack of legal motherhood or clear nationality sparked widespread debate over the rights of children born through international surrogacy, the responsibilities of surrogates, and the legal recognition of intended parents. Ultimately, humanitarian considerations led to the issuance of a Japanese one-year visa for Baby Manji, allowing her to travel to Osaka with her grandmother, Emiko Yamada. This resolution brought an end to the protracted legal and diplomatic impasse, underscoring the urgent need for comprehensive surrogacy laws to navigate the complexities of such cases.

Baby Gammy

The Baby Gammy incident in 2014 marked a critical turning point in the global conversation about commercial surrogacy. In this case, an Australian couple, David John Farnell and Wendy Li, engaged Pattaramon Chanbua, a Thai surrogate, agreeing to pay her AUD 16,000 for her services. During the pregnancy, it was discovered through an ultrasound that Chanbua was expecting twins, and she was offered an additional AUD 1,673. However, complications arose when one of the twins, a boy named Gammy, was diagnosed with Down syndrome. The couple allegedly requested that Chanbua terminate the pregnancy of Gammy, but she declined due to her Buddhist convictions and decided to raise him on her own (Cohen, 2015).

Following the birth in December 2013, the couple returned to Australia with Gammy's healthy twin sister, leaving Gammy in Thailand with Chanbua. This decision drew international criticism and media attention, especially after it was revealed that David Farnell had a history as a convicted sex offender. The public's response was substantial, with over A$250,000 raised through donations to support Gammy's medical treatments.

The incident led to significant legal repercussions in Thailand, where authorities tightened regulations on surrogacy, eventually banning commercial surrogacy for foreigners in 2015 (Stasi, 2017). This case highlighted the complexities and ethical issues surrounding commercial surrogacy, including the rights of the child, the surrogate, and the intended parents, and it spurred legal changes aimed at preventing similar cases in the future.

Baby Factory

The "baby factory" case involved a Japanese businessman, Mitsutoki Shigeta, who became infamous for fathering at least 17 babies via surrogacy in Thailand (Dolezal, 2017). This scandal came to light in 2014 when Thai authorities discovered nine babies with their nannies in a Bangkok apartment, all of whom were linked to Shigeta. Investigations revealed that Shigeta had hired multiple Thai surrogate mothers to bear his children, aiming to father as many as 20 to inherit his wealth. His actions, largely legal due to the lack of stringent surrogacy laws in Thailand at the time, sparked international outrage and highlighted the lack of regulations in the global surrogacy market. This case was instrumental in prompting Thailand to enact stricter surrogacy laws, including banning commercial surrogacy for foreigners.

High-profile surrogacy cases illuminate the multifaceted challenges and ethical questions that arise from commercial surrogacy. They expose the legal discrepancies across different countries and underscore the need for comprehensive international regulations that safeguard the rights of all parties involved—the surrogate, the intended parents, the healthcare practice, and, most importantly, the child (see Patton, 2010).

Section 3: The Global Landscape of Commercial Surrogacy

Geographical Spread

The expansion of commercial surrogacy across different regions and countries exhibits significant variations driven by cultural, legal, and economic factors. The development of commercial cross-border surrogacy typically starts in countries where such commercial practices are legally permitted. In nations with restrictive legal frameworks, concerning surrogacy treatments and eligibility, combined with a lack of expertise and resources such as donor oocytes, or absence of clinics offering ARTs, intended parents are often compelled to seek surrogacy options abroad (Gerrits, 2018). These conditions foster an environment where cross-border surrogacy flourishes, while intended parents must navigate these constraints in pursuit of fulfilling their family aspirations.

In this emerging commercial cross-border surrogacy market, entities known as "repropreneurs" and "repronubs" play pivotal roles (Whittaker et al., 2022), for profit. Repropreneurs integrate various elements of the surrogacy industry, enhancing opportunities for cross-border surrogacy and connecting patients with healthcare providers. They may manage surrogacy brokerages, link clinics with brokers, coordinate patient travel, and occasionally handle the legal requirements needed for liaising with embassies. Additionally, they assist with the local registration of births, passport applications, citizenship applications, and exit procedures (Whittaker et al., 2022). "Repronubs" are lesser-known locales that offer specialised, small-scale, cross-border gestational surrogacy services tailored to regional markets. The emergence and characteristics of various lesser-known locations across different continents that offer cross-border gestational surrogacy services are discussed below.

Asia

Previously, countries like India, Thailand, and Cambodia were major centres for commercial surrogacy. Several IVF clinics offered commercial surrogacy treatments throughout India since 2002. India, once dubbed a "rent-a-womb" hub, saw its surrogacy market estimated at over $400 million annually, involving more than 3,000 clinics (Rudrappa & Collins, 2015). The complexity of such arrangements was highlighted by the 2008 "Baby Manji" case, where a Japanese couple's divorce before the baby's birth led to legal complications and left the child stateless for months. This incident prompted India to tighten regulations, eventually banning commercial surrogacy for single parents and same-sex couples in 2013 and outlawing the practice entirely by 2018 (Saran & Padubidri, 2020). However, the industry persisted in the underground economy away from legislative protections.

As India restricted surrogacy, the industry shifted to Nepal, which briefly became a haven due to a regulatory loophole that allowed surrogacy provided the surrogate was not Nepalese. This loophole was exploited until a devastating earthquake in 2015 disrupted the operations, leading to a governmental crackdown and a total ban later that year (Attawet, 2021).

Thailand also became a key player in the market, particularly after India's 2013 restrictions. However, the industry operated in a grey area until the "Baby Gammy" scandal in 2014 spurred the Thai government to ban the practice for foreign and same-sex couples in early 2015.

The closure in Thailand redirected the market to Cambodia, where ambiguous laws initially allowed continued operations. However, Cambodia followed suit with a ban in 2016, pushing the industry into Laos (Hibino, 2022). With no specific surrogacy regulations, Laos became the next "repronub", enabling the continuation of commercial surrogacy operations from neighbouring Thailand, despite regulatory attempts elsewhere (Hibino, 2020).

Europe

Transnational commercial surrogacy, a complex and controversial practice, plays out in diverse regulatory landscapes across Europe. In Eastern Europe and Central Asia—specifically Russia, Ukraine, Georgia, and Kazakhstan—legal frameworks vary widely, reflecting differing cultural, ethical, and economic perspectives. These nations have notably served as popular destinations for those seeking surrogacy services, primarily due to their more permissive legal attitudes towards commercial surrogacy, contrasting sharply with the stringent prohibitions seen in many Western European countries.

In Russia, the surrogacy programme was implemented in 1995, and commercial surrogacy is legally permitted (Ghodrati, 2023). The framework meticulously outlines the rights and responsibilities of all parties involved, including the surrogates, the intended parents, and the donors. Russia's approach makes it one of the few places in Europe where commercial surrogacy is openly practised, thereby attracting both domestic and international intended parents. This openness is rooted in the perspective that surrogacy is a legitimate and necessary form of reproductive technology, which should be accessible within a regulated environment. Since approximately 1996, new reproductive technologies and surrogacy have been practised in Russia, reflecting a broader societal acceptance and a progressive view on reproductive rights (Mouliarova, 2019).

However, this regulatory landscape is not devoid of criticism. Critics argue that despite the robust legal framework, there are still gaps which have the potential to lead to the exploitation of surrogates and abuse of the contractual donor relationship (Mouliarova, 2019). Concerns revolve around the adequacy of the safeguards in place to protect women from being exploited by the commercial aspects of the surrogacy arrangements. Adding an additional layer of complexity, recent changes in legislation have shifted the dynamics of surrogacy in Russia. In December 2022, in response to concerns about the exploitation of the surrogacy system by wealthy foreigners, President Vladimir Putin signed new legislation that restricts the use of surrogacy services to foreigners (*The Moscow Times,* 2022). This significant legal shift now limits surrogacy services exclusively to married Russian couples and single Russian women who are unable to bear children due to medical reasons (Khazova, 2024). This move was influenced by rising apprehensions that the Russian surrogacy market was becoming a hotspot for exploitation by foreign nationals, prompting lawmakers to advocate for tighter controls. Moreover, under the new regulations, children born via surrogates in Russia are automatically granted Russian citizenship, reflecting an effort to safeguard the welfare of the children born through these arrangements and to reinforce national interests.

Prior to the geopolitical upheavals that began in 2014 and escalated with the Russian invasion, Ukraine was a major hub in the global landscape of commercial surrogacy. The country's legal framework provided well-defined protections for intended parents, including straightforward processes for establishing parental rights, which made it a favourable destination for those seeking surrogacy services. Ukraine's appeal was further enhanced by its combination of legal permissiveness, relatively lower costs, and high-quality medical services. Ukraine was one of the few countries where a surrogate cannot claim recognition of her motherhood, even in court (Reznik & Yakushchenko, 2020). The intended parents, who gave their consent to implantation to a surrogate, can request birth registration. Consequently, intended parents could be recorded as the legal parents on the birth certificate of a child born through surrogacy without the necessity of a court order, setting it apart from other jurisdictions like the United States (Reznik & Yakushchenko, 2020). This combination of factors led to Ukraine becoming the largest single-country supplier of surrogates globally, with more than 2,000 babies born each year through commercial surrogacy, according to some estimates (Stephanie & Eleanor, 2022). A significant majority of these children were born to foreign couples, who turned to Ukraine for surrogacy for various reasons, including prohibitive costs or legal restrictions in their own countries.

However, the onset of the Ukraine-Russia war has dramatically affected this industry. The conflict and resulting political instability have raised serious concerns about the safety and viability of surrogacy arrangements in the country. As the war broke out, it is reported that while some foreign couples managed to travel to Ukraine to collect their children, others were left in the care of nurses in makeshift clinics. This situation exposed the vulnerabilities of relying on international surrogacy in conflict zones (Marinelli et al., 2022).

The ongoing conflict has forced surrogates to make difficult choices: either remain in the war zone, benefiting from the legal protections surrounding surrogacy in Ukraine, or relocate to neighbouring jurisdictions where their surrogacy agreements might not be recognised or could even be prohibited. This upheaval has significantly disrupted the surrogacy sector, leading, inter alia, to a substantial drop in Ukraine's previously thriving surrogacy industry.

Georgia has established a distinctive place within the commercial surrogacy landscape since legalising the practice in 1997. In 2009, the country further solidified its position with the passage of the Embryo Adoption Act (Neel, 2019). This Act allows a legal embryo custodian to relinquish all rights and responsibilities for an embryo to the intended parents prior to the embryo transfer. Consequently, Georgia's laws grant full parental rights to intended parents immediately upon the birth of the child. Such regulations make Georgia an attractive destination for surrogacy seekers from countries with more restrictive laws.

However, Georgia does not recognise same-sex unions, including marriage, and its surrogacy law explicitly denies surrogates any legal parental rights over the delivered child. This has sparked ongoing debates about potential ethical abuses and concerns regarding the welfare of surrogates and same-sex couples (Gelashvili, 2011). Recent geopolitical shifts, notably the conflict in Ukraine, have altered the dynamics of European surrogacy. Prior to the war, Ukraine was a central hub for surrogacy in Europe, known for its relatively lax regulations and accessible medical services. But as the conflict persists, surrogacy agencies in Ukraine are operating under strained conditions, and both parents and brokers are exploring alternative destinations. In this shifting landscape, Ukrainian surrogates have begun travelling to other countries such as Greece, North Cyprus, and particularly Georgia, to fulfil surrogacy agreements. However, this increase in demand is testing Georgia's capacity to manage its surrogacy programme. In response to these pressures and broader ethical concerns, the Georgian government, led by Prime Minister Irakli Garibashvili, announced plans to ban commercial surrogacy for foreigners from 2024. The proposed ban aims to protect surrogates and children and address fears about human trafficking and the placement of babies with gay couples, which Georgian law prohibits. While altruistic surrogacy will still be permitted, it will be restricted only to Georgian nationals.

As Georgia contemplates these changes, neighbouring Armenia is emerging as a new centre for commercial surrogacy in the region. Armenian law allows commercial surrogacy and is permissible for both heterosexual and same-sex couples (Yacoubian Jr & Clements, 2014). The burgeoning surrogacy sector in Armenia is gaining momentum, partly due to the anticipated restrictions in Georgia. Many surrogacy clinics and agencies originally based in Georgia are now relocating to Armenia, establishing it as a potential new hub for international surrogacy services.

Kazakhstan has emerged as a new centre for reproductive solutions, often referred to as a "repronub" (Whittaker et al., 2022). Since legalising surrogacy in 1998 to address infertility issues, the country has meticulously crafted a comprehensive legal framework. The updated Code of the Republic of Kazakhstan "On Marriage (Matrimony) and the Family" ensures the safeguarding of surrogates' rights and well-being, including the prohibition of transferring multiple embryos to surrogates, with a limit of no more than two embryos (Ellenbogen et al., 2021). This framework demonstrates Kazakhstan's commitment to balancing regulatory rigour with accessibility to surrogacy services. Notably, Kazakhstan distinguishes itself with sophisticated regulations on reproductive technologies. It permits both domestic and international couples to utilise a broad spectrum of reproductive services, including third-party reproductive assistance. Collectively, these factors have shifted the commercial surrogacy hub to Kazakhstan, attracting individuals and couples from around the world seeking reproductive solutions.

Africa

The geographic spread of transnational commercial surrogacy in Africa reflects a complex interplay of ethical, legal, and cultural factors that vary widely across the continent. While commercial surrogacy is a common practice in parts of Asia and the Americas, its presence in Africa is relatively muted, with most countries either lacking explicit legal frameworks or outright banning the practice due to ethical and cultural concerns. However, there are exceptions where commercial surrogacy has gained a foothold, most notably in Kenya and Ghana, which have become a central node in this global network.

Kenya's emergence as a hub for commercial surrogacy is particularly significant given the general absence of clear regulatory frameworks in many African countries. The legal status of surrogacy in Kenya is not comprehensively regulated, but the practice exists in a grey area that allows it to flourish (Brandão & Garrido, 2023). This ambiguity has made Kenya an attractive destination for couples from around the world, particularly those from regions where surrogacy is heavily restricted or banned. The country's medical infrastructure, which is more developed than in many other African nations, coupled with the relatively low cost of medical procedures, adds to its appeal as a surrogacy destination.

Ghana is rapidly establishing itself as a significant hub for reproductive technologies in Sub-Saharan Africa. According to Boampong et al. (2023), it ranks among the top three countries in the region, alongside South Africa and Nigeria, in terms of the number and capabilities of IVF clinics. This growth reflects the country's increasing role as a "repronub", supported by favourable legal regulations, the availability of advanced medical infrastructure, and the growing demand for reproductive services both domestically and internationally (Hörbst & Gerrits, 2016).

In a notable advancement in 2020, Ghana implemented specific regulations under the Registration of Births and Deaths Act, 2020 (Act 1027). This legislation officially recognises surrogacy as a legitimate form of ART (Adaare, 2023). It marks a significant step in structuring the practice within the country by outlining provisions for both traditional and gestational surrogacy, the only types officially permitted in Ghana currently.

Despite these regulatory advances, Act 1027 does not make distinctions between commercial and altruistic surrogacy. This omission creates a potential gap in the legal framework, leading to ambiguity in how surrogacy agreements, whether altruistic or commercial, are applied and enforced.

As Ghana's clinics continue to cater to a diverse clientele, offering a broad spectrum of ART services, the development of Ghana's surrogacy landscape showcases a significant evolution in healthcare and legal frameworks necessary to support the growing trends in reproductive technology across Africa. However, as the industry expands, there is a clear need for further clarification and enhancement of the legal provisions governing both commercial and altruistic surrogacy. This is essential to ensure comprehensive regulation and protection for all parties involved, fostering a responsible and ethically sound surrogacy sector in Ghana.

North America

The landscape of transnational commercial surrogacy in North America is characterised by a striking contrast between the regulations and practices of its three countries: the United States, Canada, and Mexico. Each of these nations has developed its own unique approach to surrogacy, influenced by differing legal, ethical, and cultural perspectives. These diverse regulatory environments not only shape the domestic surrogacy practices but also affect their roles in the global surrogacy market.

In the United States, commercial surrogacy is widely practised and legally recognised, though the specifics can vary dramatically from state to state. Some states, like California, are known for their surrogacy-friendly laws, which provide clarity and protection for all parties involved: surrogates, intended parents, and the resulting children. These comprehensive legal frameworks make certain the United States particularly attractive destinations for international intended parents. However, this state-by-state variation can lead to complex legal challenges, particularly when surrogates and intended parents navigate across state lines or from other countries. The high cost of surrogacy in the United States is often justified by the high standards of medical care and legal protections, making it a premium market within the global surrogacy landscape.

Canada presents a contrasting model, where commercial surrogacy is illegal; surrogates may only be reimbursed for their expenses and are not paid a fee (Brandão & Garrido, 2023). This altruistic model aims to protect surrogates from potential exploitation, ensuring that the surrogate's decision is not unduly influenced by financial incentives. However, Canada's system is still open to international intended parents who seek surrogates within its borders, provided that no commercial transaction occurs. This creates a unique niche in the transnational surrogacy market, where individuals seeking less commercialised and more ethically framed surrogacy arrangements might turn.

Mexico, however, occupies a more ambiguous position. Regulations around surrogacy vary by state, and the lack of a clear national framework leads to a patchwork of local laws that can be confusing for both domestic and international intended parents. In some regions, commercial surrogacy has been accessible and relatively affordable, attracting a significant number of international clients (Schurr & Perler, 2015). However, concerns about ethical standards and the protection of surrogates' rights have led to calls for tighter regulations, with some states moving to restrict or regulate the practice more heavily.

South America

The landscape of transnational commercial surrogacy in South America presents a rich tapestry of legal, cultural, and ethical considerations. While the continent is not as prominently known for surrogacy as North America or Asia, certain countries within South America have begun to emerge as notable players in the global surrogacy market. Among these, Colombia stands out due to its relatively liberal stance towards surrogacy, contrasting with more restrictive or ambiguous legal frameworks in neighbouring countries.

Colombia has gained attention as a hub for commercial surrogacy, largely driven by its legal tolerance and progressive reproductive laws. Unlike many countries where the legalities around surrogacy are fraught with restrictions and heavy regulations, Colombia provides a more conducive environment for such practices. Surrogacy agreements, while not extensively legislated, are upheld by Colombian courts as long as the basic legal principles concerning the welfare of the child and consent of all parties involved are met. This relatively open legal environment makes Colombia an attractive destination for international intended parents who face more severe constraints in their home countries.

The practice of surrogacy in Colombia is further supported by high standards of medical care in reproductive technologies, comparable to those found in more developed surrogacy centres globally. This ensures that both surrogates and intended parents can expect a level of medical professionalism and ethical treatment aligned with international best practices. However, despite these advantages, surrogacy in Colombia—and in South America more broadly—raises substantial ethical and social concerns.

Australia/Oceania

The geographic spread of transnational commercial surrogacy in Australia and Oceania presents a complex legal and ethical landscape, heavily influenced by diverse regulatory frameworks across the region. While commercial surrogacy is generally restricted within Australia itself, other parts of Oceania, particularly New Zealand, have their own distinct legal stances. However, no country in Oceania prominently endorses commercial surrogacy on a scale seen in regions like Asia or North America.

In Australia, the legal framework governing surrogacy is both strict and fragmented. Each state and territory has its own laws, but a common thread is that commercial surrogacy is illegal and unenforceable. Australian laws only permit altruistic surrogacy. This stringent regulation aims to prevent the potential exploitation and commodification of women's bodies. However, these restrictions have led to an interesting phenomenon where Australians, unable to pursue commercial surrogacy at home, look abroad to countries with less restrictive laws (Kneebone et al., 2023).

Turning to New Zealand, the situation is somewhat similar to Australia's. New Zealand also prohibits commercial surrogacy but allows altruistic surrogacy. The country has comprehensive guidelines that ensure ethical practices are followed in all surrogacy arrangements. Surrogacy agreements themselves are not enforceable by New Zealand law, which means that the birth mother is the legal mother until and unless adoption procedures are completed. This can create a precarious situation for intended parents, as they must rely on the goodwill of the surrogate post-birth.

While neither Australia nor New Zealand supports commercial surrogacy, their rigorous regulatory environments aim to uphold high ethical standards in ART.

These laws reflect broader societal values that prioritise the welfare of all parties involved, especially the surrogate and the child. However, these same regulations also push individuals and couples towards surrogacy-friendly jurisdictions overseas, raising concerns about the potential for exploitation in less regulated environments.

Looking forward, as the demand for surrogacy continues to grow globally, countries in Australia and Oceania may need to revisit their laws and regulations. The challenge will be to find a balance between protecting the rights and welfare of everyone involved in surrogacy arrangements—particularly the surrogates and the children—and accommodating the reproductive autonomy, the right to be surrogates, and the desires of intended parents (Sifris, 2015). As such, the future of surrogacy in Australia and Oceania will likely involve ongoing legal and ethical debates, as well as potential reforms to better align domestic regulations with the realities of a globalised world where reproductive technologies and family structures are rapidly evolving.

Section 4: The Business Framework of Commercial Surrogacy

The economic and business framework of commercial surrogacy encapsulates a complex intersection of legal, ethical, medical, and financial elements. As a burgeoning industry, commercial surrogacy offers intended parents the means to start or grow families when other methods have failed or are not viable. The industry's global value is difficult to pinpoint due to varying legal statuses across countries and fluctuating market dynamics. However, the practice has been increasingly recognised not only as a personal or medical decision but also as a significant economic activity with broad implications.

Economic Impact

Surrogacy, particularly commercial surrogacy, can be a lucrative business for all parties involved, providing significant income for surrogacy agencies, legal firms, fertility clinics, and surrogates. In countries where it is legal, the industry contributes to the local economy through various services including healthcare, legal, counselling, and logistical support services. Surrogacy arrangements typically involve numerous parties: the intended parents, the surrogate, the healthcare providers, and the legal representatives, each contributing to, and benefiting economically from, the process. For instance, before India banned commercial surrogacy in 2018, it was recorded that the surrogacy industry generated more than $400 million in 2012, making it a significant contributor to the country's income (Frankford et al., 2015).

Economic Structure and Market Dynamics

The commercial surrogacy market operates within a unique economic structure shaped by demand and supply forces, cost considerations, and the influence of cultural and legal factors. Globally, the surrogacy industry has seen significant growth, driven by various factors, including medical advancements, changing societal norms around family structures, and the increasing acceptance of surrogacy as a viable means for individuals and couples to have children. Market size estimations vary, but many sources indicate substantial growth as more countries legalise or regulate surrogacy and cross-border options become accessible for intended parents from regions where surrogacy remains restricted or banned.

Global Market Size and Growth

Understanding the global surrogacy market requires an analysis of its size, growth trends, and the factors influencing its expansion. Reports indicate that the industry has been experiencing steady growth, driven largely by advancements in ART and rising infertility rates in various populations (World Health Organization [WHO], 2023). Increased societal acceptance of diverse family forms, including single parents and LGBTQ+ families, has further fuelled the demand for surrogacy. This sector is highly dynamic, with various stakeholders—fertility clinics, agencies, legal advisors, and intended parents—contributing to the industry's expansion.

Regional Demand and Supply Factors

Demand for surrogacy services varies across regions, often shaped by legal, cultural, and economic factors. In countries where surrogacy is restricted, such as parts of Europe, intended parents may seek surrogacy services abroad, creating demand in more permissive regions. For instance, surrogacy-friendly destinations like the United States, Ukraine, and Georgia attract many international clients due to their established legal frameworks and support systems for commercial surrogacy. In these regions, a robust supply of qualified surrogates and established medical facilities make the process more accessible, further driving demand.

Conversely, on the supply side, surrogates are often motivated by financial incentives or the desire to help others create families, particularly in lower-income regions where surrogacy offers a significant economic opportunity. For example, surrogates in India can earn an amount equivalent to five years of family income (Frankford et al., 2015). This financial incentive can help surrogates achieve personal and family financial goals such as paying off debt, funding education, or investing in housing.

This supply-side dynamic can lead to a concentration of surrogacy services in specific regions, forming international "surrogacy hubs" where intended parents and surrogates converge. The availability of surrogates is influenced by economic conditions, local perceptions of surrogacy, and the presence of supportive legal frameworks that protect the rights of all parties involved.

Key Players and Stakeholders

The commercial surrogacy industry involves a diverse group of stakeholders, each playing a critical role in its functioning and growth. Major players include surrogacy agencies, fertility clinics, legal professionals, and psychological support providers. Agencies often act as intermediaries, coordinating between intended parents and surrogates, managing logistics, and offering support throughout the surrogacy process. These agencies are pivotal in ensuring that arrangements are legal, transparent, and ethically sound.

Fertility clinics, particularly those specialising in IVF and ART, are essential to the surrogacy process as they provide the necessary medical support and technical expertise. Many of these clinics operate on an international level, catering to clients across borders, which has contributed to the globalisation of the surrogacy industry.

Legal professionals also play a crucial role, especially in international surrogacy arrangements where the legal rights and responsibilities of each party must be clearly defined across jurisdictions. This legal support is vital to ensure that all parties understand their rights and obligations, particularly in cases involving cross-border surrogacy.

Psychological support providers, including counsellors and therapists, are increasingly recognised as essential contributors to the surrogacy process. They offer emotional support to intended parents and surrogates alike, helping them navigate the psychological complexities associated with the surrogacy journey.

Business Framework

The business framework of commercial surrogacy is underpinned by a need for regulation and ethical considerations to prevent exploitation and ensure fair treatment of all parties involved. Different countries have adopted various models, reflecting their cultural, ethical, and economic values. The surrogacy market can be categorised into three models as follows:

Model 1: Regulated Markets

Some regions, such as certain states in the United States and Russia, have established legal frameworks that allow commercial surrogacy to operate openly under strictly regulated conditions. These regulations are designed to protect the rights of the child, the surrogate, and the intended parents while also ensuring a clear contractual framework covering consent, compensation, and the legal rights of all parties.

Model 2: Restricted or Banned Markets

In contrast, other countries, like most of the European Union, Canada, and Australia, allow only altruistic surrogacy. These regulations are intended to prevent the commercialisation of human reproduction, the potential commodification of women's bodies, and the exploitation of vulnerable parties.

Model 3: Emerging Markets

Countries such as Laos and Kazakhstan have become "repronubs" for international surrogacy tourism due to more permissive laws and lower costs. This has spurred economic growth in these regions but has also raised legal and ethical concerns about international surrogacy practices, including concerns about the exploitation of surrogates and the legal status of children born from international arrangements.

The Business Model Canvas of Commercial Surrogacy

Recent research by LIU and BICE (2021) suggests that countries with higher Gross Domestic Product (GDP) and average monthly incomes are more likely to prohibit surrogacy. This indicates that economic factors may influence a country's stance on surrogacy. As a result, the business model of commercial surrogacy tends to develop in countries with less restrictive laws, typically those with lower GDPs. In the evolving landscape of commercial surrogacy, economic impact and business frameworks are influenced by "reproprenuers". These entrepreneurs identify and capitalise on "repronubs"—key centres where surrogacy services are viable based on market size, scale, and specific focus areas, as noted by (Whittaker et al., 2022). These hubs often emerge in response to shifting market opportunities and contingencies. Depending on changes in legislation, market demands, or geopolitical situations, these hubs may either grow to become stable and important centres of the surrogacy trade or diminish and fade away. From this dynamic market environment, the commercial surrogacy framework can be visually represented using the Business Model Canvas, as illustrated in Table 1.2. It caters to the desires of intended parents and is facilitated by a network of agencies and medical practitioners. This model positions surrogates as integral workers within a global economy of reproduction, highlighting the commercial nature of surrogacy where economic transactions are central.

Table 1.2 The commercial surrogacy Business Model Canvas

Partners	**Activities**	**Value proposition**	**Customer relationships**	**Target customer**
Fertility clinics Surrogacy agencies Legal professionals Psychological support providers	Matching intended parents with a woman who has agreed to carry a foetus through pregnancy Facilitating antenatal care/birth in other jurisdictions Shifting surrogates across the border	Fulfilment of a family Screened surrogates: age, health check, history of previous pregnancy Confidentiality Affordability	Intended parents	Infertile couples, gay couples, individuals High-income countries Locations where commercial surrogacy is restricted
	Resources		**Channels**	
	Surrogates (repronubs) Assisted Reproductive Technology		Surrogacy agencies in various locations and countries Advertisement via Internet Online consultation	
Cost structure		**Revenue streams**		
Attractive prices for intended individuals/couples; one-stop services		Attractive online advertising and affordable prices maintained by recruiting surrogates from low- to middle-income countries or repronubs.		

Section 5: Conclusion

Commercial surrogacy, an increasingly prevalent method of family building, involves complex layers of emotional, ethical, legal, and economic considerations. This chapter has revealed that the surrogacy industry is not only about providing hopeful parents with the chance to have biological children but also about significant financial implications and ethical quandaries. The business model of commercial surrogacy, supported by reproprenuers, repronubs, and facilitated by specialised agencies and medical professionals, frames surrogates as key participants in a global reproductive economy. However, the practice is mired in controversy, primarily due to concerns over the exploitation of surrogates and the commodification of human life.

The economic benefits for surrogates and the healthcare industry are substantial, yet they bring to light the potential for inequity and ethical misuse, particularly in low-income countries where women may turn to surrogacy out of financial necessity, unaware of the risks. The evolution from altruistic to commercial surrogacy has prompted a re-evaluation of regulatory frameworks worldwide, aiming to protect all parties involved while acknowledging the complexities of modern reproductive technologies.

Future discussions and policies must carefully consider the balance between enabling family creation, safeguarding the rights and well-being of surrogates, and managing the commercial aspects of surrogacy. The ongoing evolution of surrogacy laws and the international nature of surrogacy arrangements may necessitate a coordinated global approach to governance. This will ensure that surrogacy practices not only meet the desires of intended parents but also respect the dignity and rights of surrogates, ultimately fostering an ethical, sustainable approach to assisted reproduction in the global landscape.

References

Adaare, K. (2023). Regulatory framework of surrogacy in Ghana. *SSRN 4355757*. http://dx.doi.org/10.2139/ssrn.4355757

Armour, K. L. (2012). An overview of surrogacy around the world: Trends, questions and ethical issues. *Nursing for Women's Health*, *16*(3), 231–236.

Armour, T., Ford, R., & Rasmussen, B. (2019). Anaesthetic nurses' perceptions of learning during interprofessional simulation education. *Clinical Simulation in Nursing*, *35*, 5–9. https://doi.org/10.1016/j.ecns.2019.06.001

Attawet, J. (2021). Mapping transnational commercial surrogacy arrangements in South and Southeast Asia. *Medico-Legal Journal*, *89*, 128–132.

Australian Government. (2022). *Freedom of information request FA 22/08/00210*. Australia: Department of Home Affairs Retrieved from https://www.homeaffairs.gov.au/foi/files/2022/fa-220800210-document-released.PDF

Bashiri, A., Cherlow, Y., & Kresch-Jaffe, T. (2024). Surrogacy: An important pathway to parenthood. A call for international standardization. *Journal of Reproductive Immunology*, *163*, 104247.

Berndt, E. (2018). Seeking surrogacy: The ethics of assisting life's creation. Brindle Award in Medical Ethics Papers. 1. http://digitalcommons.luthersem.edu/brindle/1

Boampong, O., Appiah-Boateng, S., Osei, N. Y., & Ametefe, R. (2023). Commercial surrogacy: Invisible reproductive workers in Ghana. *Global Labour Journal*, *14*(2). https://doi.org/10.1080/01459740.2017.1419223

Brandão, P., & Garrido, N. (2023). Commercial surrogacy: An overview. *Revista Brasileira de Ginecologia e Obstetrícia*, *44*, 1141–1158.

Brinsden, P. R. (2003). Gestational surrogacy. *Human Reproduction Update*, 9(5), 483–491. https://doi.org/10.1093/humupd/dmg033

Buck, W. (2019). *Mahabharata*. University of California Press.

Buster, J. E. (1998). Historical evolution of oocyte and embryo donation as a treatment for intractable infertility. In M. V. Sauer (Eds.), *Principles of oocyte and embryo donation* (pp. 1–9). Springer. https://doi.org/10.1007/978-1-4612-1640-7_1

Cohen, E. (2015). Surrogacy as international business and national disgrace of Thailand. *Asian Anthropology*, *14*(2), 115–132.

Dickinson, N. (2023, November 27th). In *Episode 30 – Is traditional surrogacy 'riskier' than Gestational surrogacy?* Retrieved from www.surrogacyaustralia.org/podcast/episode-30-is-traditional-surrogacy-riskier-than-gestational-surrogacy-narelle-dickinson-psychologist

Dolezal, L. (2017). Phenomenology and intercorporeality in the case of commercial surrogacy. In *Body/self/other: The phenomenology of social encounters* (pp. 311–336). https://www.academia.edu/34704187/Phenomenology_and_Intercorporeality_in_Commercial_Surrogacy

duBeth, D. M. (1988). Family law-surrogacy contracts-New Jersey Supreme Court offers a barren future for surrogate parenting-in re baby M, 109 NJ 396, 537 A. 2d 1227 (1988). *Seton Hall Law Review*, *18*(4), 13.

Ellenbogen, A., Feldberg, D., & Lokshin, V. (2021). Surrogacy: A worldwide demand. Implementation and ethical considerations. *Gynecological and Reproductive Endocrinology & Metabolism*, *2*, 66–73.

Frankford, D. M., Bennington, L. K., & Ryan, J. G. (2015). Womb outsourcing: Commercial surrogacy in India. *MCN. The American Journal of Maternal Child Nursing*, *40*(5), 284–290. https://doi.org/10.1097/NMC.0000000000000163

Gelashvili, I. (2011). Legal and ethical problems of surrogacy. *Journal of Law*, 77. https://heinonline.org/HOL/LandingPage?handle=hein.journals/tsujrnl2011&div=10&id=&page=

Gerrits, T. (2018). Reproductive travel to Ghana: Testimonies, transnational relationships, and stratified reproduction. *Medical Anthropology*, *37*(2), 131–144.

Ghodrati, F. (2023). A comparative study of surrogacy rights in Iran and European countries, a review article. *Ethics, Medicine and Public Health*, *27*, 100880.

Hibino, Y. (2020). Non-commercial surrogacy in Thailand: Ethical, legal, and social implications in local and global contexts. *Asian Bioethics Review*, *12*(2), 135–147. https://doi.org/10.1007/s41649-020-00126-2

Hibino, Y. (2022). Ongoing commercialization of gestational surrogacy due to globalization of the reproductive market before and after the pandemic. *Asian Bioethics Review*, *14*(4), 349–361.

Hobzová, H. (2018). Surrogate motherhood: The contradictions in terminology. *Ceska Gynekologie*, *83*(6), 464–467.

Hörbst, V., & Gerrits, T. (2016). Transnational connections of health professionals: Medicoscapes and assisted reproduction in Ghana and Uganda. *Ethnicity & Health*, *21*(4), 357–374.

Khazova, O. A. (2024). Recent changes in Russian law on surrogacy in the Eastern European context. In K. Trimmings, S. Shakargy, & C. Achmad (Eds.), *Research handbook on surrogacy and the law* (pp. 353–375). Edward Elgar Publishing.

Kneebone, E., Hammarberg, K., Everingham, S., & Beilby, K. (2023). Australian intended parents' decision-making and characteristics and outcomes of surrogacy arrangements completed in Australia and overseas. *Human Fertility, 26*(6), 1448–1458.

LIU, J., & BICE, S. (2021). Surrogacy, social policy and economic development. *Asian Journal of Advances in Medical Science, 3*(1), 72–92.

Malhotra, I., Sharma, E., & Thakur, R. (2023). Bollywood celebrities as bioconsumers of reproductive technologies in neoliberal fertility markets: A study of popular public discourse. *International Journal of Cultural Studies, 26*(5), 588–605.

Margalit, Y. (2015). From baby M to baby M (anji): Regulating international surrogacy agreements. *Journal of Law and Policy, 24*, 41.

Marinelli, S., Del Rio, A., Straccamore, M., Negro, F., & Basile, G. (2022). The armed conflict in Ukraine and the risks of inter-country surrogacy. The unsolved dilemma. *European Review for Medical and Pharmacological Sciences, 26*(16), 5646–5650.

Mouliarova, E. (2019). The legal regulation of surrogacy in Russia. *Italian Journal of Public Law, 11*, 393.

Neel, M. M. (2019). Carrying capacity: Should Georgia enact surrogacy regulation. *Georgia Law Review, 54*, 333.

Newman, J. E., Paul, R., & Chambers, G. M. (2023). *Assisted reproductive technology in Australia and New Zealand 2021*. National Perinatal Epidemiology and Statistics Unit (NPESU). Retrieved from https://www.unsw.edu.au/content/dam/pdfs/research/2023-12-npesu/2024-01-Assisted-Reproductive-Technology-in-Australia-and-New-Zealand-2021.pdf

Patel, N. H., Jadeja, Y. D., Bhadarka, H. K., Patel, M. N., Patel, N. H., & Sodagar, N. R. (2018). Insight into different aspects of surrogacy practices. *Journal of Human Reproductive Sciences, 11*(3), 212–218. https://doi.org/10.4103/jhrs.JHRS_138_17

Patton, B. A. (2010). Buying a newborn: Globalization and the lack of federal regulation of commercial surrogacy contracts. *UMKC Law Review, 79*(2), 507–534.

Points, K. (2009). *Commercial surrogacy and fertility tourism in India*. The Keenan Institute for Ethics at Duke University, 1–11.

Reznik, O. M., & Yakushchenko, Y. M. (2020). Legal considerations surrounding surrogacy in Ukraine. *Wiadomości Lekarskie, 73*(5), 1048–1052.

Rudrappa, S., & Collins, C. (2015). Altruistic agencies and compassionate consumers: Moral framing of transnational surrogacy. *Gender & Society, 29*(6), 937–959.

Saran, J., & Padubidri, J. R. (2020). New laws ban commercial surrogacy in India. *Medico-Legal Journal, 88*(3), 148–150.

Schurr, C., & Perler, L. (2015). 'Trafficked' into a better future? Why Mexico needs to regulate its surrogacy industry (and not ban it). *Open Democracy*.

Schuz, R. (2003). Surrogacy in Israel: an analysis of the law in practice. Surrogate motherhood: international perspectives (pp. 35–54). Portland: Oxford.

Sifris, R. (2015). Commercial surrogacy and the human right to autonomy. *Journal of Law and Medicine, 23*(2), 365–377. Retrieved from https://search.ebscohost.com/login.aspx?direct=true&AuthType=shib&db=mnh&AN=26939504&site=ehost-live&custid=s3684040

Söderström-Anttila, V., Blomqvist, T., Foudila, T., Hippelainen, M., Kurunmaki, H., Siegberg, R., Tulppala, M., Tuomi-Nikula, M., Vilska, S., & Hovatta, O. (2002). Experience of in vitro fertilization surrogacy in Finland. *Acta obstetricia et gynecologica Scandinavica, 81*(8), 747–752.

Stasi, A. (2017). Protection for children born through assisted reproductive technologies act, BE 2558: The changing profile of surrogacy in Thailand. *Clinical Medicine Insights: Reproductive Health, 11*, 1179558117749603.

Stephanie, H., & Eleanor, L. (2022). *Ukraine: Impossible choices for surrogate mothers and parents*. BBC. Retrieved 18 June 2024 from https://www.bbc.com/news/world-europe-60824936

Steptoe, P. C., & Edwards, R. G. (1978). Birth after the reimplantation of a human embryo. *The Lancet, 312*(8085), 366.

The Moscow Times. (2022). Putin bans surrogacy for foreigners. *The Moscow Time*. Retrieved 31 May 2024 from https://www.themoscowtimes.com/2022/12/19/putin-bans-surrogacy-for-foreigners-a79738

Trowse, P. (2011). Surrogacy: Is it harder to relinquish genes? *Journal of Law and Medicine, 18*(3), 614–633.

Utian, W. H., Sheean, L., Goldfarb, J. M., & Kiwi, R. (1985). Successful pregnancy after in vitro fertilization and embryo transfer from an infertile woman to a surrogate. *The New England Journal of Medicine, 313*(21), 1351–1352.

Whittaker, A. (2016). From 'Mung Ming' to 'Baby Gammy': A local history of assisted reproduction in Thailand. *Reproductive Biomedicine & Society Online, 2*, 71–78. https://doi.org/10.1016/j.rbms.2016.05.005

Whittaker, A. (2019). Stop Thai women's wombs from becoming the world's womb. In V. Mackie, N. J. Marks, & S. Ferber (Eds.), *The Reproductive Industry: Intimate Experiences and Global Processes*. Critical Perspectives on Psychology of Sexuality, Gender, and Queer Studies (1st ed., pp. 125–144). Lexington Books.

Whittaker, A., Gerrits, T., & Weis, C. (2022). Emerging "repronubs" and "repropreneurs": Transnational surrogacy in Ghana, Kazakhstan, and Laos. *International Journal of Comparative Sociology, 63*(5–6), 304–323.

World Health Organization (WHO). (2023). *Infertility*. WHO. Retrieved 23 June from https://www.who.int/about/contact-us

Yacoubian Jr, G. S., & Clements, L. (2014). An examination of compliance with the inter-country adoption convention: Exploring surrogacy in Armenia as a form of human trafficking. *Arizona Journal of International and Comparative Law, 31*, 811.

2 Legal Framework and Challenges

Section 1: Law and Commercial Surrogacy

The modern practice of surrogacy is driven by a variety of reasons around an inability to have a successful pregnancy (Soini et al., 2006). Surrogacy is supported by advancements in medical technology, and the availability of people willing to submit to the process, to facilitate the provision of a child to those seeking the services of surrogacy. Where this service is performed for financial gain, or profit, it is regarded as commercial surrogacy. Commercial surrogacy is only available in a small number of jurisdictions. At the time of writing, commercial surrogacy arrangements were legal in several jurisdictions,[1] although the legal structures and protections differ and may change with minimal notice.

For example, legislation supporting commercial surrogacy in South America varies widely. In Argentina it is largely unregulated, although with the intended parents' consent and the surrogate mother's waiver of rights a parenting order can be made. In Bolivia, Chile, Colombia, Ecuador, Paraguay, and Venezuela surrogacy is unregulated. Brazil and Uruguay allow altruistic surrogacy, but Brazil considers commercial surrogacy to be human trafficking, and it is prohibited. In North America, Canada, similar to Australia, permits altruistic surrogacy. The United States not only permits commercial surrogacy, but several states actively also support it. Many other states, such as Georgia, Hawaii, Idaho, Indiana, Louisiana, Maryland, Minnesota, Mississippi, Missouri, Montana, Nebraska, New Jersey, New Mexico, North Carolina, North Dakota, Oregon, Pennsylvania, South Carolina, South Dakota, Virginia, and West Virginia, basically permit altruistic surrogacy without compensation beyond normal medical expenses. In Greece, the intended parents must appear before a family court judge before commencing a surrogacy arrangement. However, once this has been approved, the surrogate mother's name does not appear on any document, and they have no rights to the child born of the arrangement.

In the realm of commercial surrogacy, what is legal is usually defined by an absence of a particular piece of proscriptive legislation. That is to say, the lower entry-level commercial surrogacy tends to proliferate in jurisdictions where there is an absence of laws banning such practices. However, the actual procurement of the services of a surrogate is only a small component of the legal considerations

DOI: 10.4324/9781003511939-2

with respect to surrogacy. The absence of legislation is often not actually a benefit but can be a substantial impediment to successful surrogacy arrangements. A plethora of legal considerations arise around nationality, heritage, inheritance, statehood, adoption, parentage, passports, visas, etc. for the parties involved. This chapter examines several jurisdictions where the practice of commercial surrogacy is widely recognised and examines the laws which promote, support, or ignore commercial surrogacy. It will also endeavour to understand the legal ramifications for parties to surrogacy arrangements and the children born from the same in these jurisdictions.

Several countries welcome the practice of commercial surrogacy, and the decision for intended parents to choose a particular jurisdiction usually depends on several socioeconomic and geographic factors. Within the United States, for example, several jurisdictions have robust commercial surrogacy industries, but these are expensive when compared to other jurisdictions, making commercial surrogacy arrangements in the United States a very expensive practice for intended parents. Accordingly, people may seek commercial surrogacy arrangements in jurisdictions which are more affordable depending on their economic circumstances or proximity to their own location. Jurisdictions permitting commercial surrogacy will be analysed in this chapter based on the legislation or legislative frameworks that apply in the circumstances. While there are many similarities between jurisdictions, small variances can make a huge difference in outcomes in states that allow commercial surrogacy. While commercial surrogacy is available in a number of countries, the risks, outcomes, and cost vary considerably depending on jurisdiction. Additionally, the rights of the intended parents and the origin of the child can have significant consequences depending on the jurisdiction selected to undertake the surrogacy arrangement. It is important to consider more than just the written surrogacy arrangement when considering surrogacy in these jurisdictions. In particular, there are significant concerns around the birth certificate, parentage, and the ability of the intended parents to leave the country with the child. Notably, some countries make this easier than others. For people seeking a more cost-effective commercial surrogacy arrangement a number of jurisdictions hold promise in this regard.[2] However, the rights of the parents and child vary considerably depending on which jurisdiction the surrogacy agreement is undertaken.

Section 2: Legal Considerations around Surrogacy Arrangements

There are several legal considerations that potentially arise around surrogacy agreements. The primary considerations centre around the laws of each jurisdiction in which surrogacy is undertaken, the terms contained within the contract, or agreement, and the responsibilities of the parties. There are quite a few secondary considerations which will also be looked at that continue to affect the parties long after the arrangement is concluded. However, notwithstanding these other considerations, the laws of each jurisdiction are paramount as they determine whether a surrogacy arrangement can be undertaken legally.

The Law of the Land

It is important to understand the overarching legal frameworks that exist in whichever jurisdiction is selected for undertaking a commercial surrogacy agreement. This is, arguably, the most crucial component of a commercial surrogacy arrangement as the relevant legal framework will have a large bearing on how the post-birth legal considerations are to be handled once the baby is born. For example, if the jurisdiction records the intended parents as the biological parents on the birth certificate, a whole myriad of problems are avoided with respect to visas, immigration, paternity, adoption, and so on. This simple step can mean the difference between a smooth transition from the surrogacy arrangement and an ongoing nightmare that may take years to resolve. If a jurisdiction is supportive of commercial surrogacy arrangements, it makes the whole process exponentially easier for the intended parents to take their new child home. For example, under the legislative framework in Belarus the rights of the intended parents were protected to a greater degree than in some other Eastern European jurisdictions. These protections extended across several separate legislative instruments.[3] Where a surrogacy contract existed,[4] the rights of the intended parent(s) were prioritised over the surrogate mother or the sperm donor. The absence of such an agreement leaves the surrogate mother as the recognised biological parent. Additionally, recognition of parenthood is also recorded on the birth certificate as being the intended parents, where a surrogacy contract exists.[5] While surrogacy is also available to foreign couples and single women, with a valid medical reason, there are age limits for surrogates and for female intended parents.[6] Accordingly, commercial surrogacy in such jurisdictions offered a notable degree of legislative protection for couples and single women who intend to undertake a surrogacy arrangement but was not available for homosexual couples or single men. Belarus thus served as the legislative benchmark for commercial surrogacy arrangements in the Eastern European states. It provided a relatively clear pathway for intended parents and surrogates and set out a process by which the child born from these arrangements could be registered as the child of the intended parents. This tended to minimise some of the usual problems associated with documentation and the subsequent legal rights and challenges parents could face in other jurisdictions. Currently, the legislation in several US states supporting commercial surrogacy represents some of the most comprehensive frameworks available for commercial surrogacy. For example, California, Connecticut, Main, New Hampshire, Rhode Island, Vermont, and Washington all have comprehensive laws supporting commercial surrogacy that, inter alia, also require the intended parents to pay for legal representation and a variety of support mechanisms for the surrogate mother throughout the surrogacy process and beyond. Other states such as Delaware, Florida, Illinois, Nevada, Oklahoma, Texas, Utah, and the District of Colombia support commercial surrogacy but do not provide that intended parents pay for the same services.

Moreover, while undertaking a commercial surrogacy arrangement in jurisdictions having supportive regulations is also likely to be significantly more expensive for the intended parents initially, and potentially more supportive of the surrogate mother, overall outcomes tend to be simpler. Where a legal vacuum exists, while it may appear easier to undertake a surrogacy arrangement due to no laws expressly banning the practice, it may actually be more difficult for the intended parents once the child is born as there may be no legal recognition whatsoever for them with respect to the child born of the arrangement (Sifris & Page, 2021). Accordingly, in jurisdictions where there are no laws it may not be, in fact, supporting commercial surrogacy and can make the whole process far more difficult and expensive. Where these practices are prohibited, it often drives commercial surrogacy arrangements underground and removes the protections for surrogates that exist in more supportive jurisdictions. Of even greater importance is the fact that a positive legislative framework also makes the contractual arrangements legislatively supported and therefore enforceable by the laws of the land. In these jurisdictions, remedies can therefore be had for a failure to perform the contract. Conversely, in jurisdictions where surrogacy is not supported, recognised, or is itself illegal, the contract of surrogacy may be unenforceable or subject to criminal penalty. In the chronology of a surrogacy arrangement, the first consideration for most intended parents is the use of a surrogacy agency, which itself necessitates a legally binding contract for the service the agency provides.

The Surrogacy Agency

In commercial surrogacy arrangements it is quite common to engage an agency to procure the surrogacy and to facilitate much of the necessary documentation. The intended parents enter into a commercial agreement with the surrogacy agency which is separate to the agreement with the surrogate mother. The surrogacy agency then acts on the intended parents' behalf with respect to many aspects of the surrogacy arrangement such as the procurement of the surrogate, visas, immigration documentation, and so on. On a legal basis, if the intended parents deal solely with a surrogacy agency, they are a third party to the contractual arrangement with a surrogate mother, whereas if the surrogacy agency merely facilitates the finding of willing surrogates, then the intended parents are parties to the contractual arrangement. Whether the intended parents are third parties to the surrogacy agreement, or parties to the contractual arrangement, can have significant follow-on ramifications and lead to cascading legal effects. This is because the rights, obligations, and responsibilities of the parties are necessarily contained within the contractual arrangement, as are remedies.

The Contractual Arrangement

The commercial surrogacy contract sets out the rights and responsibilities of each party to the surrogacy agreement. The essential terms contained within the surrogacy contract cover, or should cover, the rights and responsibilities of the intended parents, the surrogate mother, and the medical professionals involved and should clearly articulate the remuneration or consideration to be exchanged under the surrogacy arrangement. The quality of the contract of surrogacy and the specificity contained therein have an important bearing on the outcome for the intended parents. These include the parties to the contract, the procedure by which conception occurs, transfer of ova, where the medical care is to take place, and, inter alia, the rights and duties of the parties. It is important that the terms of the contract address the donation, storage, or disposal of embryos that may not need to be used in the surrogacy process. Clarifying ownership of embryos created through IVF and the legal process for transferring them to the surrogate mother is also very important. Additionally, the failure of a pregnancy, or the death of the surrogate, should also be considered. Time frames also need to be set out and understood, and some contingency for a failure of performance of any of the contractual terms. Essential terms of a contract of surrogacy have been noted in specific legislation. For example, the California Family Code sets out the following terms deemed to be essential for a contract of commercial surrogacy:

a An assisted reproduction agreement for gestational carriers shall contain, but shall not be limited to, all of the following information:

   1 The date on which the assisted reproduction agreement for gestational carriers was executed.
   2 The persons from which the gametes originated, unless donated gametes were used, in which case the assisted reproduction agreement does not need to specify the name of the donor but shall specify whether the donated gamete or gametes were eggs, sperm, or embryos, or all.
   3 The identity of the intended parent or parents.
   4 Disclosure of how the intended parents will cover the medical expenses of the gestational carrier and of the newborn or newborns. If health care coverage is used to cover those medical expenses, the disclosure shall include a review of the health care policy provisions related to coverage for surrogate pregnancy, including any possible liability of the gestational carrier, third-party liability liens or other insurance coverage, and any notice requirements that could affect coverage or liability of the gestational carrier. The review and disclosure do not constitute legal advice. If coverage of liability is uncertain, a statement of that fact shall be sufficient to meet the requirements of this section.[7]

These essential terms set out with a fairly high degree of specificity, what is expected of each party to an agreement and the minimum terms to satisfy a commercial surrogacy agreement. The contractual nature of the agreement means that once consideration has been given by either party, there are remedies at law for a failure to perform any of the essential terms to the commercial surrogacy contract. The availability of remedies in a contractual arrangement cannot be understated.[8] It gives force of law to the agreement and provides a pathway where things don't go according to the agreement for parties who suffer loss to be restored to the position that they would have been in had the contemplated loss not occurred. This gives confidence in the veracity of the arrangement and ensures a greater likelihood of compliance with the terms and conditions set out in the surrogacy arrangement. There are also a number of secondary considerations which could form part of the contractual terms but need to be examined individually to enable a better understanding of the potential risks associated with commercial surrogacy agreements.

Health and Safety Regulations

Health and safety regulations in each jurisdiction are extremely important controlling factors in the quality of health-related services and impact directly on the surrogacy process. All medical practitioners, hospitals, and healthcare providers are subject to specific legislative provisions, regulations, and internal policies that govern the way those services may be delivered, and these vary from jurisdiction to jurisdiction. They clarify what level of compliance is necessary for medical practitioners and parties involved in the delivery of gestational medical services. They set out medical standards for fertility treatments and how these may be undertaken, and in what circumstances, and with what safeguards are necessary in providing these services. In particular, they set out how the embryos are handled and the process for storage of embryos and disposition of unused embryos created during the fertility treatment. The health and safety regulations also set out the standards for hygiene, for pre and postnatal care, and what monitoring and support is required during these phases. They also set out the standards for the theatre where the childbirth occurs and the level of compliance necessary to meet the minimum industry standards for midwifery and postnatal care.

Additionally, certain policies in different hospitals may specify different processes for each component under the health and safety regulations. Hospitals vary significantly from one to another within each jurisdiction as to what is required and what levels of medical care or access should be given on completion of the birthing process. For example, hospital policy may or may not allow the intended parents to participate in the birth of the child and may limit access to the newborn child to the surrogate mother instead of intended parents. Suffice to say, the higher the general standard of medical practice in each jurisdiction the higher the likelihood of a better outcome for all parties, not least of which is the surrogate mother.

Egg/Sperm Donation and Regulation

Depending on the jurisdiction, and the rigour to which the legislative frameworks control the treatment of egg/sperm donation, handling, and use, there may be specific hurdles in relation to this component of the surrogacy arrangement.

Regulations surrounding donor conception differ significantly across the globe, with countries adopting a wide variety of approaches. In some jurisdictions, such as Greece, only strictly anonymous donation is allowed, preventing the use of known donors and limiting access to information about genetic origins. In contrast, some countries permit the release of donor information under specific conditions, such as when a donor-conceived person reaches a certain age. Meanwhile, in many regions, there are no restrictions on how many times a donor can contribute, leading to cases where donor-conceived individuals may have hundreds of half-siblings. This can make it nearly impossible for them to connect with all their biological relatives, adding layers of complexity to the donor conception experience. From a child welfare perspective, best practices increasingly advocate for information release and the use of known donors, as transparency supports the right to know one's genetic background. Yet, with the growing popularity of consumer DNA testing, many donor-conceived individuals are finding ways to trace their genetic origins, even in countries that enforce donor anonymity, rendering the concept of true anonymity increasingly difficult to maintain.

In Australia, anonymous donation is completely banned, with mandatory record-keeping for all donor-conceived individuals, ensuring that they have access to information about their biological origins when needed. Victoria has set itself apart as the most heavily regulated state, with robust policies on donor conception and stringent guidelines for maintaining records. Surrogacy laws further vary across jurisdictions, with some requiring a genetic link between the child and at least one intended parent, effectively outlawing "double-donation" where both egg and sperm come from donors. This can create legal complications surrounding parentage, particularly in cases where DNA testing is used to establish citizenship by descent, as is common in Australia. When there is no genetic link between the child and either parent, obtaining citizenship often requires navigating more complex legal pathways, such as applying for citizenship by intent, which can be a more time-consuming and uncertain process.

Termination of Pregnancy Preterm

Commercial surrogacy arrangements often contemplate contingencies where a pregnancy may not reach full term. Potential unforeseen circumstances which may impact on the ability of the surrogacy arrangements to reach full term should be considered. For example, in the event of a significant foetal abnormality, or a health risk which could threaten the surrogate mother's life, it may be necessary to terminate the pregnancy. Contractual terms contained in the commercial surrogacy agreement should address the legal considerations that may arise with respect to the rights and responsibilities of the parties. Moreover, it may be necessary to contemplate foetal reduction or selective reduction if the intended parents have not contemplated a situation where multiple pregnancies might arise. In this situation, it may be necessary to remove foetuses to satisfy the contract or to protect a surrogate mother. Multiple pregnancies sometimes pose the risk of medical complications that could be a threat to the health and safety of the surrogate mother and the other foetuses. This should be contemplated as a potential outcome in the contractual arrangement to prevent confusion. If a surrogate has carried the foetus for a substantial period of time, this needs to be contemplated with respect to compensation and support for the surrogate mother, including psychological counselling. Termination of the pregnancy affects more than just the intended parents, or the contractual arrangements, but may pose a significant risk to the surrogate mother. It is also important that these risks be the subject matter of some kind of indemnification or insurance to limit exposure to risk.

Medical Insurance

One term that should be essential to a commercial surrogacy arrangement is the responsibility to hold medical insurance. Medical insurance is essentially a contract with a third party to cover potential risks arising from the surrogacy arrangement. The third-party insurer for a fee, a premium, assumes responsibility to cover for particular losses set out in the insurance contract. It is important to clarify in the surrogacy agreement who is responsible for obtaining the medical insurance, usually the intended parents,[9] as there is often a financial asymmetry, and what is covered in the contract of medical insurance. Any contract of medical insurance should cover prenatal care, delivery, postnatal care, and any medical treatments or interventions that may be necessary, including where life-threatening problems may require immediate intervention and or termination, and all after medical care around such arrangements. Medical insurance ensures that parties are protected financially and increases the likelihood that decent medical care will be given to the surrogate mother in the event of medical complications, and it aligns with societal assumptions around the ethical treatment of surrogates. The contract of medical insurance contains within it a sunset clause that limits how long the insurance subsists with respect to the arrangement, so it's important to understand how long cover is going to be required given the circumstances may require ongoing care for several parties to the agreement after the birth of the child.

Post-Birth Legal Considerations

Once the surrogacy arrangement has been fulfilled, assuming a successful and problem-free birth of the child, the legal considerations do not end with the fulfilment of the contract of surrogacy. There may be many other legal considerations arising from the birth that continue for the parties involved, in particular the intended parents and child.

Parental Rights of the Surrogate

The surrogate, having carried the surrogate child under the arrangement of surrogacy, may have ongoing parental responsibilities for the child. A refusal of the surrogate to hand over the baby is treated at law as a breach of contract. In most jurisdictions the surrogate and her rights would take priority over that of the contractual arrangement, which would be dealt with in an award of damages in jurisdictions where commercial surrogacy is supported. In jurisdictions where commercial surrogacy is not supported, such as in Australia where it is illegal, the contract is unenforceable, and no redress is available for parties to the arrangement where such a breach occurs.[10] Accordingly, a surrogate who decides to keep the child may be allowed to do so despite any contract of surrogacy. Parental responsibilities arising following such a decision are as with any ordinary birth; however the surrogate may be subject to litigation for compensation by the intended parents or their insurance representatives should they elect to do so. With the likely financial asymmetry between the contracting parties, it would usually be a matter of the intended parents trying to recoup their payment to the surrogate, rather than seeking damages for non-financial losses. This is because the surrogate may have no capacity to pay beyond returning the money paid for the breached contract.

Birth Certificate and Legal Recognition

Many jurisdictions do not recognise the intended parents on the birth certificate of the child born out of a surrogacy arrangement. Instead, as the surrogate has given birth to the child, she may be registered as the child's mother. Depending on the jurisdiction, the father recorded on the birth certificate may be the surrogate's husband, or the male intended parent, or where same-sex couples one of the intended parents. This is where commercial surrogacy arrangements become far more complicated, depending upon the jurisdiction, as the birth certificate is effectively the legal gateway for the intended parents and the child born of the surrogacy arrangement. Essentially, absent having the intended parents on the birth certificate, once the surrogacy agreement has been concluded, the intended parents may need to apply for adoption, parentage, or parental order with respect to the child. This is so even if the embryo was produced by the intended parents, as the jurisdiction may not recognise the biological heritage of the infant child born of the surrogacy arrangement. Depending on the jurisdiction, legal processes can be difficult or streamlined and may take a great deal of time and be relatively expensive.

Adoption of the Surrogate Child

A failure of a particular jurisdiction to recognise the intended parents then means the pathway to bring their child back to their home country may require entering an adoption process in the jurisdiction where the child was born. This requires distinct legal/administrative processes and may take significant amounts of time, with the intended parents ostensibly stranded in the country where the surrogacy arrangement was made while awaiting a decision. While the processes for adoption are being undertaken the intended parents' lives and that of the child would be essentially in a legal limbo. Intended parents may also be required to extend their visas and find accommodation through a protracted time until these processes are completed. Once the adoption process has been undertaken successfully, another pressing matter remains. That is, how to get a passport or visa for entry to allow the intended parents to bring the child home to their own country.

Getting the Child Recognised by the Intended Parents' Jurisdiction

Once the adoption process is completed, the next problem that arises is that the intended parents now have a child but need a pathway to bring the child back to their home country. This may also be subject to bureaucratic delay and be time-consuming and expensive. Adoption documents will need to be tendered and identification documents of the parents, potentially affidavits need to be sworn with respect to the surrogacy arrangement, and then the intended parents will wait while this process continues. If the surrogacy arrangement and the birth were concluded in a jurisdiction that does not recognise same-sex partnerships, then one of the parties may have to be deemed the adopted parent and this will then be reflected in the travel documents, passports, and so on to bring the child home. Once the couple get home with the new child, they may have to go through the process in their own jurisdiction to have both parties recognised as the parents of the child. Depending upon the state in which they live this may be easy or quite difficult and relatively inexpensive or time-consuming and expensive. Once this process is concluded, there may still be legal issues arising around paternity, inheritance, and succession.

How the Surrogacy Arrangement Affects Inheritance Paternity and Succession Law

The surrogacy arrangement could have several effects, either beneficial or detrimental to the child of the surrogacy arrangement. They may be recognised in the home jurisdiction as the child of the surrogate mother and able to make a claim on the estate of the surrogate mother. It may be necessary for the surrogate mother to undertake a formal process of relinquishing or terminating their parental rights with respect to the child born with a surrogacy arrangement. It should be contemplated within the surrogacy agreement that the surrogate mother will relinquish their parental rights to the child and do so with minimal delay to enable the child to bond with her new parents. If such a clause is not included in the agreement, it might prove problematic later on. If the agreement already contemplates it, it may be easier to undertake the paperwork process while the surrogate mother is still pregnant. The baby may be recognised as the child of the parent named in the adoption papers in the event of a relationship breakdown. There may be recognition of the child's nationality as being in the country they were born, and they may need to seek citizenship by descent or other means in the country of the intended parents. The potential legal problems arising from the commercial surrogacy arrangements may be far-reaching over both distance and time. Some of these will be listed below. Where the embryo was implanted, and was created using genome of both intended parents, it may be possible to tender into evidence a record of genetic testing to establish the parentage and heritage of the surrogate child.

Confidentiality and Privacy of the Surrogacy Arrangement

Many intended parents and surrogates wish to maintain confidentiality of the surrogacy arrangement, often in order to protect the child born of this arrangement. Some parents want to see the child grow up without any knowledge of this, while others are more than happy to share their extended relationship with the child. When privacy is a concern, it is important to note how medical records are handled in the jurisdiction where the surrogacy arrangement is contemplated. It is important to balance the rights of the person born to access information and the rights of the parents to expect privacy and confidentiality. If it is important to the intended parents, this needs to be contemplated when selecting a jurisdiction to undertake a surrogacy agreement; however, it is generally considered in the child's best interests to know and be told of their birth and donor heritage.

Parental Orders and Legal Recognition of the Adopted Child

Once the family arrive home, it may be necessary to seek parental orders and documentation to recognise the birth of the surrogate child. It may be necessary to get a parenting order naming the parents the intended parents and the surrogate mother. Further, the agreement needs to be set out and recognised by the court so that the child can then become subject to the jurisdiction in which the intended parents live. There might be a difference, depending upon the jurisdiction, in obtaining pre-birth orders as opposed to post-birth orders and different jurisdictions may have different requirements for obtaining such orders before or after the child is born. This can also impact the intended parents and how they are recognised with respect to the child. If all goes well the transition from the surrogacy arrangement to the new intended parents can be a smooth and relatively comfortable process. A failure to adequately consider the jurisdiction in which the surrogacy arrangement is undertaken could have cascading legal effects and raised difficulties far beyond those in a more surrogacy-friendly environment.[11] As a corollary of this, the expense will also be raised as will the inconvenience and the time it takes to undertake all the processes surrounding bringing the child home.

The Best Interests of the Child

Many western jurisdictions have policies around the best interest of the child with respect to family law. In jurisdictions where this applies, the child's interests are paramount. In any disputes this is what the court will consider, and it will look at how the child may be impacted by any arrangements. For example, in the event of a relationship breakdown, the court does not look at what the parents wish but rather what is best for the child. For example, in Australia, the *Family Law Act* prioritises the best interests of the child in all deliberations and decision-making processes. In Australia, parenting disputes are resolved based on the best interests of the child. While presumptions of parentage from birth, favouring the surrogate, can be challenged, they are not always successfully rebutted, as seen in *Bernieres*.[12] Parenting orders may grant the intended parents shared parental responsibility, excluding the surrogate. The best interests of the child are determined according to section 60CC of the *Family Law Act*.[13]

Citizenship

Applications for citizenship may be undertaken on behalf of the surrogate child either by birth, in the country where the child was born, or by descent, in the intended parents' jurisdiction. In each of these situations, it will be necessary to determine some form of connection between one or more of the intended parents and the surrogate child, usually the birth certificate, even if one or both parents share genetics with the child. This will vary between jurisdictions as to whether this arrangement is recognised and whether other pathways may be needed to obtain citizenship for the child born of the surrogacy arrangement. There are two usual pathways by which this may be achieved:

1 The parents apply for a passport in the country of birth and then travel to their home country with a visa. They may then apply for citizenship in their home country when they arrive home.
2 Alternatively, they may apply for citizenship from their home country, and a passport, and then travel home with the child on that passport.

This process may take significant amount of time depending upon the jurisdiction in which this is undertaken and represents the final step in the higher legal formalities around the surrogacy arrangement. Once citizenship and recognition of the parents are completed, it may be necessary to consider other matters including healthcare and schooling. There may be conflict between federal and state laws and depending on the destination jurisdiction it may be governed by a federal law and/or by a particular state law which might impact, in a significant manner, the pathway chosen with respect to getting the child recognised for citizenship. Another important factor flowing from the birth of the child is the creation, curation, and maintenance of all the documentation necessary to give effect to the legal process required following the birth of the surrogate child. This is absolutely necessary to ensure minimal delay time and cost for the intended parents to bring the child home and for a citizenship application to be successful.

Dispute Resolution

Surrogacy agreements should outline the process and remedies to address disputes between the parties. Where disagreement exists, a robust dispute resolution process is absolutely essential. This will be set out as an essential contractual term in the surrogacy arrangement, which will deem the appropriate agreed pathway to manage disputes, disagreements, and/or breaches of the contract of surrogacy. It is not uncommon for people to misunderstand their rights and obligations or to change their mind and want something more, or something different, than that which was agreed to originally. As Yevtieieva et al. argue:

> The issues of unilateral refusal to perform the contract, refusal of parents from the born child, the fate of the child in case of death of parents or one of them, their divorce are not regulated by law. Therefore, the quality of the contract is an important aspect of using this method of reproductive medicine.
>
> (Yevtieieva et al., 2020)

Setting out unequivocally the pathways and remedies and dispute resolution process will minimise the amount of extra cost and expense, along with heartache and stress that may arise during a dispute over the surrogacy arrangement. A named dispute resolution process in the surrogacy contractual arrangement will serve as a pre-action procedure if the matter must be litigated. Many courts require a dispute resolution process to be followed as a pre-action procedure to open litigation. While litigation should always be avoided, it may be necessary to commence litigation in some circumstances. Dispute resolution processes are necessary for parties to protect their rights.

Separation of the Intended Parents

Relationship breakdown and separation of the intended parents will always have a significant legal impact on all parties including the intended parents and the child. Not only will it affect the distribution of assets and the potential outcomes arising under succession law, but it will also affect how care, living arrangements, parental care, and responsibility for the child are managed. Additionally, for same-sex partners it may be affected by the nature of the initial surrogacy arrangement if in a jurisdiction that does not recognise such unions. In these situations, the party named on the birth certificate may be recognised a priori as the relevant parent in the relationship. Additionally, in jurisdictions that do not recognise both intended parents in a same-sex relationship, one of the parties may be deemed not to be the parent. A corollary of this is that, depending on jurisdiction and the type of relationship, relationship breakdown may result in a complex and expensive litigation process to have the second intended parent legally recognised in co-parenting arrangements by the courts.

Other Considerations

Once the child arrives in the destination country there are numerous other legally related considerations to be contemplated. These are the same considerations as are necessary for a child born through traditional methods. Getting a child registered for the school system, for Medicare, or social security, and ensuring that support services are available for the child moving forward and building the usual documentary trail necessary in modern society. Ultimately, the child could seek to know and understand their heritage and the identity of their donor/surrogate families as they reach early adulthood, which may have other legal or social, or psychological consequences. These potential challenges need to be considered and addressed in an ethical manner by the intended parents.

Section 3: Conclusion

The legal landscape of commercial surrogacy is as diverse as the jurisdictions that regulate it or, in some cases, fail to regulate it adequately. While supportive legislative frameworks, such as those in certain US states, provide clarity and enforceability, jurisdictions with ambiguous or absent laws introduce significant risks for intended parents, surrogates, and children. The presence of comprehensive regulations not only facilitates smoother arrangements but also ensures better protection of rights for all parties involved. Conversely, legal vacuums or prohibitive laws often drive the practice underground, increasing vulnerability and uncertainty. This chapter highlights the importance of legislative reform and international cooperation to address disparities and ensure ethical and legally sound practices. Achieving a balance of rights, obligations, and protections is essential to safeguard the interests of all stakeholders and promote fairness and justice in reproductive healthcare.

Notes

1 These included Belarus, Georgia, Kazakhstan, Kyrgyzstan, Russian Federation, Ukraine, select US states, Quebec, Mexico, Colombia, and other South American states.
2 Australians are, presently at least, engaging in surrogacy in the United States, Canada, Argentina, Mexico, and Colombia—occasionally Georgia and Ukraine.
3 Code of the Republic of Belarus on Assisted Reproductive Technologies, 07.01.2012 № 341–343; Code of the Republic of Belarus on Marriage and Family, 09.07.1999 № 278/3; Resolution of the Council of Ministers of the Republic of Belarus "On the essential terms of the surrogacy agreement", 04.11.2006 № 1470; Resolution of the Ministry of Health of the Republic of Belarus "On approval of the list of medical indications and contraindications to surrogacy, procedure and scope of medical examination of surrogate mothers, genetic mothers and their spouses", 14.09.2006 №71.
4 Code of the Republic of Belarus on Assisted Reproductive Technologies.
5 Code of the Republic of Belarus on Marriage and Family, Art. 52.
6 For surrogates 25–35 years, and for intended parents, the female must be less than 50 years of age: Code of the Republic of Belarus on Assisted Reproductive Technologies, Arts. 6, 22.
7 California Code, Family Code §7962.
8 This is in contrast to jurisdictions where surrogacy contracts are unenforceable, such as Australia, where surrogacy arrangements are unenforceable because Australia considers the child's best interests are paramount. The agreement itself is less of a "contract" and more of a "memo of understanding" for evidentiary purposes only. This is different in other jurisdictions where enforcement is available.
9 In the United States, surrogacy arrangements frequently rely on the surrogate's existing insurance. However, insurance agencies may apply exclusions related to surrogacy, which can create challenges for both the surrogate and intended parents if not resolved before conception.
10 If the "breach" is that the surrogate refuses to relinquish the child, then the *Family Law Act 1975* (Cth) applies and "redress" may include an application to the Federal Courts. Decisions are then made based on what is in the child's best interests.
11 Note, this is not the case in all jurisdictions, although there are ongoing discussions in Ireland, New Zealand, and England about such orders. See, for example, *Re H (Surrogacy: Step-parent adoption)* [2023] EWFC 214.
12 *Bernieres v Dhopal* [2017] FamCAFC 180 ("Bernieres").
13 *Family Law Act 1975* (Cth) s 60CC.

References

Sifris, R., & Page, S. (2021). Australian surrogacy law: Recommendations for reform. *Critical Perspectives on Human Rights Law in Australia*, *2*, 81–100.

Soini, S., Ibarreta, D., Anastasiadou, V., Aymé, S., Braga, S., Cornel, M., Coviello, D. A., Evers-Kiebooms, G., Geraedts, J., & Gianaroli, L. (2006). The interface between assisted reproductive technologies and genetics: Technical, social, ethical and legal issues. *European Journal of Human Genetics*, *14*(5), 588–645.

Yevtieieva, D. P., Lapkin, A. V., & Karelin, V. V. (2020). East Slavic surrogate motherhood: State of legal regulation and risk of human rights violation. *Wiad Lek*, *73*(12), 2882–2889.

Legislation

Code of the Republic of Belarus on Assisted Reproductive Technologies, 07.01.2012 №341–343.

Code of the Republic of Belarus on Marriage and Family, 09.07.1999 № 278/3.

Code of the Republic of Belarus on Assisted Reproductive Technologies.

Code of the Republic of Belarus on Marriage and Family, Art. 52.

Code of the Republic of Belarus on Assisted Reproductive Technologies, Arts. 6, 22.

California Code, Family Code §7962.

Family Law Act 1975 (Cth) s 60CC.

Resolution of the Council of Ministers of the Republic of Belarus "On the essential terms of the surrogacy agreement", 04.11.2006 № 1470.

Resolution of the Ministry of Health of the Republic of Belarus "On approval of the list of medical indications and contraindications to surrogacy, procedure and scope of medical examination of surrogate mothers, genetic mothers and their spouses", 14.09.2006 № 71.

Cases

Bernieres v Dhopal [2017] FamCAFC 180.

Re H (Surrogacy: Step-parent adoption) [2023] EWFC 214.

3 Ethics in Commercial Surrogacy

Section 1: Ethical Foundations

Several ethical concerns arise around commercial surrogacy both internal and external to the process. Commercial surrogacy involves the carrying of a foetus to term by a person for profit. It can take on two forms, gestational surrogacy where the foetus is implanted in the surrogate's womb or traditional surrogacy where the surrogate provides her own eggs to which the genome of another donor or intended parent is added. Altruistic surrogacy, in contrast to commercial surrogacy, involves only recompense for reasonable expenses incurred by the surrogate. Similar ethical concerns also arise around altruistic surrogacy but not to the same extent, and most objections arise from personal belief systems and morality doctrines ascribed to by people within various religious communities.

Traditional surrogacy has been around human society for thousands of years and has been mentioned in many of the religious texts. Usually, this arrangement was undertaken to help a family member who could not have children. There was typically a close familial association between the surrogate and the person or persons receiving the child into their family. The rise of increasingly technologically advanced obstetric and other reproductive technologies has seen a paradigm shift in the ability to undertake gestational surrogacy. The key ethical distinctions between commercial and altruistic surrogacy are that altruistic surrogacy seeks to benefit the intended parents and only compensates the surrogate for reasonable expenses incurred and those associated expenses reasonably involved in the process, whereas commercial surrogacy does so for profit, above and beyond the expenses incurred in the surrogacy process. It is this inherent difference that gives rise to a whole range of ethical concerns. The inclusion of the profit motive shifts surrogacy into a minefield of potentially contestable ethical areas.

Foundational Ethical Theories in Commercial Surrogacy Practices

Utilitarianism

While many ethical positions may be applicable to commercial surrogacy, several foundational ethical theories may be brought to bear on analysis of the ethics surrounding this practice. The first of these is utilitarianism (Bentham, 1789).

DOI: 10.4324/9781003511939-3

Utilitarianism evaluates any action based on whether it benefits the majority and sees that an action is right insofar as it promotes happiness and that the greatest happiness of the greatest number should be the guiding principle of conduct (Mill, 2017). Commercial surrogacy, when viewed through the lens of utilitarianism, does promote an improvement in general happiness as it allows childless couples to build a family, and it allows people from lower socioeconomic positions to profit from the process. A major criticism of utilitarianism is that it fails to consider overarching considerations of justice and can overlook injustice on the individual if the greater good for the greater number is improved (Mill, 2017).

Utilitarianism can be outlined by the traditional trolley problem which describes a situation where a viewer must decide between switching tracks on a runaway railway car [trolley] that might otherwise kill five or six people, to a single track where it will most certainly kill another, with the choice to do nothing or to take the conscious action to kill the person on the single track. A utilitarian understanding would save the greater number of people at the expense of the individual. This contrasts with Deontology, where a deontological understanding of ethics involves behaviour according to a set of rules or moral standards relative to the individual. Sometimes known as duty, obligation, or rule-based ethics, it sees behaviour relative to an internal or external set of norms that govern what a person should do in making choices around their own behaviour.

Deontology

Moral absolutism is a sub-branch of Deontology, which argues there are universal moral principles by which all people's actions may be judged. However, one criticism of deontology is that by requiring people to behave according to a set of moral rules, it does not set out whose rules ought to be obeyed. This leads to disagreements as to the validity and the rightness of particular actions, and depending on the moral stance of an individual what may be right in one community could be abhorrent to another's moral standards. Deontological understandings of commercial surrogacy often lead to intense disagreements and are therefore incapable of satisfactory universal application. Another ethical approach that could be applicable to commercial surrogacy is virtue ethics. Virtue ethics arose with the Greek philosophical traditions of Plato and Aristotle and focuses on character.

Virtue

Virtue ethics does not focus on the rightness or wrongness of an action but rather on what a person's character ought to be and what qualities they should seek to develop over their lifetime. Virtues are character traits, and these include arete (excellence or virtue), phronesis (practical or moral wisdom), and eudaimonia (flourishing) (Rowe & Broadie, 2002). The character traits encouraged by virtue ethics seek to improve society by improving the individual. A branch of virtue ethics is agent-based virtue ethics. This form of ethics seeks to understand rightness or wrongness in terms of the motivation of the individual performing an action.

Actions are therefore not based solely on external rules or outcome but rather on the thought behind the deed,[1] and it is a justification to an action with a negative outcome if the motivation was good.[2] Commercial surrogacy viewed through the lens of virtue ethics would likely be considered good because the outcome benefits other people, although some may argue the profit motive, or the intent to profit, in some circumstances could outweigh the desire to help others.[3]

Feminist

A feminist approach to the ethics of surrogacy seeks to understand the power dynamics between the genders. It seeks to understand how gender power and social structures in society influence surrogacy and the compensation for surrogacy. It also looks at women's autonomy and whether they are actually free to make the decisions around entering commercial surrogacy arrangements in a society where economic inequality is driven by embedded patriarchal normativity which dominates all modern social structures (Butler & Trouble, 1990). Additionally, feminist ethics may question whether surrogacy represents empowerment of women to make choices with their own bodies, and with respect to their own reproductive ability and economic freedom, or whether it represents exploitation within existing patriarchal structures that commodify and objectify women. Accordingly, feminist understandings of commercial surrogacy may tend to favour altruism over commercial surrogacy unless adequate compensation is involved, which is itself subjective.

Section 2: Commodification of Reproduction

Ethical concerns also arise around the commodification of reproduction (Lemmens et al., 2017; Resnik, 1998). Where commercial concerns are involved and actions undertaken for profit, the physical products of these processes become in effect marketable goods (Kant & Schneewind, 2002). These include the egg, the surrogate's womb, and the child produced from the surrogacy arrangement. The categorical imperative as described by Kant argues that people should not be reduced to a means to an end but rather ends in themselves (Kant & Schneewind, 2002). Where a woman's reproductive capacities become commodified, arguably they then become a means to an end and the question then inevitably arises as to whether the use of the woman's reproductive organs for commercial reproduction or sexual gratification in prostitution is fundamentally on different ends of the same continuum (Cherry, 2014). When market forces are introduced into the commercial surrogacy field, which is unavoidable, then access to surrogacy, and in particular quality surrogacy, introduces power imbalances and favours the wealthy at the expense of those less fortunate. This can be seen most visibly in the application of commercial surrogacy in poor countries where the standards of medical care for the surrogate mother may not be to the same level as in wealthier countries, placing the surrogate mother at far greater risk of injury or death due to complications arising from the pregnancy (Jacobson & Rozée, 2022).

Another ethical concern that arises is with respect to the commodification of the child. Children, in effect, become the product of a commercial surrogacy contract which is the driving legal force behind bringing them into existence (Cutajar, 2022). Arguments around the commodification of the child inevitably lead to discussions around human trafficking and the justifications around any practice commodifying human life tend to be controversial (Abdullah, 2019).

There may also be ethical concerns around the balancing of interests between the surrogate, the intended parents, and the child born from the arrangement. As the primary driver of the arrangement with respect to commercial surrogacy, the intended parents often have a power imbalance in their favour over that of the surrogate (Panitch, 2017). Accordingly, their interests may be prioritised over those of the surrogate, reducing the surrogate's autonomy and ability to make choices around the pregnancy. Questions then arise as to whether the surrogate has entered the arrangement with fully informed consent and has the ability to make decisions about the pregnancy throughout the arrangement (Fabbo, 2020). Where these are absent it raises the question of the surrogate's reproductive freedom and personal autonomy in being able to make their own decisions.

Autonomy and Consent in Commercial Surrogacy

Informed Consent: Ethical Standards and Challenges

Most importantly, surrogates can provide informed consent with respect to the risks involved in the medical procedures and the likelihood of suffering injury or other adverse outcomes from the process (Laufer-Ukeles, 2018). As moral agents, a person should understand what they're doing and have the free will to make such a choice (Mele, 1995). If they cannot provide informed consent, it represents a form of exploitation of the woman, and places them at what could potentially be an extreme risk without their knowledge. This presents a challenge to healthcare workers and all involved to take steps to determine whether the surrogate has been adequately informed of the risks before commencing any procedures involving the surrogate. In commercial arrangements it is not unknown for salespeople to downplay risk or to not inform participants of risks involved in any endeavour and tend to focus only on the benefits or profits. When commercial surrogacy is involved and peoples' health is potentially at risk, it is absolutely necessary to know before the commencement of any procedure that the surrogate is aware of the risks involved in the process (Laufer-Ukeles, 2018).

The Autonomy of the Surrogate: Rights, Pressures, and Ethical Boundaries

A corollary of this is the question of whether the surrogate is aware of their rights, both with respect to their own person and their bodily autonomy, and also under the contract of commercial surrogacy (Frati et al., 2021). If the surrogate is unaware of their rights with respect to the arrangement, and to themselves, it also signals exploitation of the surrogate and healthcare workers need to be able to seek this information as a matter of course. Where the surrogate is unaware of her rights to have ethical boundaries which should not be intruded upon time needs to be taken to avail them of the information. In addition to knowledge and informed consent, healthcare workers need to know that surrogates have not been subject to pressure to undertake the surrogacy arrangement. Coercion or pressure to enter a surrogacy arrangement can come from many sources. For example, there may be family pressure to enter the arrangement for money, there may be pressure from the surrogacy agency to enter into the arrangement so that they may profit, and there may be pressure from the intended parents who often have an extreme financial power imbalance over the surrogate. Where poverty is a significant issue, which is not uncommon, economic forces may be driving the surrogate to undertake a process or procedure which they might otherwise not consent to or even want (Vertommen & Barbagallo, 2022). This contrasts markedly with altruistic surrogacy where the surrogate knowingly takes on the role of surrogate in order to help others. However, it is also arguable that altruistic surrogates can also be subject to coercion and control, particularly if they are feeling pressured to carry for family members (Anleu, 1992). Extended family members can place pressure on someone to carry to help out another family member. Language barriers, culture, and other power imbalances can also impact altruistic surrogacy arrangements.

Another set of potential ethical issues that may arise centre around the surrogates' rights to refuse medical treatment. As a person, with personal autonomy, a surrogate has the right to consent to or refuse any medical procedure, despite what may be contained in the contract of commercial surrogacy. Such refusal may, in certain circumstances, result in harm to both the surrogate and the as yet unborn child. In these circumstances the medical practitioners would likely be duty-bound to heed the surrogate's wishes and withhold treatment.

Ethical Considerations for Intended Parents: Rights and Responsibilities

Ethical considerations also arise for the intended parents. If the surrogacy arrangement is exploitative of the surrogate, then the intended parents are also part of that exploitation, whether they are aware of it or not (Wilkinson, 2003). The intended parents, who plan to care for the child to adulthood, also arguably have a responsibility to ensure that the surrogacy arrangement does not cause suffering to another party, the surrogate. Once the pregnancy has reached full term and the baby is born questions then arise as to whether bonding should occur between the surrogate and the child or should the child be taken directly to the intended parents (Lamba et al., 2018). Arguably, bonding post-birth may lead to increased separation anxiety for both the mother and the child when they are then separated according to the terms of the contract. Informed consent is necessary, along with an understanding of the process involved and why they are necessary, to help all parties involved navigate the post-birth separation of surrogate mother and child.

Section 3: Ethical Considerations

Exploitation and Power Dynamics in Commercial Surrogacy

As with many human interactions, the potential for exploitation arises where people seek to provide services for money to other parties. Commercial surrogacy is no exception to this, and a range of ethical concerns arise around commercial surrogacy (Writing Group on behalf of the ESHRE Ethics Committee, 2025). These include exploitation, power imbalances, vulnerability, agency, and economic inequality. Each of these raises particular ethical concerns for each party involved and are often in tension.

Ethical Concerns of Exploitation: Socioeconomic, Gender, and Racial Dimensions

Exploitation is a significant factor raised in discussions around commercial surrogacy (Wilkinson, 2003). Due to the significant power imbalance between intended parents and the parties to commercial surrogacy arrangements the commercial imperatives to undertake an arrangement may lead to deliberate exploitation of people at a socioeconomic disadvantage. Women maybe co-opted, tricked, coerced, or even forced into becoming surrogates. As with other forms of more serious human trafficking in disadvantaged countries, such as child trafficking, prostitution, or organ harvesting, it is possible that in some circumstances surrogates maybe tricked into undertaking the surrogacy arrangements. Once again it is important to understand the ethics of commercial surrogacy practice and how the agents involved in procuring surrogates undertake their screening processes, including from whom do they source surrogates or potential surrogates.

Addressing Vulnerability: Ethical Obligations and Legal Safeguards

Surrogates often represent a group of highly vulnerable people, and as vulnerable people at risk of exploitation stakeholders in surrogacy arrangements have ethical obligations to ensure that the surrogate are protected and not exploited (Ellenbogen et al., 2021). This might be particularly difficult when dealing across borders with agents whom the intended parents may have located online after reading a few testimonials which may or may not be fabricated. In US states dealing with surrogacy the rights of the surrogate are often protected to a very high degree (Hofman, 2008). This includes fully informed consent, health and medical insurance, postnatal care, and understanding the rights and obligations of all parties including the surrogate right to bodily autonomy, and how to determine the process of the pregnancy. This is often absent in surrogacy arrangements made in developing countries or countries of lower socioeconomic ability. Where poorer countries do not provide the same support either legislatively or socially it is important to understand that parties entering into a commercial surrogacy arrangement maybe putting vulnerable women at risk of exploitation (Scott, 2009).

Power Imbalances: Surrogates versus Intended Parents

Power imbalance is a significant issue between the intended parents and the surrogate. Once again, intended parents are often extremely wealthy relative to the surrogate and there is therefore a significant power imbalance between the parties. Often the agency is a mediator between the parties who takes the profit rather than the surrogate who takes the risk and the intended parents who take the child, leaving very little for the surrogate who may also have suffered social stigma in her own community due to undertaking the process of surrogacy depending upon cultural norms (Abrams, 2015; Arvidsson et al., 2017). Arguments that everybody benefits from commercial surrogacy often fail to understand the risk involved to the surrogate who is extremely vulnerable to exploitation.

Ethical Issues in Surrogate Compensation

Compensation Models: Ethical Approaches and Legal Considerations

There are two main types of compensation for surrogacy: altruistic surrogacy, where the surrogate is compensated for their medical expenses and other expenses incurred in providing the service of surrogacy; and commercial surrogacy, where the surrogate is compensated beyond the expenses incurred and enabled to make a profit from the process. Within each jurisdiction, the compensation models for surrogacy would be relative to the surrounding economic circumstances. However, when transnational or cross-border surrogacy is involved then the difference in standard of living involved in each jurisdiction and the difference in countries' economic power mean that what might be adequate remuneration in one jurisdiction may be very cheap in another, and this is the primary driver of transborder commercial surrogacy (Drabiak et al., 2007; Shapiro, 2014). Questions arise then around whether compensation models are adequate and whether the risk is adequately rewarded with respect to the surrogate. While not the same as personal injury law, in negligence, where pain and suffering are often compensated heavily, commercial surrogacy should seek to reward the surrogate for risk and for pain and suffering associated, or likely to be associated, with the pregnancy (Alghrani & Purshouse, 2019). While it remains often unsaid, it is important to understand that the separation of the surrogate from the child is also difficult and represents an extra burden on the surrogate. Debates surrounding commercial surrogacy often focus on whether substantial financial incentives are appropriate. While compensation for medical expenses and income loss is broadly viewed as a matter of justice, the provision of payment as an inducement to become a surrogate remains contested. Proponents argue that surrogacy is comparable to other forms of labor that involve physical risks and should thus be remunerated. Critics, however, raise concerns that financial vulnerability may coerce women into agreements they would not otherwise voluntarily enter, framing such practices as infringements on human dignity, the instrumentalisation of the female body, and the commodification of reproduction (Writing Group on behalf of the ESHRE Ethics Committee, 2025).

These concerns become particularly acute in cross-border arrangements, where surrogates from low-income countries may lack sufficient protections, and intended parents typically originate from wealthier nations. In such contexts, the risk of exploitation is not merely hypothetical but often substantiated by practice. While it cannot be categorically stated that ethical commercial surrogacy is impossible, it is clear that rigorous ethical safeguards and regulatory oversight are essential to ensure the protection and dignity of all parties involved.

Fairness and Equity in Compensation

Where there is a significant power imbalance there are questions around the fairness and equity in the compensation models provided to surrogate in poorer countries (Humbyrd, 2009). Does the compensation adequately cover the potential risks and fatal harm that may occur? Does the compensation include a requirement for informed consent by the surrogate and a requirement that they fully understand the terms of the contract and the risks to their bodily health involved in such an arrangement? Viewed globally, depending on which jurisdiction the surrogacy agreement is undertaken, the protections for the surrogate vary widely (Frati et al., 2021). In the United States, for example, where protections for surrogates in commercial surrogacy arrangements are among the strongest, entering into a commercial surrogacy agreement can represent a significant exercise of the surrogate's freedom of choice and bodily autonomy. However, in contrast, a woman entering into a surrogacy arrangement in a developing country may not understand the risks and implications nor have the protections around her that are offered to the surrogate in wealthier countries where the process of commercial surrogacy is legalised and protected. As a corollary of this, the protections for the child born of the commercial surrogacy arrangement also vary widely. In taking a global approach, commercial surrogacy is not a homogeneous arrangement across the globe, and the fairness and equity of compensation for surrogate mothers vary from comprehensive to almost non-existent. This raises questions around the ethical efficacy of profit-making agencies involved in the business of commercial surrogacy.

Ethical Dilemmas in Profit-Making: The Business of Surrogacy

The business of surrogacy is driven by a two-pronged concern. First is the need of the intended parents to have children and to create a family for which they are prepared to pay for a surrogate, whether that be altruistic or commercial. The intended parents are the primary drivers of commercial surrogacy and of surrogacy in general. Without intended parents there is no market, or need, for surrogacy. Where traditionally the surrogate was a family member helping out another family member, often to maintain the family bloodline, the introduction of the commercial realm and more easily available reproductive technologies have shifted this towards increasingly third-party structured arrangements. These arrangements represent the business of surrogacy, and in particular the business of commercial surrogacy. It is the business of commercial surrogacy where the greatest number of ethical concerns arise.

The ethical concerns arising from a business model that seeks to commodify both the human womb and the product thereof are inherently at odds with altruism (Kulkarni, 2015). This is because the concept of altruism is based on the motivation to help other people, in this case the intended parents, and is a selfless and generous act. While there is an argument that there is no such thing as true altruism, most altruistic surrogates report that they benefited and felt rewarded for being surrogates, even if they did not receive financial compensation. The reward is in the act itself (Jefford, 2020). In contrast, the business of commercial surrogacy is driven by the desire of the agents and affiliates to make a profit, and while the intended parents are still the consumer, it is the agents who broker the surrogate for their own personal gain, often at the expense of the surrogate's welfare and empowerment. This is where arguments around fair compensation and the ethical application of compensation with respect to commercial surrogacy, in particular for women of lower socioeconomic backgrounds, suggest that all parties involved should profit equally, including the surrogate, who often loses out in commercial surrogacy arrangements (Ber, 2000). It is undeniable that the surrogate bears the greatest risk of harm in commercial surrogacy arrangements and should therefore be the one that profits the most for taking the greatest risk.

Parentage, Identity, and the Child's Rights

Determining Legal Parentage: Ethical Challenges

The child's right to know its heritage is an important concern. As the product of a commercial surrogacy arrangement the child is often unaware, and left so, of their origins and heritage by the intended parents who seek to fully integrate them into their family and their own family narrative. The International Convention on the Rights of the Child confirms that every child has the right to know their heritage. In cases where the child is born of a donor egg and a donor sperm this may not be possible and as the surrogate has effectively incubated the foetus or the egg that was implanted in gestational surrogacy questions arise as to whether the surrogate's heritage has any bearing on the child born of the commercial surrogacy arrangement (Alexandra Harland, 2021). For traditional surrogacy, where the surrogate contributes the egg, then it is arguable that the child born of the surrogacy arrangement should have a right to know the heritage of the surrogate as part of their ancestry and lineage. In these instances, denying the child the knowledge of their heritage represents a particular ethical challenge and is arguably not advisable and ethically wrong. In contrast to this where the intended parents are the contributors of the biological genome, they may wish to forget that surrogacy was the pathway to having their child as the child is 100% the product of their biology; the intended parents may rightly ignore concerns about the ancestry and cultural heritage of the surrogate that the child may wish to know at some point in time.

Such concerns may become a problem when seeking to obtain legal recognition for the child and the intended parents may face some difficulty if the surrogate mother is recorded on the birth certificate (Albornoz, 2019). Ethical questions then arise as to the child's right to know and understand their surrogate even though there may be no biological connection beyond carrying them to term under the surrogacy arrangement. Upon reaching adulthood the child may seek to understand their heritage or to know the person who carried them to term (Goswami, 2015). However, when the child has not reached adulthood the ethical considerations and protections seek to understand what is in the best interests of the child.

Best Interests of the Child: Ethical Considerations and Legal Protections

What is in the best interest of the child usually has no bearing on what the parents may want or need. In many Western countries the rights of the child are considered by the courts to be paramount and the child's right to know the identity and origins of the surrogate mother may outweigh the parents' desire for it to remain confidential. Any circumstances that deliver withholding from the child of the heritage and the way they came into existence would represent a denial of rights and therefore an ethical concern. It would appear that the most ethically appropriate way of dealing with such a situation would be to answer the questions truthfully when, and if, asked.

Commercial Surrogacy and Social Justice

Ethical Issues of Accessibility: Who Can Afford Commercial Surrogacy?

While it may be argued that commercial surrogacy is freely available to anyone who wishes to undertake such an arrangement, it is an expensive process. The fact that commercial surrogacy is expensive means that it is not available to everybody equally. This disproportionately favours the wealthy who can afford such processes and therefore limits access based on the availability of resources and finances. Although it is likely an unintentional side effect of the commercialisation of surrogacy, the economic feature and expense create an unfair distribution of availability and access. What this in effect does is to exacerbate existing social inequalities and act as an economic barrier to access for the poor. Moreover, when the poor access commercial surrogacy, it is usually as the surrogate for financial reasons. The financial need of the surrogate is then leveraged by the other parties to the business of commercial surrogacy for their advantage (Limon, 2016). Other issues also arise around discrimination with respect to access to surrogacy. In some circumstances, discrimination based on race, sexual orientation, marital status, disability, or health may influence who can access commercial surrogacy. In particular, the sexual orientation, or marital status of individuals, often affects the ability of surrogates or intended parents to participate in surrogacy arrangements. These are often the results of moralistic judgements embedded within legislative provisions in different jurisdictions. Collectively, these issues combine to create barriers to access to commercial surrogacy based on wealth, health, race, religion, marital status, or sexual orientation, which exacerbates social inequality and reinforces social stratification in favour of the wealthy.

Potential Solutions to Disparities in Access and Social Justice

In an egalitarian society, all persons would have access on an equal basis to the things that bring fulfilment and human flourishing. In addressing the problem of social stratification one potential solution may be to regulate commercial surrogacy to enable it to be more widely available to persons who might otherwise not be able to afford it. This could come in the form of government subsidies or insurance coverage for surrogacy costs similar to the way fertility treatments are covered in various jurisdictions. Creating an ethical framework for commercial surrogacy is also advisable to address the systemic and entrenched structural problems around access and inclusion and to ensure that the surrogates are adequately compensated for not only their time and effort but also the potential risks involved in the surrogacy process. Ultimately, strong legislative support in each jurisdiction and the lowering of costs for surrogacy will stop favouring the wealthy in accessing successful surrogacy arrangements and reduce the driving of surrogacy towards more predatory and exploitative models.

Regulation and Ethical Standards in Commercial Surrogacy

The Role of Law in Regulating Ethical Conduct

In an unregulated market, where no protections are in place, relying on market forces to protect individual rights has proven ineffective over time. It would be reasonable to assume that relying solely on market forces to protect the parties involved in commercial surrogacy will also have the same outcome if the area is not adequately regulated. To ensure protection of individual rights, in particular those of the surrogate mother and child, the most appropriate pathway to achieving socially just operation within the commercial surrogacy market is the inclusion of embedded ethical controls (Drabiak et al., 2007). This can only occur if legislatures in each jurisdiction are willing to enact legislation that protects both the surrogate mother and the child born of the surrogacy arrangement and entrenches ethical principles to ensure socially just outcomes. Properly framed legislation that is based on the principles set out in the International Convention on the Rights of the Child (Unicef), and International Covenant on Civil and Political Rights, would represent a movement towards a more ethically aligned commercial surrogacy industry. This is because following the principles set out in these international treaties automatically prioritises the rights of vulnerable persons and individuals and would help foster a safer industry for all involved.

Best Practices and Ethical Guidelines: Ensuring Ethical Surrogacy Arrangements

In the absence of supportive legislative frameworks, it may be possible to develop a set of universal best practice guidelines for use by medical practitioners and those involved in healthcare around surrogacy. While not providing an overarching protective framework as achievable with a solid legislative framework, best practice guidelines could help create safer spaces within hospitals to facilitate the practice of surrogacy, and in particular the surrogate. Any reform, or creation, of best practice guidelines around commercial surrogacy should include ethical considerations around bodily autonomy, informed personal consent, self-determination, coercion, and the surrogate ability to choose what direction the healthcare around the pregnancy should follow. Additionally, the surrogate should have the right at any point to withdraw from the contract and keep the child born of the agreement.

Section 4: Conclusion

Commercial surrogacy presents a multifaceted ethical landscape that demands a nuanced and holistic approach. At its core, the practice challenges traditional notions of autonomy, informed consent, and the commodification of human reproductive capacities. While surrogacy offers intended parents a pathway to parenthood, it often exposes surrogates to vulnerabilities shaped by socioeconomic inequalities, power imbalances, and inadequate legal protections. These ethical dilemmas are further compounded in transnational arrangements, where disparities in healthcare standards and compensation amplify risks to the surrogates and children.

Addressing these challenges requires a balance between ensuring reproductive freedom and safeguarding against exploitation. Ethical frameworks must incorporate principles of justice, equity, and autonomy, while recognising the cultural, economic, and gendered dynamics that underpin surrogacy practices. Regulatory mechanisms, both national and international, are essential to standardise protections, ensure fair compensation, and prevent exploitation, particularly in economically disadvantaged contexts. Moreover, the development of best practices and ethical guidelines can provide clarity and support to healthcare professionals and stakeholders engaged in surrogacy arrangements.

Ultimately, the ethical viability of commercial surrogacy hinges on its ability to respect the dignity and rights of all involved—surrogates, intended parents, and the children born from these arrangements. By fostering a collaborative, equitable, and transparent approach, society can navigate the complex ethical terrain of commercial surrogacy while promoting social justice and human flourishing.

Notes

1. This has some correlation with the criminal law concept of *Mens Rea*, where the guilty mind must have had the intent to do wrong, and absent intent there can be no guilt for non-strict liability offences.
2. This is still applied when assisting an injured person if some harm is done accidentally there is no liability.
3. Some studies have found that in some commercial settings (the United States in particular) the motive to become a surrogate is altruistic, not financial.

References

Abdullah, F. M. (2019). Legal and ethical aspects beyond commercial surrogacy: Modern form of human trafficking. *Journal of Legal, Ethical and Regulatory Issues*, *22*, 1.

Abrams, P. (2015). The bad mother: Stigma, abortion and surrogacy. *Journal of Law, Medicine & Ethics*, *43*(2), 179–191.

Albornoz, M. M. (2019). Chapter 33, Parentage and international surrogacy-common solutions for a contentious issue? In T. John & R. Gulati, & B. Koehler (Eds.), *The Elgar Companion to the Hague Conference on Private International Law*. Edward Elgar Publishing. https://ssrn.com/abstract=3396176

Alexandra Harland, J. (2021). Surrogacy, identity, parentage and children's rights–Through the eyes of a child. *Family Court Review*, *59*(1), 121–130.

Alghrani, A., & Purshouse, C. (2019). Damages for reproductive negligence: Commercial surrogacy on the NHS? *The Law Quarterly Review, 135, 405.*

Anleu, S. R. (1992). Surrogacy: For love but not for money? *Gender & Society*, *6*(1), 30–48.

Arvidsson, A., Vauquline, P., Johnsdotter, S., & Essén, B. (2017). Surrogate mother – Praiseworthy or stigmatized: A qualitative study on perceptions of surrogacy in Assam, India. *Global Health Action*, *10*(1), 1328890. https://doi.org/10.1080/16549716.2017.1328890

Bentham, J. (1789). *An introduction to the principles of morals and legislation*. Clarendon Press. http://dx.doi.org/10.1093/oseo/instance.00077240

Ber, R. (2000). Ethical issues in gestational surrogacy. *Theoretical Medicine and Bioethics*, *21*, 153–169.

Butler, J., & Trouble, G. (1990). Feminism and the subversion of identity. *Gender Trouble*, *3*(1), 3–17.

Cherry, A. L. (2014). The rise of the reproductive brothel in the global economy: Some thoughts on reproductive tourism, autonomy, and justice. *University of Pennsylvania Journal of Law and Social Change*, *17*, 257.

Cutajar, J. (2022). The commodification of family: The multilayered harms of surrogacy. In R. Baikady, S. Sajid, J. Przeperski, V. Nadesan, M. R. Islam, & J. Gao (Eds.), *The Palgrave handbook of global social problems* (pp. 1–20). Palgrave Macmillan. https://doi.org/10.1007/978-3-030-68127-2_88-1

Drabiak, K., Wegner, C., Fredland, V., & Helft, P. R. (2007). Ethics, law, and commercial surrogacy: A call for uniformity. *Journal of Law, Medicine & Ethics*, *35*(2), 300–309.

Ellenbogen, A., Feldberg, D., & Lokshin, V. (2021). Surrogacy: A worldwide demand. Implementation and ethical considerations. *Gynecological and Reproductive Endocrinology and Metabolism*, *2*, 66–73.

Fabbo, A. (2020). Legal issues (surrogacy laws, informed consent). In A. Esquinas & N. Vargas (Eds.), *Ventilatory support and oxygen therapy in elder, palliative and end-of-life care patients* (pp. 325–336). Springer. https://doi.org/10.1007/978-3-030-26664-6_37

Frati, P., La Russa, R., Santurro, A., Fineschi, B., Di Paolo, M., Scopetti, M., Turillazzi, E., & Fineschi, V. (2021). Bioethical issues and legal frameworks of surrogacy: A global perspective about the right to health and dignity. *European Journal of Obstetrics & Gynecology and Reproductive Biology*, *258*, 1–8.

Goswami, G. K. (2015). The genetic truth of surrogate parentage. *Medico-Legal Journal*, *83*(4), 188–193.

Hofman, D. L. (2008). Mama's baby, daddy's maybe: A state-by-state survey of surrogacy laws and their disparate gender impact. *William Mitchell Law Review*, *35*, 449.

Humbyrd, C. (2009). Fair trade international surrogacy. *Developing World Bioethics*, *9*(3), 111–118.

Jacobson, H., & Rozée, V. (2022). Inequalities in (trans) national surrogacy: A call for examining complex lived realities with an empirical lens. *International Journal of Comparative Sociology*, *63*(5–6), 285–303.
Jefford, S. (2020). *More than just a baby*.
Kant, I., & Schneewind, J. B. (2002). *Groundwork for the metaphysics of morals*. Yale University Press.
Kulkarni, R. (2015). Ethical dilemmas in surrogacy. *Journal of Medical Humanities*, *7*(1). https://hekint.org/2017/01/30/ethical-dilemmas-in-surrogacy/
Lamba, N., Jadva, V., Kadam, K., & Golombok, S. (2018). The psychological well-being and prenatal bonding of gestational surrogates. *Human Reproduction*, *33*(4), 646–653.
Laufer-Ukeles, P. (2018). The disembodied womb: Pregnancy, informed consent, and surrogate motherhood. *North Carolina Journal of International Law*, *43*, 96.
Lemmens, T., Martin, A. F., Lee, I. B., & Milne, C. (2017). *Regulating creation: The law, ethics, and policy of assisted human reproduction*. University of Toronto Press.
Limon, C. (2016). From surrogacy to ectogenesis: Reproductive justice and equal opportunity in neoliberal times. *Australian Feminist Studies*, *31*(88), 203–219.
Mele, A. R. (1995). *Autonomous agents: From self-control to autonomy*. Oxford University Press.
Mill, J. S. (2017). *Utilitarianism: With related remarks from mill's other writings*. Hackett Publishing.
Panitch, V. (2017). Global surrogacy: Exploitation to empowerment. In *Gender justice and development: Vulnerability and empowerment* (pp. 97–112). Routledge.
Resnik, D. B. (1998). The commodification of human reproductive materials. *Journal of Medical Ethics*, *24*(6), 388–393.
Rowe, C. J., & Broadie, S. (2002). *Nicomachean ethics*. Oxford University Press.
Scott, E. S. (2009). Surrogacy and the politics of commodification. *Law & Contemporary Problems*, *72*, 109.
Shapiro, J. (2014). For a feminist considering surrogacy, is compensation really the key question. *Washington Law Review*, *89*, 1345.
Unicef. Convention on the rights of the child. https://www.unicef.org/child-rights-convention/convention-text-childrens-version
Vertommen, S., & Barbagallo, C. (2022). The in/visible wombs of the market: The dialectics of waged and unwaged reproductive labour in the global surrogacy industry. *Review of International Political Economy*, *29*(6), 1945–1966.
Wilkinson, S. (2003). The exploitation argument against commercial surrogacy. *Bioethics*, *17*(2), 169–187.
Writing Group on behalf of the ESHRE Ethics Committee, Shenfield, F., Tarlatzis, B., Baccino, G., Bounartzi, T., Frith, L., Pennings, G., Provoost, V., Vermeulen, N., & Mertes, H. (2025). Ethical considerations on surrogacy†. Human reproduction (Oxford, England), 40(3), 420–425. https://doi.org/10.1093/humrep/deaf006

4 Surrogacy Practice Healthcare Guidelines and Policies

Section 1: The Importance of Surrogacy Practice Healthcare Guidelines

Surrogacy is a multifaceted arrangement that involves medical, legal, ethical, and emotional considerations. Given its complexity, the success of a surrogacy arrangement relies on well-established surrogacy regulations, policies, and protocols. In the healthcare sector, the surrogacy practice healthcare guidelines, policies, and/or protocols also play a crucial role in shaping regulations and laws, affecting the protection and well-being of all parties to the process. Surrogacy practice guidelines in the healthcare sector are designed to support, protect, and promote the health and welfare of everyone involved, whether in altruistic or commercial surrogacy arrangements, making them a standard across all surrogacy types. Strict adherence to the surrogacy practice healthcare guidelines is essential for the success and safety of surrogacy arrangements. Current standard surrogacy practice healthcare guidelines include:

- The Code of Practice by the Human Fertilisation and Embryology Authority (HFEA) in the United Kingdom
- Practice Guidance by the American Society for Reproductive Medicine (ASRM) in the United States
- Ethical Guidelines on the Use of Assisted Reproductive Technology by the National Health and Medical Research Council (NHMRC) in Australia
- Advice and Guidelines for Gamete and Embryo Donation and Surrogacy by the Advisory Committee on Assisted Reproductive Technology (ACART) in New Zealand
- Surrogacy Guidelines by The Australian and New Zealand Infertility Counsellors Association (ANZICA).

The primary goal of the surrogacy practice healthcare guidelines is to effectively govern the complex process of arranging surrogacy for surrogates, intended parents, and surrogate children.

Ensuring the Health and Safety of the Surrogate

The health and safety of surrogates is the subject of much global debate. Several studies have highlighted the potential health risks faced by surrogates, often linked

DOI: 10.4324/9781003511939-4

to financial exploitation (Panitch, 2013; Trowse & Cooper, 2018). For instance, a study by Attawet, Wang, and Sullivan (2022) found that surrogates in developing countries agreed to carry embryos inseminated with HIV-positive sperm in exchange for double pay, compared to carrying uninfected embryos. Although the advanced ART process shows a reduction and low risk of HIV transmission to surrogates and embryos (Khawcharoenporn & Sha, 2016), there remains a possibility of infection (Wang et al., 2011). This highlights the medical risks surrogates are willing to take for financial compensation. Evidently there is an urgent need to protect surrogates from financial exploitation and ensure that health professionals clearly explain the potential risks involved.

Other studies also suggest that surrogates are willing to take higher risks for the right price. Attawet, Wang, Farquhar, et al. (2022) highlighted the practice of offering additional compensation for multiple embryo implantation, typically requested by intended parents. This practice significantly increases the physical health risks associated with multiple pregnancies, including complications and long-term health consequences. It is imperative that surrogates are fully aware of these risks, which should be clearly explained by healthcare professionals.

Additionally, while some research suggests that surrogates may experience low emotional attachment to the baby, there is still the risk of resultant psychological issues. Beyond attachment, surrogates can encounter emotional and psychological challenges that must be acknowledged and addressed. These challenges may include stigmatisation due to cultural norms and lack of social acceptance and support, which can lead to depression and isolation (Arvidsson et al., 2017; Attawet, 2022). Stress is also a significant concern, particularly when surrogates are under pressure from financial responsibilities, the demands of the surrogacy process, or even the potential failure of the pregnancy, which could impact compensation in commercial arrangements (Attawet, Wang, & Sullivan, 2022).

The points mentioned above highlight the necessity of stringent health guidelines to safeguard the well-being of surrogates and ensure they are not exposed to undue harm. Comprehensive surrogacy practice healthcare guidelines are essential for preparing surrogates both physically and mentally for the demands of pregnancy and childbirth.

Key aspects of surrogacy practice healthcare guidelines to ensure the health and safety of surrogates include:

- **Pre-Surrogacy Health Screening**: Comprehensive medical and psychological screenings are conducted to ensure that the surrogate is in optimal health and capable of carrying a pregnancy to term. This includes testing for infectious diseases, genetic conditions, and overall health assessments to prevent any complications during pregnancy.
- **Surrogacy Medical Procedures**: Health practice guidelines in surrogacy ensure adherence to standard medical protocols. For instance, embryo transfer procedures and oocyte/sperm/embryo donation must comply with national health and medical standards in the respective country.

- **Ongoing Medical Care**: Throughout the pregnancy, surrogates require regular prenatal care in the same manner as non-surrogates. Health guidelines ensure surrogates receive routine check-ups, ultrasounds, and any necessary medical interventions. Continuous monitoring helps detect and manage potential health issues early, safeguarding both the surrogate's safety and foetal development.
- **Support Services**: Surrogacy can be emotionally demanding. Providing access to counselling and support groups for surrogates is crucial. These services help surrogates manage the emotional challenges of carrying a child for another family and ensure their mental health is supported throughout the process.
- **Ethical Oversight**: Ethical considerations are integral to the surrogacy process. Health guidelines must enforce ethical standards to ensure that surrogates are treated with respect and dignity. This includes informed consent, the right to autonomy, and protection against any form of coercion or exploitation.

Safeguarding the Interests of Intended Parents

Surrogacy practice healthcare guidelines are not only vital for the surrogate but also play a crucial role in protecting the interests of the intended parents. The surrogacy practice healthcare guidelines ensure that the entire surrogacy process is carried out in a safe, ethical, and transparent manner, providing intended parents with confidence and peace of mind. By adhering to surrogacy practice protocols, intended parents can be assured that the surrogate's well-being, the health of the baby, and the legal and ethical aspects of the arrangement are being carefully managed. This structured approach minimises potential risks and uncertainties, allowing intended parents to focus on their journey to parenthood with greater assurance and confidence. Key aspects of surrogacy practice healthcare guidelines designed to safeguard the interests of intended parents include:

- **Screening Intended Parents**: Screening is conducted to assess intended parents' physical, emotional, and financial readiness for the surrogacy journey. This screening helps to ensure that intended parents are fully prepared for the responsibilities of parenthood and capable of providing a stable and supportive environment for the child.
- **Ensuring the Health and Safety of the Surrogate**: Surrogacy practice healthcare guidelines ensure that the surrogate undergoes thorough medical and psychological screening, receives proper prenatal and postnatal care, and follows best practices throughout the pregnancy. This safeguards both the surrogate's health and the well-being of the baby, giving intended parents peace of mind.
- **Minimising Legal and Ethical Risks**: Surrogacy practice healthcare guidelines help navigate the complex legal and ethical landscape of surrogacy. They ensure that all parties are informed and that the process adheres to the legal requirements, reducing the risk of disputes or legal complications.
- **Protecting the Health of the Baby**: Adhering to surrogacy practice healthcare guidelines ensures that the pregnancy is managed according to the highest

available medical standards, reducing the risk of complications and raising the likelihood that the baby will be born healthy.

- **Managing Expectations and Responsibilities**: Guidelines help clearly outline the roles and responsibilities of both the surrogate and the intended parents. This includes managing expectations around the medical process, communication, and post-birth arrangements.
- **Supporting Emotional and Psychological Well-Being**: Surrogacy can be emotionally complex for all parties involved. Guidelines ensure that intended parents and surrogates receive the necessary psychological support, which can help in managing the emotional challenges and stress associated with the surrogacy journey.
- **Ensuring Ethical Practices**: Health guidelines help maintain ethical standards in surrogacy arrangements, ensuring that the surrogate is treated with respect, fairness, and dignity and that her rights are protected throughout the process. This ethical oversight is crucial for intended parents to feel confident in the integrity of the surrogacy arrangement.

Protecting the Health of the Child

The health and well-being of the child is a paramount concern in any surrogacy arrangement, making it crucial to adhere to surrogacy practice healthcare guidelines. These guidelines ensure that the medical practices involved in conception, pregnancy, and childbirth are of the highest standard, minimising risks to the child. Important elements include:

- **Genetic Screening of Donors and Intended Parents**: If the surrogacy involves egg or sperm donation, it is important the parties are provided with options for screening and sufficient information to make informed decisions. This can help to minimise the risk of passing on negative hereditary conditions or infections to the child.
- **Embryo Transfer Protocols and Procedures**: Creating and transferring embryos must adhere to strict medical protocols. This includes using ARTs and ensuring the laboratory environment is sterile and optimised for embryo development. The number of embryos transferred must also comply with the guidelines to minimise the risk of multiple gestations, which could impact the health of both the surrogate and the child.
- **Prenatal Care and Monitoring**: Regular prenatal check-ups and monitoring of foetal development are crucial. Health guidelines ensure that the surrogate receives appropriate medical care, including nutritional advice and supplements, to support a healthy pregnancy.
- **Birth Planning**: Planning for the birth is an integral part of the surrogacy process. Health guidelines ensure that a comprehensive birth plan is in place, considering the surrogate's health, the intended parents' preferences, and the baby's safety. This includes decisions about delivery methods, pain management, emergency procedures, and whether the intended parents are involved.

Studies have shown that in transnational commercial surrogacy arrangements, there is often a preference for caesarean sections (C-sections). This practice may become standard to accommodate the intended parents' schedules, especially if they need to plan their return journey to their home country (Attawet, Wang, & Sullivan, 2022; Hovav, 2020). However, the health and well-being of the child and surrogate should take precedence over contractual demands. Healthcare professionals should advocate for the health of both the child and the surrogate, while also respecting their autonomy. Ensuring that medical decisions are made based on health benefits rather than convenience is essential for maintaining ethical standards in surrogacy arrangements.

The Role of Health Professionals

Health professionals, including fertility specialists, obstetricians, and psychologists, play a critical role in the surrogacy process. Their expertise and adherence to surrogacy health guidelines ensure that the surrogacy journey is safe, ethical, and successful. Key responsibilities include:

- Medical Oversight: Fertility specialists and obstetricians provide essential medical oversight, ensuring that all procedures are performed correctly and that the health of both the surrogate and the baby is monitored throughout the pregnancy. Healthcare staff must also be knowledgeable about the specific procedures and care requirements associated with surrogacy during delivery and hospitalisation, which can differ from those of non-surrogate pregnancies. This specialised awareness is crucial for providing appropriate care and support throughout the surrogacy journey for surrogates, intended parents, and surrogate babies.
- Counselling and Support: Psychologists and counsellors offer emotional support to surrogates and intended parents, helping them navigate the complex emotions associated with surrogacy.
- Adherence to Ethical Guidelines: Health professionals are bound by a code of ethics and professional practice that governs their conduct throughout the surrogacy process. This includes ensuring informed consent, maintaining confidentiality, and upholding the highest standards of care. Their commitment to these ethical principles is crucial for protecting the rights and well-being of all parties involved and for fostering trust in the surrogacy process.

Comprehensive surrogacy practice healthcare guidelines are indispensable in creating a supportive and secure environment for surrogates and intended parents. The surrogacy practice healthcare guidelines ensure the success and ethical integrity of surrogacy arrangements, ultimately contributing to the birth of healthy children and the well-being of all parties involved (Figure 4.1).

The surrogacy practice healthcare guidelines may be categorised into three distinct phases: pre-surrogacy (discussed in Section 2: Surrogacy Practice Healthcare Guidelines: Pre-Surrogacy Arrangements), during surrogacy (discussed in Section 3: Surrogacy Practice Healthcare Guidelines: During-Surrogacy Arrangement), and

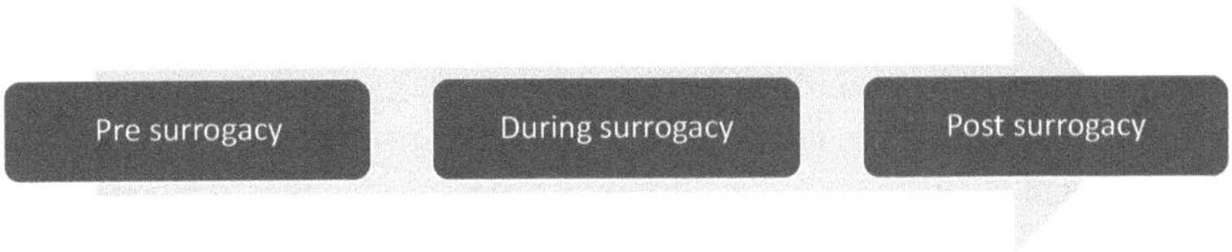

Figure 4.1 The phrase of surrogacy practice health guideline

post-surrogacy (discussed in Section 4: Surrogacy Practice Healthcare Guidelines: Post-Surrogacy), as outlined by the HFEA, ASRM, NHMRC, ACART, and ANZICA surrogacy practice guidelines. The details and requirements of each phase will be discussed in the following section, offering a systematic approach to safeguard health and ensure the success of surrogacy arrangements.

Section 2: Surrogacy Practice Healthcare Guidelines: Pre-Surrogacy Arrangements

Pre-Surrogacy Arrangement for Surrogates

The medical aspects of pre-surrogacy arrangements are crucial for safeguarding the health and well-being of all parties involved, including the surrogate, the intended parents, and the future child. Comprehensive medical assessments are essential to identify and mitigate potential health risks, ensuring a smooth and successful surrogacy journey. These assessments encompass a wide range of evaluations and screenings designed to ensure the physical and mental suitability of both surrogates and intended parents and/or genetic contributors.

Eligibility Criteria for Surrogates

Before the detailed medical assessments, surrogates must meet specific eligibility criteria to ensure they are suitable candidates for the surrogacy process. Each country has specific criteria with respect to surrogacy regulation and consequent eligibility to undertake the process. The main eligibility criteria across jurisdictions include:

AGE

Surrogates are generally required to be between the ages of 21 and 40, though this can vary depending on the specific legal requirements of each jurisdiction. For example, in most Australian states, surrogacy laws mandate a minimum age of 25 for surrogates (see the supplementary page for information on Surrogacy Act in Australia), while in the United States, the legal age range is typically from 21 to 45 years (Legal Professional Group [LPG], 2024). In Thailand, the age requirement for surrogates is between 20 and 40 years old (Tapiromkul & Wongbandit, 2014). The age ranges are considered optimal to ensure the surrogate's physical health and to support a successful pregnancy outcome.

CITIZENSHIP OF SURROGATES

Surrogates are generally required to be citizens or legal residents of the country where the surrogacy arrangement is taking place. This is to ensure that the surrogate is protected under local laws and that the surrogacy process adheres to the country's legal, ethical, and moral standards. Some jurisdictions may also require that the surrogate has lived in the country for a certain period before entering into a surrogacy agreement.

REPRODUCTIVE HISTORY

- **Previous Pregnancy**: in countries where surrogacy is legal, such as Australia, the United States, the United Kingdom, and Canada, surrogacy laws typically require that surrogates have successfully completed at least one prior pregnancy. Some jurisdictions may specifically require that the surrogate has given birth to her own child, while others do not impose this requirement (see the supplementary page for information on Surrogacy Act in Australia). Therefore, it is essential to verify the eligibility criteria in the relevant jurisdiction before proceeding with the surrogacy arrangement. This provision is a well-highlighted component of surrogacy laws, supporting surrogacy practice healthcare guidelines to ensure that surrogates have demonstrated their ability to carry a pregnancy to term without significant complications. This requirement is crucial for safeguarding the health and well-being of both the surrogate and the intended child and aims to provide a strong foundation for safe and effective surrogacy practices.
- **Uncomplicated Pregnancy History**: it is essential that surrogates have a history of carrying a pregnancy to term without complications. This is not merely a recommendation but rather a critical requirement emphasised in the pre-screening process of surrogacy practice healthcare guidelines. Ensuring an uncomplicated pregnancy history is vital for minimising risks and ensuring a smooth surrogacy journey. This measure significantly enhances the safety and effectiveness of the surrogacy process, protecting the health of both the surrogate and the intended child.

Pre-Surrogacy Arrangement: Medical Assessment for Surrogates

Medical assessment of surrogates before entering into a surrogacy arrangement is vital to ensuring their readiness for a successful surrogacy outcome. A comprehensive medical history review and physical examination are essential to identifying any potential health risks that could impact the surrogacy process. Typically, the pre-surrogacy medical assessment in surrogates includes the following key components:

Pre-Surrogacy Medical Screening

- **Screening for Sexually Transmitted Infections (STIs)**: Testing for STIs such as HIV, hepatitis B and C, syphilis, chlamydia, and gonorrhoea is crucial to prevent transmission to the foetus or to the intended parents.

- **Genetic Disorders**: Assessing for any genetic disorders that could pose a risk during pregnancy or affect the child's health.
- **Infectious Diseases**: Screening for other infectious diseases to ensure the surrogate is in optimal health.

REPRODUCTIVE HISTORY EXAMINATION

Evaluating the surrogate's reproductive history provides insight into her ability to carry a pregnancy to term without complications. Key considerations include:

- **Previous Pregnancies**: Medically, surrogates should ideally have had at least one uncomplicated, term pregnancy to demonstrate their capacity for a successful pregnancy. However, this considered ideal is not always a requirement under surrogacy laws. Therefore, from a personal autonomy perspective, anyone can choose to be a surrogate without having had a child previously.
- **Pregnancy Outcomes**: Analysing the outcomes of previous pregnancies helps in predicting potential complications and ensuring the surrogate's suitability.

PRECONCEPTION TESTING

Preconception testing involves several crucial assessments to confirm the surrogate's readiness for pregnancy:

- **Blood Type and Rh Factor**: Determining blood type and Rh factor is essential for managing potential Rh incompatibility issues.
- **Cervical Cancer Screening**: Regular screenings for cervical cancer are necessary to ensure reproductive health.
- **Mammogram**: Conducting mammograms helps in detecting any breast abnormalities that could affect pregnancy.
- **Titres for Varicella and Rubella**: Ensuring immunity to varicella (chickenpox) and rubella is vital to protect the foetus from congenital infections.
- **Urine Drug Screen**: Screening for drug use is important to maintain a healthy environment for the developing foetus.

UTERINE EVALUATION

Assessing the surrogate's uterine cavity is crucial to confirm its suitability for pregnancy. This may involve procedures such as hysteroscopy or ultrasound to detect any abnormalities that could affect oocyte implantation or pregnancy maintenance.

PSYCHOLOGICAL READINESS

Most surrogacy laws outline key requirements for surrogates, such as age and a history of previous pregnancies. Although psychological readiness is not a legal requirement, it plays a crucial role in the surrogacy process and is strongly recommended in the pre-screening guidelines for surrogacy practice. This screening is essential for preparing surrogates to maintain mental and emotional stability, ensuring they are equipped to manage the psychological demands of the surrogacy journey.

Although screenings are recommended to safeguard surrogates, their implementation will depend on the jurisdiction and the decision-making of the involved parties.

Pre-Surrogacy Arrangement for Intended Parents

Eligibility Criteria for Intended Parents

Intended parents must also meet certain criteria to ensure they are prepared for the surrogacy process and the responsibilities of parenthood. These criteria should include:

AGE

Intended parents must be of legal age to enter into a surrogacy agreement and should demonstrate the maturity and stability required for parenting. While surrogacy laws typically mandate a minimum age of 25 for both the surrogate and the intended parents, some jurisdictions do not specify this condition. Therefore, it is advisable to consult with a legal expert before proceeding with the surrogacy arrangement to ensure compliance with local regulations.

CITIZENSHIP OF INTENDED PARENTS

- **Domestic Surrogacy**: In many countries, surrogacy is primarily available to citizens or legal residents. Intended parents are often required to be citizens of, have a connection to, or have permanent residency in the country where the surrogacy is to occur. This ensures that the intended parents are subject to local laws and that the child born through surrogacy will have a recognisable citizenship status.
- **International Surrogacy**: For intended parents engaging in international surrogacy, citizenship requirements can be more complex. Some jurisdictions restrict surrogacy to their citizens only, while others may allow foreign nationals to engage in surrogacy under specific conditions. For example, Ukraine is one of the few countries that permit commercial surrogacy for foreign intended parents. The legal framework stipulates that intended parents must be a heterosexual married couple to be eligible for commercial surrogacy in Ukraine. In Thailand, surrogacy is prohibited for foreign intended parents; however, if one member of the couple is Thai, they may be eligible, provided they have been married for at least three years. Engaging in international surrogacy can exponentially complicate the child's citizenship status. Therefore, careful legal planning is required to ensure the child's citizenship and legal parentage are properly recognised.

HEALTH STATUS

- **Physical Health**: Intended parents should be in good physical health, ensuring they can provide a healthy environment for the child.
- **Mental Health**: Intended parents should be mentally and emotionally stable and prepared to handle the stresses and responsibilities of parenting.

Pre-Surrogacy Assessment: Medical Assessment for Intended Parents and Genetic Contributors

MEDICAL HISTORY AND PHYSICAL EXAMINATION

Intended parents and genetic contributors undergo comprehensive medical evaluations to ensure they are in good health and capable of proceeding with ART procedures. This includes a detailed review of their medical histories and physical examinations.

INFECTIOUS DISEASE SCREENING

Screening for infectious diseases is essential to minimise the risk of transmission to the surrogate or foetus. Tests for HIV, hepatitis, syphilis, and other relevant infections are conducted to ensure a healthy surrogacy process.

GENETIC SCREENING

Genetic screening is crucial for identifying potential genetic risks that could affect the child's health. This includes:

- **Common Genetic Disorders**: Screening for disorders such as cystic fibrosis, spinal muscular atrophy, and thalassemia.
- **Expanded Carrier Screening**: Recommended to identify carriers of genetic conditions, helping to assess and mitigate potential risks.

PSYCHOLOGICAL READINESS

Similar to surrogates, intended parents undergo psychological assessments to ensure they are emotionally prepared for the surrogacy process and the responsibilities of parenting a child born through surrogacy.

Pre-surrogacy medical assessments for both surrogates and intended parents are a critical component of the surrogacy process, designed to ensure the health and well-being of surrogates, intended parents, and the future child. Through comprehensive screenings and evaluations, potential health risks can be identified and managed effectively, increasing the likelihood of a successful surrogacy outcome. These assessments, coupled with psychological and legal counselling, provide a solid foundation for a positive and well-supported surrogacy experience, ensuring that all parties are prepared for the emotional, physical, and legal challenges that may arise.

Section 3: Surrogacy Practice Healthcare Guidelines: During-Surrogacy Arrangement

Medical Procedures in a Surrogacy Process

The core procedure in a medical surrogacy process consists of informed consent, IVF procedures, and the protocols for embryo transfer (Figure 4.2).

Informed Consent

A crucial aspect of the medical surrogacy process is obtaining informed consent, which serves as a cornerstone of ethical surrogacy practices. Surrogacy health practice guidelines stress the importance of making sure that both surrogates and intended parents are fully informed about the medical, psychological, and ethical dimensions of surrogacy before any agreements are made. This process includes comprehensive counselling sessions where healthcare providers thoroughly explain the procedures, potential risks, benefits, and responsibilities involved in a surrogacy arrangement. It is essential that surrogates give their consent voluntarily, free from any form of coercion, and with a clear understanding of their rights and the implications of the surrogacy arrangement. Informed consent ensures that all parties involved are making well-informed decisions and are adequately prepared for the journey ahead. An example of comprehensive surrogacy guidelines is the HFEA Code of Practice from the United Kingdom (hfea-draft-code-of-practice-9th-edition-consultation-version.pdf [https://www.hfea.gov.uk/media/2565/hfea-draft-code-of-practice-9th-edition-consultation-version.pdf]). The HFEA guidelines emphasise the importance of informed consent, thorough medical screening, and ongoing psychological support. They require that surrogates undergo rigorous medical evaluations to ensure their suitability for pregnancy and mandate regular prenatal care to monitor the health of the surrogate and the foetus. The HFEA guidelines also stress the importance of ethical practices, ensuring that surrogates participate voluntarily and receive fair compensation.

Another example is the guidelines issued by the ASRM (ASRM Practice Guidance | American Society for Reproductive Medicine | ASRM [https://www.asrm.org/practice-guidance/]) in the United States, which emphasise medical standards,

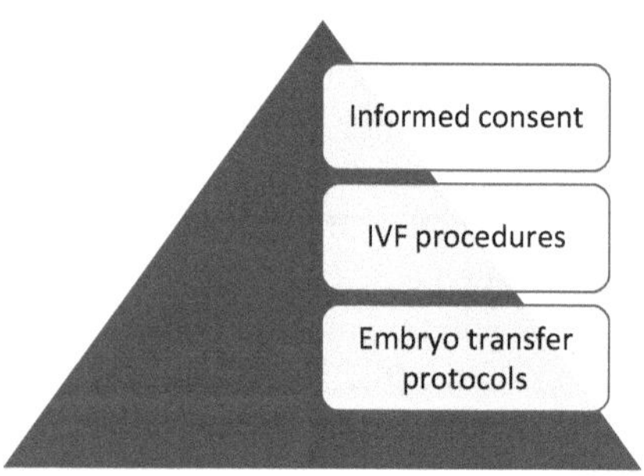

Figure 4.2 Procedures in the surrogacy process

ethical considerations, and the importance of psychological support. These guidelines mandate comprehensive medical screening and ongoing care for surrogates, aligning closely with the standards set by the HFEA. Informed consent is emphasised, with detailed counselling provided to ensure that surrogates and intended parents understand the medical procedures, risks, and ethical implications. The ARSM guidelines also stress the importance of protecting the surrogate's autonomy and ensuring fair compensation practices.

In Australia, NHMRC (Ethical guidelines on the use of assisted reproductive technology | NHMRC [https://www.nhmrc.gov.au/about-us/publications/art]) provides ethical guidelines on the use of assisted reproductive technology, including surrogacy. These guidelines emphasise informed consent, requiring comprehensive counselling for surrogates and intended parents. Medical care is a priority, with detailed protocols for screening and monitoring surrogates to ensure their health and the health of the foetus. The NHMRC guidelines also highlight the importance of ethical considerations, ensuring that surrogacy arrangements are conducted with respect for the dignity and autonomy of all parties involved.

In New Zealand, ACART provides the Advice and Guidelines for Gamete and Embryo Donation and Surrogacy (https://acart.health.govt.nz/assets/Uploads/ACART/Publications/Advice-and-Guidelines-for-Gamete-and-Embryo-Donation-and-Surrogacy.pdf), which focus on the ethical and legal aspects of surrogacy. These guidelines stress the importance of informed consent and comprehensive counselling for both surrogates and intended parents. Detailed medical care protocols are outlined to ensure the health and safety of the surrogate and the child. Ethical considerations are integral to the consent process, with guidelines designed to protect the surrogate's autonomy and rights in making decisions about procedures conducted on them.

In Australia and New Zealand, ANZICA offers the Surrogacy Guidelines (ANZICA-SURROGACY-GUIDELINES-OCTOBER-2022.pdf [fertilitysociety.com.au] [https://www.fertilitysociety.com.au/wp-content/uploads/ANZICA-SURROGACY-GUIDELINES-OCTOBER-2022.pdf]), which place significant emphasis on counselling procedures. Informed consent and best practices are key components of the counselling process, ensuring that surrogates and intended parents fully understand the procedures, are aware of the associated risks, and receive ongoing support throughout their surrogacy journey.

In Vitro Fertilisation (IVF) Surrogacy Procedures

The process of IVF in surrogacy is similar to conventional IVF, but it includes additional steps to accommodate the involvement of both the surrogate and the intended parents. It is a carefully coordinated journey that begins with an initial consultation involving all parties. During this consultation, thorough medical evaluations are conducted to assess the health and suitability of everyone involved. These evaluations are crucial for identifying any potential issues that could impact the success of the IVF process (see the supplementary page). Alongside these medical assessments, legal consultations are held to establish clear agreements that protect the rights and responsibilities of all parties, ensuring a smooth and well-understood process from the outset.

Once the legal and medical groundwork is established, the surrogate's body is prepared for embryo transfer. This preparation involves administering hormone treatments such as oestrogen and progesterone to build a thick and receptive uterine lining, which is essential for successful embryo implantation. While the surrogate is being prepared, the intended mother or an egg donor undergoes ovarian stimulation. This process involves taking fertility medications to stimulate the ovaries to produce multiple eggs, increasing the chances of retrieving viable eggs for fertilisation.

The next step is the egg retrieval process, where the matured eggs are collected from the intended mother or donor through a minor surgical procedure known as transvaginal ultrasound aspiration. This procedure is typically performed under sedation and involves using a needle to extract the eggs from the ovarian follicles.

Once the eggs are retrieved, they are fertilised with sperm from the intended father or a sperm donor in a laboratory setting. This fertilisation can occur through conventional IVF, where the eggs and sperm are combined and allowed to fertilise naturally, or through a more precise method called intracytoplasmic sperm injection (ICSI), where a single sperm is injected directly into an egg. The fertilised eggs, now embryos, are then cultured in a controlled environment for several days, usually until they reach the blastocyst stage, which is around five days after fertilisation.

During this time, intended parents may choose to have the embryos undergo preimplantation genetic testing (PGT). PGT is a sophisticated screening process that checks for genetic abnormalities, helping to ensure that only the healthiest embryos are selected for transfer. This step can be particularly important for parents who are concerned about hereditary conditions or who have experienced previous failed pregnancies.

When the embryos are ready, the actual embryo transfer to the surrogate's uterus is performed in accordance with the established embryo transfer protocol. This procedure is relatively simple and involves placing the selected embryo or embryos into the surrogate's uterus using a thin catheter. Despite its simplicity, this step is a critical moment in the surrogacy process, as it determines whether the establishment of the pregnancy will be successful.

The IVF process, as mentioned, is essentially the same for both surrogates and non-surrogates. Since IVF protocols are well established in assisted reproductive technology (ART), this book will not explore them in detail. Rather, it offers a brief overview of the key steps involved.

Embryo Transfer Protocols

It is not uncommon for intended parents, driven by a strong desire to achieve a successful pregnancy, to request the transfer of multiple embryos into the surrogate's uterus. Historically, it has been believed that transferring more than one embryo could enhance the likelihood that at least one will successfully implant and result in a viable pregnancy (Price, 1989). However, research has shown that this practice does not necessarily lead to better outcomes. Studies have demonstrated that the transfer of multiple embryos does not significantly increase the likelihood of achieving pregnancy compared to elective or single embryo transfer (eSET/SET) (Ma et al., 2022; Monteleone et al., 2018). Moreover, transferring multiple embryos increases the risk of multiple pregnancies, which can lead to complications such as preterm birth, low birth weight, and increased strain on the surrogate's health. In contrast, SETs have been found to offer similar pregnancy rates with far fewer complications, making it a safer and more effective approach in many cases. The standard practice of eSET/SET has been widely recommended by leading ART organisations, including the ASRM, NHMRC, HFEA, the Southern African Society of Reproductive Medicine and Gynaecological Endoscopy (SASREG), and others. This approach is advised, not only for non-surrogate pregnancies but also for surrogate pregnancies, as it optimises the health and well-being of both the surrogate and the child. However, the belief that transferring multiple embryos increases the chances of pregnancy may still persist, particularly in commercial surrogacy arrangements (Attawet, Wang, Farquhar, et al., 2022; White, 2017). It is therefore crucial for healthcare professionals and surrogacy guidelines to uphold ethical practices that prioritise the best outcomes for all parties involved.

Following the embryo transfer, the surrogate is provided with additional hormone support, typically in the form of progesterone, to help maintain the early stages of pregnancy. About two weeks after the transfer, a blood test is conducted to measure the levels of human chorionic gonadotropin (hCG), a hormone produced during pregnancy, to confirm whether the procedure was successful.

During the surrogacy process, informed consent is the cornerstone of the surrogacy process, requiring comprehensive counselling to ensure that all parties fully understand the medical, legal, and ethical aspects involved. This foundational step is not just a one-time event but part of an ongoing dialogue and collaboration among healthcare professionals, ethicists, and policymakers. This continuous exchange is vital for improving surrogacy practices and adapting to new challenges and advancements in the field. The IVF surrogacy journey, therefore, is not just about the initial agreements but also about the careful planning, coordination, and support that follow. With a multidisciplinary team guiding them, intended parents and surrogates can navigate this complex process, ultimately working together to achieve a successful and fulfilling surrogacy experience. Establishing and following comprehensive surrogacy practice healthcare guidelines are vital to optimise the surrogacy journey and ensure the health and well-being of the surrogate, intended parents, and children.

Pregnancy Surrogacy Monitoring and Care

Once a pregnancy is confirmed, the surrogate begins a phase of regular prenatal care, which is essential for monitoring the health of both them and the developing baby, much like in a non-surrogacy pregnancy. This care includes scheduled obstetric appointments, routine ultrasounds, and a variety of diagnostic tests to ensure the pregnancy is progressing normally. These check-ups are not just routine; they are vital touchpoints where healthcare providers can identify potential complications, such as gestational diabetes or pre-eclampsia, which require immediate attention and management through carefully crafted emergency protocols and contingency plans.

In addition to medical monitoring, the surrogate is guided through nutritional and lifestyle adjustments that support a healthy pregnancy. Healthcare providers offer detailed dietary recommendations to ensure that the surrogate is receiving the necessary nutrients, while also advising on physical activity and lifestyle modifications to promote overall well-being. This aspect of care is critical, as it helps to maintain the surrogate's health throughout the pregnancy and mirrors the care provided in non-surrogacy pregnancies. However, in surrogacy, there is an added layer of psychological counselling to address the unique emotional challenges that may arise, ensuring that the surrogate is supported holistically.

A key component of the surrogacy process is the ongoing emotional support provided to the surrogate. A fundamental element of the surrogacy process is the provision of ongoing emotional support to the surrogate. Research consistently highlights the importance of the relationship between the surrogate and the intended parents, noting that it plays a pivotal role in the surrogate's emotional well-being. This relationship is often viewed as a key determinant of the surrogate's experience, influencing not only her emotional state but also the perceived success of the surrogacy journey as a whole. The positive experiences that arise from a strong, supportive relationship can foster a sense of fulfilment and accomplishment for both the surrogate and the intended parents (Kneebone et al., 2022; Silvern & Cojocaru, 2022).

While the relationship between the surrogate and the intended parents is significant, it is crucial to recognise and address the broader context in which this relationship exists, including personal circumstances, societal attitudes, and cultural norms. These factors can profoundly impact the surrogate's emotional experience and overlooking them may result in insufficient support being received by the surrogate. Therefore, it is essential that healthcare professionals ensure that the emotional support and counselling provided to surrogates are comprehensive and responsive, addressing the full spectrum of their needs within this complex landscape.

Section 4: Surrogacy Practice Healthcare Guidelines: Post-Surrogacy

As the pregnancy reaches its conclusion, preparations for the surrogate's delivery are carefully coordinated, ensuring that all medical and logistical aspects are in place for a smooth and safe birth. Following the birth, the focus shifts to the legal aspects of the surrogacy arrangement. It is crucial to complete the legal process to ensure that the intended parents are recognised as the legal guardians of the child (see Chapter 2). Depending on the jurisdiction, this may involve additional steps such as obtaining court orders or finalising adoption procedures, which are vital for securing the intended parents' rights.

Throughout the surrogacy journey, strict adherence to legal agreements and guidelines is recommended. This ensures transparency and accountability, which are key to maintaining trust and ensuring the process unfolds smoothly. Detailed documentation of all medical and psychological care provided during the pregnancy must be meticulously maintained, serving legal purposes and ensuring the well-being of all parties involved—the surrogate, the intended parents, and the baby.

Post-Delivery Care

After childbirth, prioritising postpartum care for surrogates is just as important as it is for non-surrogates. This care includes regular medical check-ups to monitor physical recovery, address any complications, and provide necessary treatments. Guidelines for physical recovery, such as rest, nutrition, and appropriate medical care, are followed closely to ensure the surrogate's physical well-being. Beyond physical recovery, psychological support is crucial during this phase, helping the surrogate process the emotional aspects of relinquishing the baby. Interestingly, research has shown that many surrogates experience little to no struggle with this relinquishment (Yee & Librach, 2019). However, ongoing access to counselling and support networks is essential for managing any long-term emotional challenges.

After relinquishing the baby, research found that same-sex male couples and single men often develop long-lasting relationships with their surrogates, more so than heterosexual couples or single mothers (Yee & Librach, 2019). Maintaining a connection with the intended parents has been shown to contribute positively to the experiences of both parties and can be beneficial if the intended parents choose to disclose the surrogacy to their children in the future (Jefford, 2020).

The newborn also receives immediate and ongoing neonatal care, including initial health assessments, routine examinations, and vaccinations. These health guidelines ensure that the baby's development is regularly monitored from the outset. For the intended parents, this period is critical as they transition into their new roles. Adjustment counselling helps them bond with the newborn child and navigate the challenges of early parenthood, fostering a healthy parent-child relationship.

Long-Term Follow-Up and Support

The care provided during the post-surrogacy phase extends beyond the immediate post-birth period. Typically, women receive long-term follow-up after delivery, including periodic health check-ups to monitor their ongoing physical and emotional well-being. Generally speaking, the same approach can be applied to surrogates, ensuring that their health and well-being are consistently supported throughout the post-surrogacy phase. Continued access to support groups and counselling services ensures they have the necessary resources to manage any challenges that arise as they transition out of the surrogacy role. However, it is important to note that there are currently no reports or studies that provide findings on the utilisation or effectiveness of long-term follow-up services for surrogates.

For the intended parents and the child, regular check-ups are scheduled to ensure the child's development is on track and to address any health or developmental concerns, mirroring the care provided for non-surrogate babies. However, challenges can arise in cases where the surrogate baby is born overseas or through commercial surrogacy arrangements. In such situations, the child's welfare might be at risk due to not being fully recognised in the intended parents' country (Rotabi et al., 2017), which could lead to delays in accessing child benefits and healthcare services. The process of obtaining recognition for the child may therefore require legal steps to secure citizenship, adding complexity to ensuring the child's rights and status are properly secured (see Chapter 2). During this critical period, resources and support, including counselling if needed, must be provided to assist the family.

Legal and Ethical Oversight

The post-delivery phase also includes completing essential legal procedures to ensure the seamless transfer of parental rights from the surrogate to the intended parents. All necessary legal paperwork and court procedures need to be lodged, including detailed records maintained to ensure transparency and accountability. Ethical oversight remains in place throughout this phase to protect the rights and well-being of all parties involved. Mechanisms are established for resolving any conflicts or disputes promptly and fairly, ensuring that the process concludes smoothly.

In cases of commercial surrogacy, the complexity of these processes increases, particularly when considering the best interests of the child. Ensuring that all legal and ethical standards are met becomes even more critical in such situations, emphasising the importance of careful planning and professional support throughout the entire surrogacy process. Further details regarding the ethical and legal aspects of healthcare and commercial surrogacy are discussed in the following chapters.

Section 5: Best Practices and Recommendations

Research demonstrates that surrogates and intended parents often encounter significant challenges with healthcare providers, particularly within maternal and birth care services, primarily due to the lack of recognition of the legitimacy of surrogacy arrangements (Kneebone et al., 2024). These challenges are evident in healthcare settings where surrogacy services are either non-existent or inadequately supported, leading to instances where services are denied at the time of surrogacy delivery. In cases where hospitals proceed without specific surrogacy policies, the hospital system and healthcare staff frequently experience confusion regarding the appropriate care protocols. For example, Kneebone et al. (2024) highlights significant gaps in hospital policies in Australia. The study found that some hospitals have refused to provide services for surrogacy pregnancies, preventing the delivery of the baby, and there have been cases where a surrogate could not be discharged from the hospital without the baby, further complicating the care process. This confusion likely stems from a lack of understanding of surrogacy care or recognition of the complexity of the arrangement among healthcare providers, exacerbated by the absence of organisational surrogacy policies, leading to confusion or negative outcomes in the surrogacy care process. Other evidence, such as in the United Kingdom, shows that despite the Department of Health & Social Care establishing guidance to support healthcare professionals in the care of surrogates and intended parents during surrogacy births (Department of Health & Social Care, 2024), gaps in healthcare practice remain. These gaps have turned what should be a joyful event into a source of distress, leaving involved parties facing emotional strain and unresolved dilemmas (Edwards et al., 2023).

These issues underscore a critical gap in the education and training of healthcare professionals regarding surrogacy, which may have profound implications for the families involved. While national policy debates on surrogacy laws often dominate the discourse, the downstream effects, such as hospital policies and practices, merit equal attention. A more informed and supportive healthcare system, particularly within maternal and birth care services, could significantly enhance the experiences of both surrogates and intended parents and safeguard surrogates from unnecessary post-birth emotional trauma. Additionally, improved support within the healthcare system. within maternal and birth care services, could positively influence related areas such as healthcare funding and insurance, potentially leading to better rebate options and public sentiment towards surrogacy. Moreover, a well-educated healthcare system could facilitate more domestic surrogacy arrangements, thereby reducing the reliance on commercial surrogacy overseas.

By educating both the public and healthcare providers about surrogacy, we can create a supportive environment that benefits all parties involved.

To address these challenges, the following actions are recommended:

1 **Development of National Guidelines**: Establish comprehensive national guidelines for surrogacy healthcare policies, particularly within maternal and birth care services, clearly outlining the roles and responsibilities of healthcare providers, surrogates, and intended parents.
2 **Training and Education**: Implement targeted training programmes for healthcare professionals on surrogacy-related issues to ensure they are equipped to deliver appropriate and respectful care.
3 **Policy Implementation**: Advocate for hospitals to adopt and implement these national guidelines, with adjustments made to suit specific institutional contexts while maintaining core principles around healthcare delivery.
4 **Regular Review and Update**: Ensure that surrogacy policies are subject to regular reviews and updates to reflect evolving best practices and legal requirements.

Section 6: Conclusion

This chapter examined the essential aspects of healthcare in the surrogacy process, focusing on the intersection of medical practices, guidelines, and medico-ethical considerations. It examined the significant role that healthcare professionals play in the surrogacy process, addressing the responsibilities they hold in safeguarding the well-being of surrogates, intended parents, and the unborn child. It then explored the standard medical practices and guidelines that govern surrogacy, highlighting the importance of adherence to established protocols to ensure the health and safety of all parties involved.

This chapter also touched on the ethical dilemmas inherent in surrogacy, emphasising the need for a balanced approach that respects the autonomy and rights of surrogates while prioritising the welfare of the child. The lack of recognition and clear guidelines in healthcare settings often leads to confusion and challenges for surrogates and intended parents, pointing to a significant gap in the education and training of healthcare professionals.

To address these challenges, we recommend the development of national surrogacy guidelines, the implementation of targeted training programmes for healthcare providers, and the adoption of policies that reflect current best practices. We also make the case for regular reviews and updates to surrogacy policies, ensuring they remain relevant and effective in supporting the evolving needs of surrogates, intended parents, and healthcare providers.

References

Arvidsson, A., Vauquline, P., Johnsdotter, S., & Essén, B. (2017). Surrogate mother–Praiseworthy or stigmatized: A qualitative study on perceptions of surrogacy in Assam, India. *Global Health Action*, *10*(1), N.PAG-N.PAG. https://doi.org/10.1080/16549716.2017.1328890

Attawet, J. (2022). The nexus between self-perception and behavioural responses of gestational surrogates' risk experiences. *Human Fertility (Cambridge, England)*, *25*(3), 562–568. https://doi.org/10.1080/14647273.2020.1870171

Attawet, J., Wang, A., & Sullivan, E. (2022). 'Womb for work' experiences of Thai women and gestational surrogacy practice in Thailand. *Human Fertility (Cambridge, England)*, *25*(5), 912–923. https://doi.org/10.1080/14647273.2021.1937716

Attawet, J., Wang, A. Y., Farquhar, C. M., Jordan, V., Li, Z., & Sullivan, E. A. (2022). Pregnancy and birth outcomes of single versus multiple embryo transfer in gestational surrogacy arrangements: A systematic review and meta-analysis. *Human Fertility (Cambridge, England)*, *25*(2), 217–227. https://doi.org/10.1080/14647273.2020.1785643

Department of Health & Social Care. (2024). *Guidance care in surrogacy: Guidance for the care of surrogates and intended parents in surrogate births in England and Wales*. GOV.UK. Retrieved 2 Sep from https://www.gov.uk/government/publications/having-a-child-through-surrogacy/care-in-surrogacy-guidance-for-the-care-of-surrogates-and-intended-parents-in-surrogate-births-in-england-and-wales#annex-b-checklist-of-information-to-be-included-in-surrogacy-birth-plan

Edwards, E., Jones, S., Kenwright, E., Hennessy, F., Horsey, K., Mahmoud, Z., & Marway, H. K. (2023). Care in surrogacy: Practice, ethics and regulations. *International Journal of Birth and Parenting Education*, 13. Retrieved from https://ijbpe.com/journals/supplements

Hovav, A. (2020). Cutting out the surrogate: Caesarean sections in the Mexican surrogacy industry. *Social Science & Medicine*, *256*, 113063.

Jefford, S. (2020). *More than just a baby*.

Khawcharoenporn, T., & Sha, B. (2016). HIV infection and infertility. In A. M. Darwish (Ed.), *Genital infections and infertility* (pp. 178–199). IntechOpen.

Kneebone, E., Beilby, K., & Hammarberg, K. (2022). Experiences of surrogates and intended parents of surrogacy arrangements: A systematic review. *Reproductive BioMedicine Online*, *45*(4), 815–830. https://doi.org/10.5772/62390

Kneebone, E., Hammarberg, K., & Beilby, K. (2024). Surrogates', intended parents', and professionals' perspectives on ways to improve access to surrogacy in Australia. *International Journal of Law, Policy and the Family*, *38*(1), ebae009. https://doi.org/10.1093/lawfam/ebae009

Legal Professional Group (LPG). (2024). *Surrogacy laws by state*. ARSM. Retrieved 15 Aug from https://connect.asrm.org/lpg/resources/surrogacy-by-state?ssopc=1

Ma, S., Peng, Y., Hu, L., Wang, X., Xiong, Y., Tang, Y., Tan, J., & Gong, F. (2022). Comparisons of benefits and risks of single embryo transfer versus double embryo transfer: A systematic review and meta-analysis. *Reproductive Biology and Endocrinology*, *20*(1), 20.

Monteleone, P. A., Peregrino, P. F., Baracat, E. C., & Serafini, P. C. (2018). Transfer of 2 embryos using a double-embryo transfer protocol versus 2 sequential single-embryo transfers: The impact on multiple pregnancy. *Reproductive Sciences*, *25*(10), 1501–1508.

Panitch, V. (2013). Global surrogacy: exploitation to empowerment. *Journal of Global Ethics*, *9*(3), 329–343. https://doi.org/10.1080/17449626.2013.818390.

Price, F. (1989). Establishing guidelines: Regulation and the clinical management of infertility. In *Birthrights* (pp. 63–80). Routledge.

Rotabi, K. S., Mapp, S., Cheney, K., Fong, R., & McRoy, R. (2017). Regulating commercial global surrogacy: The best interests of the child. *Journal of Human Rights and Social Work*, *2*(3), 64–73.

Silvern, R., & Cojocaru, S. (2022). Interaction between surrogate mother and intended mother: Sociological aspects in surrogacy. *Revista de Cercetare si Interventie Sociala*, *77*, 89–105. https://www.rcis.ro/images/documente/rcis77_06.pdf

Tapiromkul, A., & Wongbandit, A. (2014). *Legal problems on commercial surrogacy in Thailand under the protection of children born from assisted reproductive technologies act, BE 2558*. Thammasat University.

Trowse, P., & Cooper, D. (2018). The agony and the ecstasy: Sacrifice and pain for financial gain: Have Indian surrogate mothers been exploited by their intended parents in commercial surrogacy arrangements? *Journal of Law and Medicine*, *25*(2), 388–407. Retrieved from https://search.ebscohost.com/login.aspx?direct=true&AuthType=shib&db=mnh&AN=29978644&site=ehost-live&custid=s3684040

Wang, D., Li, L.-B., Hou, Z.-W., Kang, X.-J., Xie, Q.-D., Yu, X.-j., Ma, M.-F., Ma, B.-L., Wang, Z.-S., & Lei, Y. (2011). The integrated HIV-1 provirus in patient sperm chromosome and its transfer into the early embryo by fertilization. *PLoS One*, *6*(12), e28586.

White, P. M. (2017). "One for Sorrow, Two for Joy?": American embryo transfer guideline recommendations, practices, and outcomes for gestational surrogate patients. *Journal of Assisted Reproduction and Genetics*, *34*(4), 431–443. https://doi.org/10.1007/s10815-017-0885-7

Yee, S., & Librach, C. L. (2019). Analysis of gestational surrogates' birthing experiences and relationships with intended parents during pregnancy and post-birth. *Birth*, *46*(4), 628–637.

5 The Role of Healthcare Providers in Commercial Surrogacy

Section 1: Setting the Ethical Landscape of Surrogacy Care

The international landscape of surrogacy is marked by a lack of cohesive and universally accepted guiding principles, making it challenging for healthcare practitioners to establish standardised treatment and care protocols. While no overarching international framework currently exists to regulate the quality and safety of international surrogacy practices (Fenton-Glynn, 2016; Trimmings & Beaumont, 2011), efforts such as the Verona Principles—a set of human rights-based guidelines aimed at protecting the rights and well-being of all parties involved in surrogacy arrangements, including surrogates, intended parents, and the child—and the ethical standards set by the Society for Ethics in Egg Donation and Surrogacy (SEEDS) are steps towards addressing these gaps.

The Verona Principles, published by the International Social Services (ISS) in 2021, were developed through a comprehensive consultation process involving over 100 stakeholders across various disciplines, regions, and perspectives. These principles were designed to safeguard the rights of children born through surrogacy. Recognised by the United Nations (UN) Committee on the Rights of the Child, the Verona Principles offer guidance for legislative and policy reforms that prioritise the best interests of the child, ensuring their protection from discrimination and guaranteeing their human rights in surrogacy arrangements. While there is still no global consensus on surrogacy, the need to address the rights of children born through these arrangements is becoming increasingly urgent.

In parallel, SEEDS—a US-based nonprofit organisation—aims to self-regulate surrogacy and egg donation practices by establishing ethical standards for agencies, clinics, lawyers, and mental health professionals. SEEDS focuses on promoting ethics within the surrogacy industry, ensuring that all parties, including surrogates, donors, and intended parents, engage in ethical practices.

While these efforts contribute to a more ethically informed and regulated environment, significant ethical and legal concerns remain (González, 2020). The lack of uniform international standards continues to present risks, particularly in cross-border surrogacy, underscoring the necessity for global initiatives that prioritise the rights and well-being of all parties involved, especially the children born from these arrangements.

DOI: 10.4324/9781003511939-5

In the management of surrogacy, healthcare providers occupy a crucial and intricate role, one that is delicately balanced between the well-being of the surrogate mother and child and the expectations of the intended parents. Traditionally, the primary duty of care has been oriented towards the surrogate, recognising them as the central figure undergoing the physical and psychological challenges of pregnancy and childbirth. This approach is underscored by ethical considerations and supported by legal frameworks and health policies that validate the prioritisation of the surrogate's health and autonomy.

However, the existence of commercial surrogacy complicates this dynamic. Commercial contracts, which underpin many surrogacy arrangements, can alter the power dynamics and potentially impact the provision of healthcare to the surrogate. In commercial surrogacy, the surrogate may face pressure to prioritise the wishes of the intended parents over their own health and well-being. This imbalance can manifest in various ways, from the choice of delivery method to the timing of post-birth separation from the baby.

For instance, commercial surrogacy contracts may stipulate practices such as multiple embryo transfer (MET) and caesarean sections for convenience, often disregarding the potential risks to the surrogate. MET, which has become standard practice in many surrogacy arrangements, is associated with an increased risk of multiple pregnancies and subsequent pregnancy and perinatal complications (Attawet, Wang, Farquhar, et al., 2022). Additionally, immediate removal of the baby after birth, often mandated by commercial agreements, can exacerbate emotional distress for the surrogate, who may not receive adequate psychological support post-birth.

The challenge for healthcare providers lies in navigating these ethical dilemmas while upholding their duty of care to the surrogate and the baby. It is imperative that healthcare providers advocate for the surrogate's health and autonomy, ensuring that decisions regarding their health and the birthing process are respected. At the same time, they must also recognise the rights and emotional needs of the intended parents, supporting their involvement in the pregnancy and birth while preparing them for their future role as parents. This requires a nuanced understanding of the complexities inherent in all forms of surrogacy and a commitment to providing equitable and compassionate care.

In this context, robust professional guidelines and specialised training are essential to equip healthcare providers with the knowledge and skills necessary to navigate the complexities of both altruistic and commercial surrogacy. Providers must be adept at upholding ethical standards while safeguarding the physical, emotional, and psychological well-being of the surrogate, the intended parents, and the child. By adhering to ethical frameworks — particularly the four main principles of biomedical ethics: autonomy, non-maleficence, beneficence, and justice — healthcare professionals can help mitigate the potential distortions inherent in commercial surrogacy arrangements (Feiglin & Savulescu , 2018). These principles are deeply informed by broader ethical theories (see chapter 3): deontological ethics emphasises the duty to respect autonomy and prevent harm; utilitarianism prioritises maximising beneficence and minimising harm for all parties; virtue ethics encourages compassionate and just conduct rooted in moral character; and feminist ethics highlights the importance of relational autonomy and addressing systemic inequalities in care.

Ideally specialised training would ensure that healthcare providers are prepared to address the surrogate's health and autonomy and enable them to manage the legal and emotional dimensions of the intended parents' involvement. A comprehensive approach helps ensure that all parties receive the care, support, and respect they deserve, fostering a more just and compassionate surrogacy experience.

Surrogacy necessitates consideration for the surrogate, the child, and the intended parents, and due to its relative rarity, it remains poorly understood by many healthcare professionals (Armuand et al., 2018). As a result, healthcare professionals require clear guiding principles of care. There are widely diverse and generally inadequate policies and approaches to surrogacy where most hospitals lack adequate training or guiding policies on the subject (Frati et al., 2021). For this reason, it is necessary for healthcare professionals to consider the overarching ethical principles that can be universally applied. These principles will provide consistent guidance and support across all surrogacy scenarios.

The following sections explore how healthcare providers can rely on the four main principles in biomedical ethics of Autonomy, Beneficence, Non-Maleficence, and Justice. All these are essential to ethical practice across all forms of surrogacy. This should help clarify the role of healthcare providers in the landscape of both commercial and altruistic surrogacy, providing clear guidance on their responsibilities and ethical dilemmas. And lastly this chapter will also discuss strategies for implementing these principles effectively in practice.

Section 2: Surrogacy—Global Trends and Context

The demand for commercial surrogacy has surged significantly in recent years, driven by various factors such as advancements in reproductive technologies, changing family dynamics, and broader societal acceptance of diverse parenting models (Brandão & Garrido, 2022).

Many high-income countries, including Australia and European nations, have seen an increase in the number of individuals and couples, including same-sex couples and single men, opting for surrogacy as a means to build their families. As maternal age continues to rise, infertility treatments, including surrogacy, have become a more sought-after solution for intended parents who face challenges in conceiving naturally. Transnational surrogacy has grown rapidly, with intended parents seeking surrogacy arrangements in countries where legal frameworks are more favourable or the costs are significantly lower. Despite many nations like India, Nepal, Thailand, and Cambodia implementing stricter regulations or outright bans on commercial surrogacy, the demand persists and has led to a shift towards alternative destinations (Attawet, 2021). This rising trend underscores the global nature of the surrogacy industry and reflects the continued demand despite evolving legal and ethical landscapes (Brandão & Garrido, 2022).

In countries where surrogacy is prohibited or heavily restricted, the practice often continues through "reproductive tourism", where intended parents seek surrogacy services in countries with more permissive or unregulated environments.

This demand is driven by factors such as rising maternal age, same-sex couples seeking parenthood, and the availability of medical technology.

The legal landscape is fragmented, and efforts such as those by the Hague Conference on Private International Law (HCCW) aim to standardise international guidelines, but no uniform global regulation exists. Cultural, religious, and ethical factors also play significant roles in shaping national policies on surrogacy, with some countries and religious groups rejecting the practice, while others allow it under specific conditions.

Thus, while the trend in certain regions may lean towards stricter regulation or banning, there is no clear global movement towards the total prohibition of commercial surrogacy. Instead, the landscape reflects a mix of approaches, ranging from bans to regulated commercial surrogacy to unregulated, informal practices.

There are several salient challenges with informed consent in commercial surrogacy. Healthcare providers should be aware of these issues, ensuring adherence to universal medical ethical standards, regardless of their practice location.

Section 3: Autonomy in Commercial Surrogacy—Balancing Rights and Realities

Autonomy is a cornerstone of medical ethics, embodying the principle that individuals should have the freedom to make informed decisions about their own bodies and healthcare. In commercial surrogacy the application of this principle becomes profoundly complex, as healthcare providers must navigate the often-conflicting interests of surrogates and intended parents. This section explores the multifaceted nature of autonomy in commercial surrogacy, examining how it can be both upheld and compromised.

Understanding Autonomy in the Context of Surrogacy

In healthcare, autonomy signifies the right of patients to make choices about their medical care without external coercion. This right is especially pertinent in reproductive health, where decisions have deeply personal and often long-lasting implications. For surrogates, autonomy involves having the agency to make decisions about their health, the pregnancy, and the birth process.

In commercial surrogacy, surrogates agree to carry and deliver a child for another individual or couple, often under the constraints of a legal contract. These agreements can place surrogates in a position where their personal health decisions may be influenced, or even overridden, by the expectations and desires of the intended parents, creating a potential conflict between contractual obligations and the surrogate's autonomy (Pande, 2014a; Tanderup et al., 2015a).

In this complex dynamic, healthcare providers play a crucial role in safeguarding the autonomy and well-being of the surrogate mother. It is the duty of medical professionals to ensure that the surrogate, as their patient, receives care that prioritises their health, respects their autonomy, and supports their ability to make informed decisions about their body and medical care throughout the surrogacy process.

It is essential that surrogates fully understand their rights and the potential implications of the surrogacy contract on their health and autonomy. This includes clear communication about their options and the legal and medical aspects of the surrogacy agreement.

Ensuring that the surrogate's consent to medical procedures is truly informed and voluntary is paramount. This means providing comprehensive information about risks, benefits, and alternatives and making sure that informed consent is given freely, without undue pressure from the intended parents or other parties involved.

While respecting the desires of the intended parents, healthcare providers must advocate for the surrogate's right to make decisions about their own body. This involves navigating the delicate balance between honouring the surrogate's personal health choices and the contractual obligations under the contract. Ultimately, healthcare providers' primary duty is always to the surrogate and the child (Bhatia et al., 2009). Any medical treatment decisions for a surrogate or the unborn child should be made as though the contractual surrogacy agreement does not exist.

Surrogacy can be emotionally and psychologically challenging. Healthcare providers should offer or facilitate access to counselling and support services to help surrogates navigate these challenges and maintain their autonomy and well-being throughout the process.

At all stages of the surrogacy journey, from pre-conception to postpartum care, healthcare providers must continuously advocate for the surrogate's rights and needs (Bhatia et al., 2009). This includes monitoring for any undue influence or coercion and intervening when necessary to protect the surrogate's autonomy.

Protecting the Child's Future Autonomy

While the primary focus in surrogacy often centres on the surrogate's autonomy and the intended parents' desires, it is crucial to also consider the future autonomy of the child born through surrogacy. Although infants and young children lack the capacity to make autonomous decisions, ethical surrogacy practices should consider the future rights and autonomy of the child.

The child's autonomy can be impacted by decisions made long before they have the capacity to express their own will. This includes considerations about their origins, their relationship with the surrogate, and their knowledge of the circumstances of their birth. It is ethically significant to ensure that the child, once capable, has access to truthful information about their genetic and gestational background. This access respects the child's right to an informed understanding of their identity, which is a critical aspect of their future autonomy.

Additionally, decisions made during the surrogacy process, such as the use of genetic material or the selection of specific traits, could have long-term implications for the child's life and well-being. The child's future autonomy should be a guiding principle, ensuring that they are not unfairly burdened by the choices made by the adults involved in the surrogacy arrangement.

Ethically, surrogacy agreements and practices should strive to balance the personal autonomy of the surrogate with the long-term autonomy of the child. This balance is essential in crafting fair and respectful surrogacy arrangements that consider the rights and well-being of all parties involved.

The Influence of Commercial Contracts

Commercial surrogacy agreements often contain detailed stipulations regarding medical care and the birthing process. For instance, contracts may specify the method of delivery—sometimes favouring caesarean sections for reasons of scheduling convenience or perceived safety, despite the surrogate's preferences or medical advisability for a vaginal delivery. This imposition can significantly impact the surrogate's autonomy, placing them in a position where the surrogate must navigate between their own health needs and the contractual expectations.

A concrete example can be seen in cases where surrogates are pressured to undergo caesarean sections (Attawet, Wang, & Sullivan, 2022), which can pose additional risks and longer recovery times compared to vaginal births (Bodner et al., 2011; Gregory et al., 2012). Here, the surrogate's ability to make an autonomous choice is constrained by the commercial nature of the agreement, highlighting a key ethical dilemma for healthcare providers who must advocate for the surrogate's health and well-being regardless of the terms of the contract.

Ensuring Informed Consent

Informed consent is a foundational element of medical ethics, ensuring that patient is fully aware of the risks, benefits, and alternatives to any medical procedure before they agree to it. This principle is crucial in any medical setting but becomes particularly complex in the context of commercial surrogacy. Here, the dynamics involve not just the surrogate but also the intended parents, healthcare providers, and often commercial agencies.

Informed consent in commercial surrogacy involves a complex web of ethical considerations, particularly when addressing critical decisions such as embryo transfer and foetal reduction. Foetal reduction refers to a medical procedure used to reduce the number of foetuses in a multiple pregnancy, often performed to decrease health risks for both the surrogate and the remaining foetus(es). While informed consent ideally ensures that all parties involved—especially surrogates—are fully aware of the risks, benefits, and alternatives to any medical procedure, studies show that this process is often insufficiently conducted. A study conducted in Delhi, India, by Tanderup et al. (2015a) highlight significant gaps in the informed consent process in fertility clinics and surrogacy agencies. The research, which included interviews with doctors, surrogates, and agents, revealed that none of the 14 surrogates interviewed were able to explain the risks involved in procedures like embryo transfer and foetal reduction (Tanderup et al., 2015a). Worryingly they also found that most decisions about embryo transfer and foetal reduction were made unilaterally by doctors, often without the full participation or understanding of the surrogates. Intended parents were generally only indirectly involved, which raises concerns about autonomy and the decision-making dynamics in the surrogacy process. The qualitative analysis pointed to significant ethical concerns, including the difficulties in explaining complex medical procedures to surrogates, the financial and social pressures they face, and potential conflicts of interest among the involved parties.

Although such practices may not be as prevalent in more regulated surrogacy markets like the United States, where stricter legal frameworks and ethical guidelines are in place, they are characteristic of the conditions that often arise in poorly regulated markets. In these less regulated environments, the absence of oversight can lead to significant power imbalances, where surrogate mothers may be left uninformed or pressured into procedures without fully understanding the risks or having the ability to participate meaningfully in the decision-making process. There is no doubt that robust regulatory frameworks are required to protect the rights and autonomy of surrogates; however, healthcare professionals can ensure that informed consent is not only a legal formality but also a true ethical practice.

Whatever the regulatory environment in which healthcare providers may operate, doctors and nurses have a professional duty to uphold ethical principles such as autonomy, regardless of external pressures or limitations. Even in poorly regulated surrogacy markets, where the system might not fully safeguard surrogates' rights, healthcare professionals can and should act in accordance with higher ethical standards. By prioritising the surrogate's autonomy and ensuring they are fully informed and empowered to make decisions about their own bodies, medical practitioners demonstrate that ethical obligations transcend the regulatory landscape. Upholding these principles not only protects individuals but also reinforces the integrity of the medical profession.

Navigating Conflicts between Contracts and Health Decisions

When the terms of a surrogacy contract conflict with the surrogate's health interests or their wishes, particularly regarding delivery methods or other critical medical decisions, healthcare providers may be placed in a complex and ethically charged position. These situations demand a careful and principled approach to ensure the surrogate's rights and health are protected.

The fundamental ethical obligation of healthcare providers is to prioritise the health and well-being of their patients, in this case, the surrogate and child. If the contractual terms stipulate a medical procedure that is not in the surrogate's best interest or against their wishes—such as a mandated caesarean section—the healthcare provider must advocate for their right to make an autonomous decision based on their health and personal circumstances.

Healthcare providers must actively intervene to protect the surrogate from any pressures that compromise their health. This includes advocating for their right to choose the safest and most appropriate delivery method, as determined by medical advice and their own informed preferences, regardless of contractual stipulations. Healthcare providers should seek to mediate between the surrogate and the intended parents to find a solution that respects their autonomy and well-being.

Healthcare providers may also need to facilitate access to legal and ethical guidance to assist the surrogate in understanding their rights within the surrogacy agreement. This support can help surrogates navigate situations where contract terms may not align with their health needs or wishes, empowering them to assert their autonomy.

Open and transparent communication is essential. Healthcare providers should facilitate discussions that involve all parties—the surrogate, intended parents, and legal representatives—to address and resolve conflicts related to health decisions. This communication should emphasise the surrogate's right to make informed choices about their body and health. It is also crucial to recognise the potential influence that the intended parents and their legal representatives can exert on the surrogate's health decisions. In particular, the dynamics of commercial surrogacy often create a power imbalance (Attawet et al., 2024) where the surrogate might feel pressured to conform to the desires and expectations of the intended parents, especially when they are present during medical consultations.

To safeguard the surrogate's autonomy and ensure that their decisions are truly voluntary and informed, healthcare professionals should take specific measures to ensure this. Suggested measures include:

Private Consultations with the Surrogate

Healthcare providers should have one-on-one consultations with the surrogate, excluding the intended parents and their legal representatives from these initial discussions. This private setting allows the surrogate to freely express their concerns, preferences, and any hesitations without any immediate influence or pressure from external parties.

Obtaining Surrogate's Consent

Only after these private consultations and with the surrogate's explicit consent should the intended parents and their representatives be included in discussions. This approach respects the surrogate's right to privacy and autonomy in making health decisions.

Assessing Influence Dynamics

Providers should be vigilant in assessing whether the surrogate feels unduly influenced or coerced during shared discussions. This vigilance ensures that their consent remains informed and voluntary, reflecting their genuine preferences and best interests.

Providing Support and Advocacy

In cases where the surrogate expresses concern or resistance to the contractual terms, healthcare professionals should offer additional support and advocate on their behalf. This may involve mediating between the surrogate and the intended parents or referring the surrogate to independent legal counsel to reinforce their decision-making autonomy.

As illustrated above, these are complex and sensitive situations, and it is hard to expect the healthcare providers to feel confident managing them without clear policies and ethical guidelines that prioritise the surrogate's health and autonomy. Such policies should be available to guide providers in handling conflicts between contractual obligations and medical best practices, ensuring that the surrogate's rights are protected throughout the process.

Relational Autonomy: A Broader Ethical Perspective

The concept of relational autonomy extends beyond the traditional, individualistic view of decision-making to consider the broader social and economic contexts in which decisions are made. This perspective is particularly relevant in commercial surrogacy, where surrogates often make choices influenced by their financial situations, family dynamics, and societal expectations.

For many surrogates, the decision to enter into a surrogacy agreement is driven by financial needs. This economic motivation can affect their autonomy, as the decision to become a surrogate may be less about personal choice and more about necessity. Healthcare providers must recognise these broader influences and support surrogates in making health decisions that truly reflect their well-being and values, rather than merely fulfilling contractual obligations.

Global Disparities in the Practice of Surrogacy

Autonomy in surrogacy is experienced differently across the globe. In the Global North, surrogates typically have greater access to resources, information, and support, which can empower them to make more informed and voluntary decisions. Research suggests that surrogates in these regions often feel respected and valued, experiencing a higher degree of autonomy throughout the surrogacy process (Kneebone et al., 2022).

In contrast, in the Global South, economic disparities and limited access to healthcare can severely constrain the surrogate's autonomy (Kneebone et al., 2022). People in these regions may enter into surrogacy agreements out of economic necessity, with fewer safeguards and less support to ensure their decisions are genuinely voluntary and informed. For instance, some surrogates in India were subjected to medical procedures without their consent, including foetal reduction and caesarean sections (Gupta & Prasad, 2019; Munjal-Shankar, 2015; Saravanan, 2013). This disparity raises significant ethical concerns about exploitation and the adequacy of consent.

Healthcare providers working in these contexts must be particularly vigilant in advocating for the surrogate's rights and autonomy, ensuring that their medical and ethical obligations are not overshadowed by the commercial aspects of surrogacy arrangements.

Altruistic Surrogacy

The lack of financial incentives in altruistic surrogacy can help maintain the surrogate's autonomy by reducing external pressures and motivations. The surrogate's decisions are more likely to be driven by personal values and altruistic motives, potentially fostering a more supportive and consensual environment. However, even in altruistic arrangements, there can be implicit expectations and emotional pressures from the intended parents, family members, or friends, which may affect the surrogate's autonomous decision-making. For instance, surrogates often require social support and may disclose their decision to close friends and immediate family to gain emotional support and assistance with their own family during pregnancy (Gupta & Prasad, 2019; Karandikar et al., 2014; Taebi et al., 2020). This reliance on social networks can influence the surrogate's autonomy, as the surrogate may feel obligated to meet others' expectations.

Commercial Surrogacy

Commercial surrogacy, in contrast, involves significant financial compensation for the surrogate. This compensation is often a primary motivation for surrogates in low- to middle-income countries, where the ability to financially support their own families is a crucial factor. While this financial incentive can empower surrogates economically, it also introduces complex dynamics that can compromise their autonomy.

The presence of financial incentives may create a power imbalance between the surrogate and the intended parents. Commercial surrogates may face pressures to comply with the demands and expectations of the intended parents and surrogacy agencies, potentially limiting their ability to make independent health and medical decisions, highlighting the risks to autonomy in commercial surrogacy arrangements.

Additionally, commercial surrogates often encounter societal stigma and may keep their decision a secret to avoid negative perceptions (Attawet, 2022; Gupta & Prasad, 2019; Munjal-Shankar, 2015). This secrecy can further isolate surrogates and limit their access to necessary emotional and social support, adversely affecting their autonomy.

In both altruistic and commercial surrogacy arrangements, healthcare practitioners must navigate the delicate balance between supporting the surrogate's autonomy and addressing the expectations and needs of the intended parents. Clear ethical guiding principles are essential to ensure that surrogates are empowered to make informed and independent decisions throughout the surrogacy process, regardless of the nature of the arrangement. In the absence of a unified international framework regulating surrogacy practices, these principles provide crucial guidance to uphold the surrogate's rights and well-being amidst varying motivations and pressures.

The Role of Healthcare Providers as Advocates

Healthcare providers play a pivotal role in upholding the surrogate's autonomy within the commercial surrogacy framework. They must navigate the ethical tension between respecting the surrogate's right to make informed decisions about their health and fulfilling the contractual expectations imposed by surrogacy agreements. This role requires a deep commitment to the surrogate's health and well-being, as well as a robust understanding of the contractual and ethical landscape of surrogacy.

Healthcare providers should act as advocates for the surrogate's autonomy, ensuring that their choices about medical care and the birthing process are respected and supported. This advocacy includes resisting pressures to prioritise contractual terms over medical and ethical considerations. For example, if a surrogate expresses a preference for a vaginal delivery but the contract stipulates a caesarean section for convenience, healthcare providers should support the surrogate's choice unless there are compelling medical reasons to recommend otherwise.

Furthermore, healthcare providers must offer comprehensive support, including psychological care, to help surrogates manage the physical and emotional demands of surrogacy. This holistic approach is essential in empowering surrogates to make decisions that align with their personal health and well-being.

Complex Medical Procedures and Risks

Surrogates often undergo complicated medical procedures such as IVF and foetal reduction, which carry inherent risks (Kamphuis et al., 2014). These procedures require a detailed explanation for informed consent to be truly meaningful. However, the medical terminology and intricacies of these processes can be daunting and difficult to grasp for many surrogates, especially if they have limited education or health literacy. However, informed consent cannot be considered fully given if surrogates do not have crucial information such as the number of embryos implanted or potential complications. Studies of commercial surrogacy arrangements showed that surrogates are often poorly informed, and that most cannot specify how many embryos were transferred or describe the potential complications of multiple pregnancies and foetal reduction (Attawet, Wang, & Sullivan, 2022). It's important to understand that in the context of surrogacy, there can be a significant disparity between perceived and actual informed consent. Surrogates often believe they have been fully informed about the procedures and risks involved, yet they may be unaware of crucial details that could impact their health and the outcome of the pregnancy.

A study by Tanderup et al. (2015) illuminates this gap vividly. The researchers found that while all interviewed surrogates felt adequately informed, none were able to accurately explain the number of embryos that had been transferred or articulate the potential complications associated with multiple pregnancies and foetal reduction. This finding highlights a troubling disconnect: surrogates may feel confident in their understanding yet remain ignorant of vital information that could influence their decision-making and consent.

This disconnect can stem from several factors, including complex medical jargon, insufficient explanations from healthcare providers, and the emotional and psychological pressures faced by surrogate mothers. In the context of commercial surrogacy in developing countries, there often exists a significant power dynamic between the authority-wielding doctors and often near-illiterate surrogates, which exacerbates this issue. Many surrogates may feel it is inappropriate to question the expertise of their doctors, viewing such inquiries as disrespectful or unnecessary. This perception can prevent them from seeking crucial elaboration on medical procedures and risks.

The consequences of such gaps in understanding can be profound, affecting both the surrogate's health and the ethical integrity of the surrogacy process. Additionally, there is often reluctance among surrogates to request detailed information on medical procedures they perceived as solely the domain of doctors or agencies (Tanderup et al., 2015b).

This underscores the critical need for healthcare providers to proactively disclose all relevant medical details, encourage questions, and ensure surrogates are fully informed participants in their own care, aligning with ethical standards of transparency and patient-centred care. Healthcare providers can improve communication by using plain language, visual aids, and allowing ample time for discussions. Maintaining best practices includes ensuring thorough understanding through multiple consultations and providing ongoing support throughout the process.

Educational, Socioeconomic Disparities and Cultural and Linguistic Barriers

Many surrogates come from economically disadvantaged backgrounds and have limited access to education, as evidenced by emerging dynamics such as "repronubs" and "repropreneurs" (Whittaker et al., 2022). These socioeconomic factors can hinder their ability to fully understand medical information and the associated risks. The financial incentives in surrogacy can also pressure these women into agreeing to procedures without fully understanding the implications, further complicating the consent process. Surrogates often come from diverse cultural and linguistic backgrounds. Communication barriers can make it challenging for healthcare providers to convey complex medical information effectively. In many cases, the surrogate may not fully understand the language used by the medical staff, leading to a significant gap in comprehension and, consequently, informed consent.

Healthcare professionals can mitigate these challenges by prioritising comprehensive education and counselling sessions. This includes using culturally sensitive and plain language explanations, ensuring adequate time for discussions, and providing written materials in accessible formats. Empowering surrogates with information and support can help them make informed decisions aligned with their best interests and well-being.

Doctor-Dominated Decision-Making

The decision-making process in many surrogacy arrangements is often dominated by doctors and medical professionals (Tanderup et al., 2015a). Surrogates may feel intimidated or reluctant to question the authority of these professionals, leading to a scenario where consent is more assumed than actively obtained. This paternalistic approach undermines the surrogate's autonomy and fails to respect their right to be an informed participant in their own care. To avoid a paternalistic approach in surrogacy arrangements, healthcare professionals should prioritise shared decision-making and collaboration with surrogate mothers. This involves fostering open dialogue where the surrogate is encouraged to actively participate in discussions about treatment options, risks, and benefits. Respecting the surrogate's autonomy is crucial, emphasising their right to make informed decisions regarding their own healthcare journey.

Conflicts of Interest

The commercial nature of surrogacy introduces conflicts of interest that can impact the quality and honesty of the consent process. Clinics and agencies often have financial motivations to maximise success rates and minimise costs, which can influence medical decisions that prioritise economic outcomes over the surrogate's health and well-being. This can lead to pressures on surrogates to accept METs or high-risk procedures without fully understanding the potential consequences. Healthcare providers, particularly treating doctors, are ethically bound by principles such as non-maleficence to prioritise the well-being of the patient above financial considerations. They must advocate for practices that minimise risks and ensure informed consent, providing transparent information about the risks and benefits of procedures and offering alternatives that prioritise the surrogate's health. This commitment to ethical standards will strengthen trust and integrity in surrogacy arrangements while safeguarding the health and rights of surrogates.

Power Imbalances and Agency Control

The relationships in surrogacy are often marked by significant power imbalances. Surrogates may feel subordinate to the commissioning parents and agencies, fearing repercussions if they voice concerns or ask for more information (Tanderup et al., 2015b; Triviño-Caballero, 2023). This dynamic can inhibit open communication and lead to situations where surrogates consent to procedures without fully understanding their rights or the medical implications. Healthcare professionals should provide comprehensive information about procedures, risks, and alternatives in a clear and accessible manner, using plain language and visual aids as needed. They should also ensure that surrogates have adequate time to consider their options and seek independent advice if desired.

Duties of Healthcare Providers

Commercial arrangements create several unique ethical challenges and healthcare providers need to navigate these challenges while upholding the ethical principle of autonomy in commercial surrogacy. To do this, healthcare providers must adopt a comprehensive and empathetic approach to informed consent. Their duties include:

Providing Clear and Accessible Information

Healthcare providers must ensure that all medical information is presented in a way that is understandable and accessible to surrogate mothers. This includes simplifying medical jargon, using visual aids, and providing information in the surrogate's preferred language. Providers should take extra time to explain procedures and their associated risks, ensuring that surrogates have a thorough understanding before giving consent.

Verifying Understanding and Voluntary Consent

It is essential for healthcare providers to verify that surrogate mothers genuinely understand the information provided and that their consent is given freely and voluntarily. This can be done through follow-up discussions, asking surrogates to describe the procedures and their risks in their own words and providing opportunities for questions and clarifications. Ensuring that surrogates are not pressured or coerced into consenting is a critical aspect of this duty.

Involving Surrogates in Decision-Making

Surrogates should be active participants in all decisions regarding their medical care. Healthcare providers must foster an environment where surrogates feel empowered to express their preferences and concerns. This participatory approach respects the surrogate's autonomy and ensures that their voice is central in the decision-making process. Providers should facilitate a balanced discussion that includes the surrogate's perspective on all medical interventions.

Balancing Interests without Bias

While it is important to involve the intended parents in discussions, the healthcare provider's primary duty is to the surrogate. Healthcare providers must advocate for the surrogate's best interests, ensuring that their health and well-being take precedence over contractual obligations or the desires of the commissioning parents. Medical decisions should be guided by what is best for the surrogate, regardless of financial or contractual pressures.

Ensuring Ethical and Regulatory Compliance

Healthcare providers should adhere to both local and international ethical guidelines governing surrogacy practices. They should advocate for and support the development of robust regulatory frameworks that protect the rights and autonomy of surrogates. Healthcare providers must stay informed about best practices and continuously strive to align their care with ethical standards, ensuring that surrogates are treated with dignity and respect throughout the process.

Addressing Power Dynamics and Providing Support

Recognising the inherent power dynamics in surrogacy arrangements, healthcare providers should offer additional support to surrogates. This includes providing access to counselling services, ensuring surrogates have independent advocates to support their decision-making, and fostering an environment of respect and dignity throughout the surrogacy process. Providers should be aware of and mitigate any potential exploitation or undue influence.

Informed consent in commercial surrogacy is fraught with challenges that stem from complex medical procedures, educational and socioeconomic disparities, and the commercial nature of the arrangement. Healthcare providers play a crucial role in navigating these challenges by ensuring that surrogate mothers are fully informed, active participants in their own care. By providing clear and accessible information, verifying understanding, involving surrogates in decision-making, balancing interests without bias, ensuring ethical compliance, and addressing power dynamics, providers can uphold the principle of autonomy and safeguard the rights and well-being of surrogates in commercial surrogacy arrangements.

Moving towards Ethical Surrogacy Practices

To foster an ethical practice of surrogacy that respects the surrogate's autonomy, it is crucial to establish robust regulatory frameworks and professional guidelines. These should protect surrogates against coercion and exploitation, ensuring they have the freedom to make informed choices about their health and the birthing process.

Healthcare providers should be equipped with specialised training to understand and navigate the unique challenges posed by commercial surrogacy. This training should encompass not only the medical aspects of surrogacy but also the ethical considerations and the socioeconomic factors that influence surrogates' decisions.

By embracing a comprehensive, relational approach to autonomy and advocating for the rights and well-being of surrogate mothers, healthcare providers can help mitigate the ethical complexities of commercial surrogacy. This approach ensures that surrogacy practices respect the dignity and autonomy of all parties involved, contributing to a more ethical and equitable framework for reproductive healthcare.

Section 4: Non-Maleficence (Do No Harm)

The principle of non-maleficence, often summarised by the phrase "do no harm", is a fundamental tenet of medical ethics. It emphasises the responsibility of healthcare providers to avoid causing unnecessary harm to patients. In the context of surrogacy, whether commercial or altruistic, this principle takes on added significance, given the complex interplay of medical, ethical, and contractual factors involved. This section explores how the principle of non-maleficence is applied differently in commercial and altruistic surrogacy arrangements and the challenges healthcare providers face in upholding this ethical standard.

Non-Maleficence in Commercial Surrogacy

In commercial surrogacy, where financial compensation is exchanged, the potential for harm can be exacerbated by the pressure to fulfil contractual obligations and the desires of the intended parents. These dynamics can sometimes lead to medical interventions that prioritise convenience or contractual terms over the health and safety of the surrogate and the baby.

Guarding Against Unnecessary Medical Interventions

Commercial surrogacy agreements often include specific requirements about the pregnancy and delivery process. For example, some contracts may mandate a caesarean section for the convenience of scheduling or perceived control over the birthing process. While caesarean sections can be life-saving when medically necessary, they are also associated with increased risks, such as infections, blood clots, and longer recovery times for the surrogate (Mascarello et al., 2017). Several Indian studies found that surrogates were subjected to medical procedures like foetal reduction and caesarean sections without having a say in these decisions (Gupta & Prasad, 2019; Munjal-Shankar, 2015).

Healthcare providers must critically evaluate these contractual stipulations against the medical necessity of the interventions. The ethical duty to "do no harm" means that providers should resist unnecessary medical interventions that are driven by the desires of the intended parents or the terms of the contract rather than by the health needs of the surrogate and the baby.

For instance, if a surrogate is capable of safely delivering vaginally, healthcare providers should advocate for this option, aligning with the least harmful approach unless a caesarean section is medically indicated. This stance protects the surrogate from unnecessary surgical risks and supports a more natural and potentially less traumatic birthing process.

Balancing Non-Maleficence and Multiple Embryo Transfer in Surrogacy

In surrogacy, the principle of non-maleficence—avoiding harm—is central to clinical decision-making, particularly when considering MET. MET is often driven by intended parents' preferences, financial pressures, or traditional beliefs, but it significantly increases the risks associated with multiple pregnancies. In contrast, elective/single embryo transfer (eSET/SET) is widely recognised as a safer approach (Practice Committee of the American Society for Reproductive Medicine and the Practice Committee for the Society for Assisted Reproductive Technologies, 2021), supported by evidence-based guidelines and ethical standards such as those established by the SEEDS (SEEDS Agency Standards – Seeds Ethics [https://seedsethics.org/seeds-agency-standards/]). eSET/SET minimises health risks for surrogates and future children and is promoted as best practice in assisted reproduction.

This tension between intended parents' preferences and the ethical obligation to prioritise safety creates a complex dilemma for healthcare providers. While MET may seem appealing to intended parents, healthcare professionals must navigate these pressures by advocating for safer practices like eSET/SET. Addressing this challenge requires balancing the rights and needs of all parties involved while upholding non-maleficence as a guiding principle. Achieving this balance is critical to ensuring ethical and safe surrogacy care.

Ensuring Non-Maleficence in the Selection of Surrogates and Intended Parents

A pivotal component of upholding the principle of non-maleficence in surrogacy care lies in the careful selection of intended parents and surrogates. Ensuring that candidates meet well-defined criteria, as outlined in Chapter 4, is not merely procedural but fundamental to safeguarding the physical, emotional, and ethical integrity of all parties involved. This process minimises potential risks, such as psychological distress, coercion, or unmet expectations, which could lead to harm during or after the surrogacy journey.

By implementing rigorous assessment protocols, healthcare providers ensure that the surrogacy arrangement begins on a foundation of mutual understanding, preparedness, and informed consent. This approach not only minimises harm but also upholds the surrogate's and intended parents' autonomy, as it fosters transparent decision-making and mutual trust. Ultimately, integrating these measures reflects a deeper commitment to ethical practice, reinforcing the dual priorities of protecting individuals and promoting positive outcomes in surrogacy care.

Managing Post-Birth Expectations and Care

Another area where the principle of non-maleficence is crucial in surrogacy is the post-birth period. Commercial contracts may stipulate an immediate handover of the baby to the intended parents, potentially neglecting the surrogate's emotional well-being. The abrupt separation can be psychologically distressing, especially without adequate emotional support and time to process the separation.

Healthcare providers have an ethical obligation to minimise this harm by ensuring that surrogates receive comprehensive post-birth care, including psychological support. They should advocate for practices that consider the surrogate's emotional health, such as allowing for a brief period of bonding if desired by the surrogate and providing counselling to help manage the transition (Goli et al., 2022).

Supporting the Surrogate's Emotional and Physical Well-Being

Non-maleficence in surrogacy extends to providing holistic care that addresses both physical and emotional well-being. Surrogates should receive thorough prenatal care tailored to their individual needs and preferences, free from the pressures of fulfilling contractual obligations.

Moreover, healthcare providers should ensure that surrogates have access to comprehensive postpartum care, including support for any emotional challenges they may face after the birth. This support is crucial in preventing long-term psychological harm and fostering a positive surrogacy experience (Goli et al., 2022).

Supporting a surrogate's emotional well-being includes several unique challenges, and some important considerations are given below.

COUNSELLING

Psychological and ethical counselling is a vital responsibility of healthcare providers during the pre-surrogacy stage. Both the surrogate and the intended parents should receive psychological counselling to prepare them emotionally and mentally for the journey ahead. This counselling helps manage expectations, address potential emotional concerns, and ensure that all parties understand the process and their roles within it. Counselling sessions should include an exploration of the broader ethical implications of surrogacy and outline the responsibilities and expectations of all involved parties. This ensures that everyone is fully informed and that the ethical dimensions of surrogacy are thoroughly considered. In practice this is not uniformly applied and can be impacted by commercial arrangements.

ADDRESSING FEELINGS OF ATTACHMENT

One of the critical aspects of counselling for surrogates is addressing the complex and often intense feelings of attachment they may develop towards the foetus during pregnancy. Non-maleficence in this context should be applied by addressing the emotional attachment that surrogates often develop towards the foetus during pregnancy. This attachment is a universal sentiment experienced by many surrogates, and it should be an integral part of routine counselling (Ferolino et al., 2020; Goli et al., 2022; Yee et al., 2020). Despite being fully aware that they will separate from the baby after birth, many surrogates experience profound emotional bonds with the child they carry. This attachment can lead to feelings of sadness, anxiety, and grief at the prospect of separation (Ferolino et al., 2020; Goli et al., 2022; Yee et al., 2020). These feelings are natural and must be openly acknowledged and managed with sensitivity. Surrogates may need to discuss their feelings of attachment and healthcare providers need to be aware of this. The healthcare providers' duty of care includes actively managing emotional distress and maintaining an ongoing dialogue that ensures the surrogate mothers are not left to navigate their feelings of attachment alone.

ADDRESSING THE IMPACT OF TABOOS AND STIGMA ON THE SURROGATE

Surrogacy, despite its growing acceptance in some parts of the world, remains a socially stigmatised practice in many communities. This stigma can profoundly impact surrogates, particularly in societies where traditional social networks play a critical role in providing emotional and practical support. The potential impacts of these taboos include social isolation, emotional distress, and a lack of support, which can complicate the surrogacy journey significantly (Goli et al., 2022; Rozée et al., 2020). Surrogacy is often viewed as a deviation from traditional norms of family and motherhood. This perception leads to significant judgement and stigma, causing surrogates to hide the true nature of their pregnancy. This fear of social ostracism and dishonour compels many surrogates to limit their social interactions and conceal their surrogacy. This concealment can lead to a range of emotional and practical challenges. Social networks, including family, friends, and community, play a crucial role in providing psychological support during pregnancy (Goli et al., 2022; Rozée et al., 2020). This support may not be available to surrogates who face judgement, rejection, or misunderstanding from those they would typically rely on for emotional and practical help. As a result, the stigma surrounding surrogacy can lead to a lack of support from their social networks at the very moment when surrogates most need it. Additionally, divorced mothers or those in less stable social situations are particularly vulnerable to heightened stigma and blame. These individuals may be more exposed to societal judgement and have fewer resources to cope with the emotional and practical demands of surrogacy. The lack of support can exacerbate feelings of isolation and distress, making the surrogacy experience more challenging. It is therefore imperative that regular counselling sessions address the emotional impact of stigma and provide strategies for coping with societal judgement. Counselling can offer a safe space for surrogates to express their fears and anxieties. Healthcare providers need to be aware of the impact of surrogacy concealment and adequate counselling and support provided.

COUNSELLING AND EDUCATION ON POTENTIAL FAMILY DISTURBANCES IN SURROGACY

Surrogacy can significantly impact family dynamics, marital relationships, and future childbearing plans (Kneebone et al., 2022; Rozée et al., 2020). Therefore, comprehensive counselling and education are essential both before and during the surrogacy process to prepare and support surrogate mothers and their families.

Throughout the pregnancy, continuous marital support is essential. Counselling should address how the process may affect marital relationships. Healthcare providers should offer counselling sessions to help couples navigate the emotional and physical changes they experience. This support can include guidance on maintaining intimacy, communication strategies to manage frustration and anger, and tools for emotional support. Ensuring that both partners feel heard and supported can mitigate the strain on their relationship. Surrogates often face concerns about sexual activity during pregnancy, fearing it might harm the foetus (Goli et al., 2022). Therefore, pre-surrogacy counselling should consider discussions about potential sexual health concerns and their impact on marital intimacy. Couples could be provided with strategies to maintain their relationship and manage any sexual health issues that may arise during the pregnancy.

The implications on family planning should also be considered. Surrogates who have their own children often plan to expand their families after completing a surrogacy. However, complications from the surrogacy process can disrupt these plans. Pre-surrogacy counselling should thoroughly discuss potential long-term reproductive health impacts. Women should be informed about the risks associated with multiple caesarean sections and other potential complications.

An important but often overlooked aspect of supporting surrogates is providing guidance on how to introduce and explain surrogacy to their own children. Many surrogates struggle with this aspect and often resort to telling their children that the pregnancy is their own and, after childbirth, that the baby has died (Goli et al., 2022; Rozée & Unisa, 2015). This approach can lead to confusion and emotional distress for the children. Therefore, it is crucial for counsellors to provide surrogates with appropriate strategies to manage this complex issue. There is little literature on best practice to support these conversations with the surrogates' children, but some general guidelines are appropriate. Counsellors should encourage surrogates to have early and age-appropriate conversations with their children about surrogacy. These discussions should be tailored to the child's level of understanding and maturity. For younger children, simple explanations using basic concepts can be effective, while older children can handle more detailed and nuanced discussions. Counsellors should guide surrogates to use a positive and straightforward language. Explaining that the surrogate is helping another family who cannot have a baby on their own can frame the surrogacy in a positive light. Emphasising the altruistic aspect of surrogacy can help children appreciate the significance of their mother's decision. Counsellors can provide surrogates with resources and tools to facilitate these discussions. If available, storybooks, educational materials, and videos designed for children can be valuable aids in explaining surrogacy.

The principle of non-maleficence underscores the ethical duty of healthcare providers to avoid causing harm to surrogates and their babies. In the complex landscape of surrogacy, this principle serves as a guide, directing medical practitioners to prioritise health and safety over contractual or convenience-based considerations.

By steadfastly adhering to the commitment to "do no harm", healthcare providers can navigate the ethical challenges of commercial and altruistic surrogacy, ensuring that their care fosters the best possible outcomes for both surrogates and the babies they carry. This dedication to non-maleficence not only protects the health of surrogates but also contributes to a more ethical and compassionate framework for surrogacy practices worldwide.

Section 5: Beneficence

Healthcare providers often find themselves navigating a complex web of ethical obligations. Traditionally, the principle of non-maleficence—"do no harm"—has been a central focus, ensuring that the surrogate and the child are protected from any undue risks or harm. However, the ethical principle of beneficence—"do good"—which calls for proactive efforts to promote the well-being of all parties involved, is equally crucial but frequently underemphasised.

Beneficence in surrogacy requires healthcare providers to go beyond mere harm prevention, actively engaging in practices that enhance the physical, emotional, and psychological welfare of the surrogate, the intended parents, and the future child. This includes comprehensive pre-surrogacy counselling and holistic care for the surrogate, ensuring fair compensation and support and promoting positive relationships between all parties involved. Moreover, healthcare providers must consider the long-term well-being of the child, advocate for ethical practices, and provide continued postpartum care and psychological support.

Despite its importance, the application of beneficence in surrogacy is often overshadowed by the dominant focus on non-maleficence. This tendency may result in missed opportunities to support the surrogate and the intended parents fully, particularly in managing the emotional complexities and ethical dilemmas that arise throughout the surrogacy journey. As such, there is a pressing need for healthcare providers to balance these ethical principles, ensuring that beneficence is given due consideration in their care practices.

To illustrate, studies have shown that comprehensive pre-surrogacy counselling significantly enhances the surrogate's and intended parents' preparedness, reducing psychological distress and improving satisfaction with the surrogacy process (Khalaf et al., 2008). Moreover, ensuring that the surrogate has access to holistic care—including mental health support—has been shown to mitigate the emotional burden and potential attachment issues that can arise during and after pregnancy (Imrie & Jadva, 2014).

Furthermore, the ethical principle of beneficence is reflected in advocating for fair compensation and robust support systems for surrogates, which help protect against exploitation and promote their financial and emotional security (Armuand et al., 2018). The role of healthcare providers in facilitating positive relationships between surrogates and intended parents also exemplifies beneficence, as these relationships can significantly influence the overall surrogacy experience and outcomes (Golombok et al., 2013).

Fiduciary Duty and Conflict of Interest

A critical dimension of beneficence in this context is the conflict of interest that arises when a single physician is responsible for both the surrogate and the intended parents. Surrogacy is a highly medicalised process, involving extensive clinical interactions between doctors and surrogates, which establishes a clear doctor-patient relationship. This relationship is central to the surrogacy experience, encompassing a range of medical treatments and interventions. The surrogate may undergo various procedures, such as taking birth control pills or hormone injections to synchronise cycles with the oocyte provider and undergoing embryo transfer and blood tests to confirm pregnancy. Additional medical interventions may include amniocentesis or chorionic villi sampling to test for chromosomal abnormalities or foetal infections, as well as procedures like selective foetal reduction in cases of multiple pregnancies, and possibly caesarean sections. Given the intensity and scope of these medical interactions, it is evident that a doctor-patient relationship is established, one that inherently carries a fiduciary duty. This duty is based on the trust and vulnerability inherent in the relationship, where the doctor is entrusted with the surrogate's health and well-being throughout the complex and medically intensive surrogacy process.

The fiduciary duty of a physician, especially the duty of loyalty, is central to ensuring that the surrogate receives care that is in their best interest. According to Frankel (2010), the duty of loyalty in fiduciary relationships comprises two essential components: the requirement that fiduciaries exercise their discretionary power exclusively for the benefit of their beneficiaries and the prohibition against actions that conflict with the interests of their beneficiaries (Frankel, 2010). In the context of surrogacy, this means that a physician's primary responsibility is to act in the best interest of the surrogate, ensuring that their health, autonomy, and well-being are prioritised. This principle aligns with the guidelines established by the Royal College of Midwives (RCM), which provide clear directions for midwives caring for surrogates during pregnancy (Royal College of Midwives [RCM], 1997). In cases of conflict or disagreement, a midwife's legal duty of care is owed to the surrogate and their child rather than the intended parents—a principle that applies equally to obstetricians (Bhatia et al., 2009).

However, when a physician is simultaneously managing the desires of the intended parents and the care of the surrogate, a conflict of interest arises. The intended parents may have preferences or demands—such as decisions regarding embryo transfer or foetal reduction—that might not align with the best medical or psychological outcomes for the surrogate. This dual responsibility places the physician in a precarious position, where the duty of loyalty to the surrogate could be compromised by the competing interests of the intended parents.

The reason fiduciaries, such as physicians and other healthcare workers, are obligated to act loyally and avoid conflicts of interest is closely tied to the inherent power imbalance in fiduciary relationships. The duty of loyalty is founded upon the beneficiary's vulnerability to the fiduciary. In a fiduciary relationship, the beneficiary must depend on the fiduciary's exercise of discretionary power, and this power, if misused or abused, can severely harm the beneficiary's interests. The duty of loyalty is a protective measure, designed to respond to and mitigate this structural vulnerability. It ensures that the fiduciary's power is exercised solely for the benefit of the beneficiary, safeguarding the surrogate from any exploitative or self-serving actions by the physician.

The duty of loyalty in a fiduciary relationship is not just a precautionary measure but a necessary condition to prevent the misuse of discretionary power. It recognises that conflicts of interest pose a significant threat not only to the fiduciary's willingness to act in the beneficiary's best interests but also to their capacity to do so. This is because, as Irit Samet (2008) points out, moral psychology suggests that even well-intentioned fiduciaries may be vulnerable to self-deception, wherein a secondary interest could unconsciously influence their judgement and actions (Samet, 2008). Therefore, avoiding conflicts of interest is essential to ensure that the fiduciary—here, the physician and healthcare worker—remains fully committed to the surrogate's welfare.

Influence of Intended Parents

Tanderup et al. (2015) observed that intended parents often exert considerable pressure on doctors, influencing decisions about the mode of delivery and other aspects of care. In some cases, this influence is direct, such as when intended parents demand caesarean sections for surrogates and offer additional payments for such procedures. In other cases, the influence is more indirect but still significant.

For instance, doctors may pre-emptively accommodate the preferences of intended parents, believing those align with their interests and avoids potential complications (Tanderup et al., 2015b). This dynamic underscores a fundamental conflict of interest, where the priorities of intended parents can overshadow the medical and ethical considerations of surrogate care.

Medical Decision-Making and Financial Incentives

Financial conflicts of interest further complicate the scenario. In the commercial surrogacy industry, doctors may face pressure to make decisions that maximise profitability rather than prioritise surrogate health. As noted by Pande (2014b), some surrogates are pressured into undergoing medically unnecessary caesarean sections or other interventions to meet the preferences of intended parents or to fit clinic schedules (Pande, 2014b). The financial motivations for doctors—whether through clinic ownership or increased business generated by higher pregnancy success rates—can lead to practices that are not always aligned with the best interests of surrogates. For example, clinics with high success rates use these metrics as a marketing tool, potentially incentivising the transfer of multiple embryos to achieve higher pregnancy rates (Gruben, 2013). This practice not only increases the risk of multiple pregnancies but also imposes additional physical and emotional stress on surrogates (Pande, 2014b).

Ethical Implications of Dual Treatment

The potential for conflicts of interest is also evident in cases where doctors manage the care of both surrogates and intended parents. Teman (2010) observed that doctors often mediate conflicts between surrogates and intended parents, such as disagreements over travel during pregnancy (Teman, 2010). In such situations, doctors' loyalties may be divided, leading to decisions that favour the intended parents' interests over the surrogate's well-being. The ethical complexity of dual treatment situations highlights the need for clear boundaries and impartiality in medical care.

Global Perspectives on Surrogacy Practices

These conflicts of interest are exacerbated in international contexts where commercial surrogacy practices vary. While developed countries often have guidelines or regulations to manage these conflicts, many developing countries lack such stringent oversight. For instance, the American College of Obstetricians and Gynecologists (ACOG) strongly advises against doctors treating both surrogates and intended parents due to the inherent conflicts of interest (American College of Obstetricians Gynecologists [ACOG], 2016). However, in many developing countries, where commercial surrogacy is often less regulated, these standards are rarely enforced. As a result, the lack of regulatory frameworks in these regions can lead to practices that prioritise financial gains over the health and rights of surrogates.

The commercial surrogacy industry is fraught with conflicts of interest that can compromise the ethical and medical integrity of care. The significant influence of intended parents, combined with financial incentives and inadequate regulatory oversight in some regions, underscores the need for rigorous ethical standards and practices that prioritise the health and well-being of surrogates. Addressing these conflicts is crucial for ensuring that surrogacy practices are conducted with the utmost respect for all parties involved.

BEST PRACTICE RECOMMENDATIONS

To address this ethical dilemma, an important aspect of beneficence in surrogacy is the separation of care between different physicians—one for the surrogate and another for the intended parents. This separation ensures that each party's interests are independently represented, thus upholding the surrogate's rights and well-being without the risk of bias or conflicting interests. By assigning separate physicians, the surrogate is assured of receiving care that is genuinely aligned with their best interests, free from the influence of the intended parents' desires.

This approach not only reinforces the principle of beneficence by actively promoting the surrogate's welfare but also preserves the fiduciary duty of loyalty that physicians owe to their patients. It is through such careful consideration and management of ethical principles that healthcare providers can navigate the complex dynamics of surrogacy, ensuring that all parties are treated with fairness, respect, and care.

This following discussion outlines a series of recommendations for healthcare practitioners involved in commercial surrogacy, drawing on the ethical principle of beneficence. Beneficence, in this context, necessitates that healthcare practitioners prioritise the surrogate's well-being and act in their best interests.

AVOIDING DUAL TREATMENT

There is growing consensus against a single physician treating both the surrogate and the intended parent(s) (dual treatment) (Triviño-Caballero, 2023). In several developed countries, organisations such as ACOG, the European Society of Human Reproduction and Embryology (ESHRE), and the Royal College of Obstetricians and Gynaecologists (RCOG) advocate for the separation of care providers to mitigate conflicts of interest. Although not all these bodies explicitly mandate this separation, their guidelines emphasise the importance of impartiality and the avoidance of dual treatment scenarios. The American Society for Reproductive Medicine (ASRM) is particularly explicit in its recommendations against dual roles for physicians in surrogacy arrangements, highlighting the potential for conflicts that could compromise the surrogate's care and the ethical integrity of the process.

Conversely, in many developing countries where commercial surrogacy practices are prevalent, these standards are typically disregarded. The rapid expansion of commercial surrogacy in these regions frequently outpaces the development and implementation of robust ethical guidelines and regulatory frameworks. As a result, the principles endorsed by established international bodies are rarely applied, leading to situations where the same physician will simultaneously manage the care of both the surrogate and the intended parents. This lack of separation not only raises significant ethical concerns but also underscores the disparity between the regulatory practices of developed and developing nations. The absence of such safeguards in developing countries often results in compromised care and heightened risks for surrogates, highlighting a critical gap in the ethical oversight of global surrogacy practices.

This practice generates significant conflicts of interest, as the physician is obligated to act in the best interests of both parties, which may not always align. For instance, the intended parent(s) might prioritise a MET to increase the chances of a successful pregnancy, even though this carries higher health risks for the surrogate (Kneebone et al., 2022; Munjal-Shankar, 2015; Saravanan, 2013). This directly contradicts the principle of beneficence, which requires prioritising the patient's (in this case, the surrogate's) well-being.

SEPARATE ADVOCATE TEAMS

Taking inspiration from guidelines for live organ donation, where similar concerns about conflicting interests exist, one recommendation is for separate advocate teams for surrogates and intended parents. These teams, potentially comprising psychologists, social workers, fertility doctors, and obstetricians, can guide their respective client/patient through the process and advocate for their interests. This separation helps ensure that medical decisions are made with the surrogate's best interests at the forefront, aligning with the principle of beneficence, while also safeguarding the intended parents by providing them with focused advocacy that addresses their specific needs and concerns.

FINANCIAL INDEPENDENCE

Maintaining financial distance between the intended parents and the surrogate's doctor is crucial to prevent conflicts of interest. Direct payment from the intended parents to the surrogate's doctor creates a financial conflict of interest, potentially compromising the doctor's commitment to the surrogate's well-being. For instance, if the doctor receives payment directly from the intended parents, there might be subtle pressure to prioritise their wishes—such as speeding up the process or taking medical risks that could endanger the surrogate—over the surrogate's health. Mediating payment for the surrogate's medical treatment through the surrogate herself helps ensure the doctor's primary financial responsibility is to her, reinforcing the principle of beneficence in the doctor-surrogate relationship and reducing the risk of compromising their care.

ELECTIVE/SINGLE EMBRYO TRANSFER (ESET/SET)

eSET/SET is increasingly being enforced as the standard of care in surrogacy arrangements (Cutting, 2018). While METs can boost pregnancy success rates, this practice exposes surrogates to unnecessary health risks, such as complications from multiple pregnancies, including preterm birth, gestational diabetes, and pre-eclampsia (Attawet, Wang, Farquhar, et al., 2022). These risks directly conflict with the principle of beneficence, which obligates medical professionals to act in the best interest of their patient and to minimise harm wherever possible.

By enforcing eSET/SET, medical professionals remove this ethical conflict, ensuring that the surrogate's well-being is not compromised in pursuit of higher success rates. This helps to protect the surrogate from avoidable medical complications and reinforces the medical professional's commitment to beneficence. It is a crucial practice for those who wish to uphold the highest ethical standards in their care, prioritising the health and safety of the surrogate over other considerations. Adhering to this standard is a clear demonstration of the medical professional's dedication to placing patient welfare at the forefront of clinical decision-making.

INDEPENDENT DECISION-MAKING

Medical decisions about the surrogate's care should be made independently by the surrogate and their physician, free from undue influence from the commissioning couple. While the surrogate can choose to involve the commissioning couple in these decisions, the ultimate authority should rest with the surrogate and their healthcare team. This autonomy for the surrogate regarding their own medical care aligns directly with the principle of beneficence.

Upholding the principle of beneficence within commercial surrogacy necessitates a restructuring of current practice. By avoiding dual treatment, establishing separate advocate teams, ensuring financial independence, implementing SET as standard, and protecting independent decision-making, healthcare practitioners can ensure they are acting in the best interests of the surrogate.

Section 6: Justice in Surrogacy

The Principle of Justice in Surrogacy: Ethical Guidance for Healthcare Professionals

The principle of justice, a fundamental tenet of medical ethics, demands fairness in medical care delivery, equitable distribution of resources, and the safeguarding of rights. In the context of surrogacy, justice ensures that all parties involved—the surrogate, the intended parents, and the child—are treated fairly and equitably. However, the application of this principle in surrogacy is complex, given the diverse legal, cultural, and socioeconomic landscapes that define surrogacy practices around the world. For healthcare professionals, upholding justice involves navigating these complexities to provide ethically sound and equitable care.

Both altruistic and commercial surrogacy models are subject to scrutiny regarding exploitation, albeit in different ways. Altruistic surrogacy, while avoiding direct financial transactions, can still be influenced by emotional and relational dynamics that might lead to exploitation. Commercial surrogacy, with its financial incentives, faces criticism for potentially exploiting economic vulnerabilities and commodifying reproduction.

Effective regulation and ethical oversight are crucial in both models to address these concerns. For altruistic surrogacy, ensuring that surrogates are not subjected to emotional manipulation and power imbalances is vital. In commercial surrogacy, robust safeguards are necessary to protect surrogates from economic coercion and to address concerns about commodification.

Ultimately, both models require careful consideration of ethical principles and regulatory frameworks to balance the interests and well-being of all parties involved. Addressing these issues thoughtfully can help mitigate the risks of exploitation and ensure that surrogacy practices are conducted with respect and fairness.

Exploring Exploitation and Power Imbalances in Surrogacy

Discourse on surrogacy, in particular commercial surrogacy, consistently highlights the ethical principle of justice as a major point of concern. The potential for exploitation stems from power imbalances. This is especially relevant when significant economic disparities exist between the surrogate, who is often from a low-income background, and the intended parents, who tend to have greater financial resources (Blazier & Janssens, 2020).

Exploitation occurs when one party unfairly benefits at the expense of another, often involving coercion, manipulation, or taking advantage of someone's vulnerability. In surrogacy, there are various ways in which exploitation can manifest.

Financial coercion is one area of concern. Offering large sums of money for surrogacy, particularly in resource-poor countries, can create a coercive environment where women may feel compelled to become surrogates out of financial desperation rather than genuine choice. For instance, studies describe how surrogates in India felt pressured to accept lower payments or silence their concerns due to their precarious economic situations (Gupta, 2012; Pande, 2010).

There is also the issue of unequal bargaining power. The inherent power differential between surrogates and intended parents, often amplified by socioeconomic disparities, can result in unfair contract terms or a lack of agency for the surrogate throughout the process. Several studies found that contracts included restrictive measures that limited the surrogate's autonomy, such as imposing specific lifestyle requirements, restricting information sharing, mandating certain prenatal tests, or even requiring compulsory C-sections (Blazier & Janssens, 2020).

Another point of contention is the assertion from some researchers that commercial surrogacy is the commodification of women and reproductive labour, particularly in commercial arrangements where the focus shifts from altruism to financial transaction (Pande, 2010; Wilkinson, 2003). Pande (2010) recounts the experiences of surrogates in India who were housed in hostels and treated as mere "vessels" for carrying foetuses, their autonomy and emotional needs disregarded for the sake of profit. Some argue that this can be dehumanising and undermine the inherent dignity of women (Anderson, 2020; Satz, 1992; Wilkinson, 2003).

Mitigating Exploitation and Promoting Justice in Healthcare

To address the disparity, healthcare professionals can take several steps aligned with the principle of justice. Healthcare providers should push for surrogates' access to independent legal counsel, particularly in international arrangements where surrogates may not fully understand their rights. They should ensure that the surrogate is fully informed of the legal risks and obligations in a language and context the surrogate understands, facilitating true informed consent.

Justice also demands particular attention to the surrogate's well-being, especially in cross-border surrogacy, where economic inequalities may result in undue pressure on people to enter agreements out of financial necessity. Healthcare professionals have an ethical duty to recognise and address these imbalances by ensuring surrogates are not exploited and have agency in the process.

While laws may differ from country to country, justice requires healthcare professionals to uphold consistent ethical standards that protect surrogates, intended parents, and children. This includes following best practices in surrogacy care, even if not mandated by local law, and advising against arrangements that do not meet these standards.

Ultimately, justice in surrogacy requires healthcare professionals to take a proactive role in ensuring fair treatment for all parties involved, particularly surrogates, who are often at a disadvantage due to legal or economic disparities. This may involve advocating for stronger international regulations, contributing to public policy, or refusing to participate in surrogacy arrangements that fail to meet basic ethical and legal standards.

Empowerment and Support

The healthcare worker plays a critical role in empowering surrogates and ensuring they have agency throughout the surrogacy journey. This involves providing comprehensive information, facilitating access to support networks, and promoting respectful communication between all parties.

It is recommended that healthcare professionals prioritise transparent communication as a fundamental aspect of ethical surrogacy care. This includes using a clear, non-technical language to explain medical procedures, ethical considerations, and the legal implications of surrogacy. Such an approach enables surrogates and intended parents to make informed decisions, fostering autonomy and ensuring that surrogates are not subjected to pressure or coercion when making medical choices.

Healthcare professionals are also encouraged to facilitate access to psychological support for surrogates and intended parents. Providing access to psychological counselling for all parties involved addresses the emotional complexities of surrogacy, promoting mental well-being throughout the process.

Another recommended practice is to support surrogates by linking them with peer networks of other surrogates. These networks offer a safe space for sharing experiences, voicing concerns, and receiving emotional support, which can enhance surrogates' sense of empowerment and autonomy. Likewise, intended parents benefit from participation in support groups, where they can prepare for the emotional and practical realities of parenting through surrogacy.

Although often overlooked, healthcare workers are a critical point of contact between the intended parents and the surrogate and therefore must endeavour to foster open, respectful communication between the surrogate and the intended parents. This includes ensuring that the surrogate's opinions and feelings are heard and respected at every stage of the process. Healthcare workers should act as neutral facilitators, promoting mutual respect and ensuring that power imbalances do not lead to the surrogate feeling dominated or undervalued. In this delicate position healthcare workers will also play a key role in mediating potential conflicts between surrogates and intended parents, particularly around medical decisions. By promoting constructive dialogue and providing neutral advice, healthcare workers can help resolve misunderstandings or differences in expectations in a fair manner.

Despite this role as a mediator healthcare professionals must ensure full medical autonomy, and surrogates should have control over decisions about their health and well-being during the pregnancy. Healthcare workers can empower surrogates by thoroughly explaining medical procedures, offering options, and ensuring that they are the primary decision-makers in matters affecting their bodies. This includes their right to refuse certain treatments or medical interventions if they are not comfortable with such procedures.

The significant ethical dimensions of surrogacy require regular, proactive communication with the surrogate throughout the pregnancy to ensure the surrogate feels supported and informed. Healthcare workers should initiate conversations about their well-being, emotional state, and any concerns the surrogate may have, ensuring they know they have a voice in every part of the process.

The importance of cultural sensitivity cannot be understated, particularly in the context of commercial surrogates where the intended parents and surrogate mother are typically from vastly different socioeconomic and cultural backgrounds. Healthcare workers should be aware of the cultural and socioeconomic backgrounds of both surrogates and intended parents. Providing culturally sensitive care ensures that surrogates are not misunderstood, manipulated, marginalised, or discriminated against due to their background, particularly in cross-border surrogacy.

Although the focus of the healthcare worker is primarily on the surrogate, empowerment extends to intended parents as well. Healthcare workers should offer guidance on navigating the medical process, legal obligations, and emotional aspects of surrogacy. This includes preparing them for their parental roles, while also ensuring they are respectful of the surrogate's boundaries and autonomy.

Healthcare workers should advocate for the adoption of best practices and ethical standards in surrogacy care, even in countries or regions where laws may be insufficient or unclear. By adhering to international standards of care, they can ensure that surrogates are protected from exploitation and that intended parents receive ethical guidance.

In situations where healthcare workers observe unethical practices—such as pressuring surrogates to undergo unnecessary procedures or withholding critical information—it is essential that they support the surrogate's right to autonomous decision-making. When direct advocacy may not be possible due to professional constraints or fear of job loss, healthcare workers can contribute by fostering a culture of ethical practice within their scope of influence. This might include promoting informed consent, encouraging transparent communication, and highlighting ethical concerns through appropriate internal reporting channels. By doing so, they play a vital role in upholding the surrogate's rights while protecting their own professional well-being.

Healthcare workers play a crucial role in supporting the future well-being of the child during the surrogacy process by helping intended parents prepare for their role as primary caregivers. This support is provided through clear, concise communication about parental rights and responsibilities, key medical considerations for newborn care, and access to relevant support services or community resources. Practical actions may include offering brief guidance, addressing questions, and providing informational materials to ensure intended parents have the foundational knowledge and resources they need. By facilitating a smooth transition post-birth, healthcare workers contribute to positive outcomes for the child, the surrogate, and the intended parents.

Examining Equitable Access to Surrogacy

The principle of justice in surrogacy examines the fairness and equity of access to surrogacy services, considering both intended parents and potential surrogates. This analysis is particularly relevant when evaluating the implications of restrictions on commercial surrogacy and their impact on access to reproductive services.

Access for Intended Parents

Restrictions on commercial surrogacy often aim to prevent exploitation and ensure ethical practices, but they can also inadvertently affect the equitable access of intended parents. Commercial surrogacy provides an avenue for those who may not have access to altruistic surrogates, due to geographical, social, or personal reasons. For many intended parents, particularly those with high medical needs, financial constraints, or specific legal barriers, commercial surrogacy represents a viable path to parenthood.

However, the high costs associated with commercial surrogacy can be prohibitive, leading to a situation where only those with substantial financial resources can afford it. In regions where commercial surrogacy is highly regulated or banned, intended parents might face significant barriers, including lengthy wait times, limited availability of altruistic surrogates, and increased costs associated with navigating complex legal frameworks. This can create inequities where access to surrogacy becomes a privilege of the wealthy, while others are effectively excluded from this reproductive option.

In countries with strict restrictions, intended parents may find themselves unable to pursue surrogacy, due to either the prohibitive costs of legal and medical services or the scarcity of altruistic surrogates willing to participate. Such restrictions, while intended to protect surrogates and ensure ethical practices, can disproportionately affect those with fewer financial resources or those who do not have access to alternative reproductive options.

Access for Potential Surrogates

For potential surrogates, the principle of justice also requires examination. In some jurisdictions, restrictions on commercial surrogacy aim to safeguard against the exploitation of surrogates, but they can also limit opportunities for people who might wish to participate in a surrogacy arrangement for financial reasons or personal motivations. Altruistic surrogacy, while ethically sound in many respects, may not provide the same level of support and compensation that commercial surrogacy offers. This can impact those who are economically disadvantaged or who view surrogacy as an opportunity for financial improvement.

Moreover, altruistic surrogacy might not be feasible for all women, particularly those who do not have a personal connection to intended parents or who are unwilling to participate without financial compensation. Restricting commercial surrogacy can thus limit the options available to potential surrogates, potentially excluding those who could benefit from the financial support and structure that commercial arrangements provide.

Balancing Justice and Regulation

The challenge lies in balancing the principle of justice with the need to regulate surrogacy practices to prevent exploitation. Effective regulation should aim to protect surrogates from coercion and ensure fair compensation while also considering the needs and rights of intended parents. This includes addressing the financial barriers that can limit access to surrogacy services for those with fewer resources.

A fair and equitable approach would involve creating regulatory frameworks that not only protect surrogates but also provide pathways for intended parents to access surrogacy without prohibitive costs. This might involve implementing measures to ensure that surrogacy remains a viable option for a broader range of individuals, such as subsidising costs for lower-income intended parents or supporting programmes that facilitate altruistic surrogacy without undermining the financial stability of surrogates.

Equitable access to surrogacy requires a nuanced understanding of the principle of justice, balancing the need to prevent exploitation with the need to ensure that surrogacy remains accessible to all individuals. By addressing the financial and regulatory barriers faced by both intended parents and potential surrogates, it is possible to create a more just and inclusive system that respects the rights and needs of all parties involved.

Fairness in Medical Care Delivery

Fairness in medical care delivery is central to the principle of justice in surrogacy. It involves providing all necessary medical services to surrogate mothers to ensure their health and safety throughout the surrogacy process. Fairness is compromised when surrogates do not receive the care they are promised or when their medical needs are inadequately addressed.

Significant issues have been found in international surrogacy arrangements. Despite assurances from surrogacy agencies, many surrogate mothers faced inadequate medical care (Brandão & Garrido, 2022). One reported case involved a surrogate who underwent three cycles of embryo transfers, each with a triple-embryo transfer attempt, before becoming pregnant. At an early check-up, the absence of the baby's heartbeat led to an emotionally and physically taxing Dilation and curettage (D&C) procedure. The surrogate experienced severe pain and a lengthy recovery, yet her compensation was reduced as she did not complete the pregnancy and delivery (Attawet, Wang, & Sullivan, 2022). This case underscores a troubling trend where the financial and emotional costs borne by surrogates are grossly disproportionate to the inadequate care they receive and the limited compensation provided.

Adequate Health Monitoring for Surrogates

In various surrogacy arrangements, particularly within lower-income settings, surrogates may experience infrequent and substandard medical monitoring compared to those in wealthier regions. Evidence indicates that surrogates in developing countries often have limited access to comprehensive care, which jeopardises both their own health and that of the foetus (Gupta & Prasad, 2019; Munjal-Shankar, 2015; Saravanan, 2013). This lack of control over their medical care contributes to a broader issue of inadequate health monitoring and care. A quantitative study revealed that surrogates in India exhibited higher levels of depression compared to a group of expectant mothers, highlighting significant psychological distress resulting from these care inadequacies (Lamba et al., 2018). Moreover, postnatal care is a particularly important consideration in surrogacy arrangements, and some surrogates have reported feelings of emotional attachment to the babies they carried, exacerbated by circumstances where they were required to care for the child post-birth due to delays or specific demands from the intended parents (Karandikar et al., 2017; Saravanan, 2013). Further compounding these issues, reports from Ukraine and Kenya describe oppressive living conditions, poor surrogate healthcare, and instances of forced late-term abortions where international surrogacy practices remain largely unregulated (Lepapa, 2021; Marinelli et al. 2022; Tanderup et al., 2023). These disparities underscore the urgent need for standardised care protocols to ensure that all surrogates, regardless of geographic location, receive equitable monitoring and support throughout the surrogacy process.

Equal Access

The principle of justice, when applied to surrogacy, emphasises the imperative of equal access to reproductive opportunities for every individual. This principle suggests that surrogacy should not be restricted or influenced by factors such as marital status, ethnicity, religion, or sexual orientation (Mackenzie et al., 2020; Smith et al., 2013). Justice in this context is not merely about offering surrogacy services but ensuring that such services are available to a diverse array of individuals, including infertile couples, singles, and same-sex couples. However, this does not imply that having a child is an inherent right. Equal access to surrogacy is appropriate only when there is assurance that the child will be raised in an environment where their physical, emotional, and developmental needs will be adequately met. Additionally, while the principle of justice advocates for equal access to surrogacy, healthcare providers also have an ethical responsibility to ensure that the welfare of the child remains central throughout the process. Equal access should be balanced with a consideration of the child's best interests, ensuring that intended parents have the capacity to provide a stable, loving, and supportive environment. Justice, therefore, involves not only fairness in offering reproductive options but also safeguarding the well-being of the future child in these arrangements.

The application of justice requires a system that transcends discriminatory barriers, providing equitable opportunities for all who seek to build their families through surrogacy. By aligning surrogacy practices with the principle of justice, it may facilitate a move towards a more inclusive and fair reproductive landscape where every individual has the chance to access this service without prejudice or exclusion.

Discharge and Handover: Navigating Legal Complexities

One significant issue healthcare providers must address is the legal parentage of the child at the time of discharge. In many jurisdictions, intended parents do not have immediate legal rights to the child upon birth. Typically, legal parentage is only granted once a parentage order is issued, which may occur weeks or even months after birth. Until that time, the surrogate is considered the legal parent, even though they may have no intention of caring for the child post-birth. This creates a dilemma for midwives and hospitals, who, in many cases, are reluctant or refuse to discharge the child directly to the intended parents due to legal concerns.

In some hospitals, the policy is that the child must be discharged with the surrogate, who then transfers the child to the intended parents outside of the hospital setting. While this ensures adherence to legal protocols, it can be a distressing process for all involved, particularly for the intended parents who are eager to assume their role as caregivers from the moment of birth.

A potential recommendation to address this issue is for healthcare providers to accept written consent from the surrogate, explicitly allowing the handover of the child to the intended parents. This approach, however, must be balanced against hospital policies and legal frameworks, which vary widely across regions and institutions. It is crucial for healthcare practitioners to be aware of the specific regulations governing surrogacy in their hospital and jurisdiction, while also advocating for processes that respect the rights of the child and the intentions of the surrogate and intended parents.

Ultimately, justice in this context demands that the child is not subjected to unnecessary disruptions or delays in receiving care from their intended parents.

Healthcare providers should work to facilitate a smooth transition while complying with legal obligations, recognising that the intended parents, though not yet the legal parents, are the child's future caregivers.

Including Intended Parents in Newborn Care: A Justice-Based Approach

Justice also requires that children born through surrogacy receive the same level of care as any other child, which includes the involvement of their intended parents in crucial aspects of newborn care. While the surrogate retains legal rights immediately after birth, it is typical for them to give consent for the intended parents to participate in the care of the child. Once this consent is given, healthcare providers should actively involve the intended parents in early bonding activities, such as skin-to-skin contact and breastfeeding support, ensuring that the child benefits from the presence and care of those who will ultimately raise them.

Including intended parents in the care process may seem counterintuitive to traditional notions of motherhood in healthcare settings, where the birth mother is viewed as the primary caregiver. However, justice requires a broader understanding of "parenthood" in surrogacy contexts. The intended parents, even if not biologically or legally connected to the child at birth, will assume the full parental role. Therefore, healthcare providers must recognise them as key figures in the child's care and encourage their participation in the newborn's early life.

For instance, skin-to-skin contact, known for its numerous health benefits to newborns—including regulating temperature and heart rate and promoting bonding—should be facilitated between the intended parents and the child, provided the surrogate mother has given their consent. Similarly, intended parents should be offered the same guidance and support on breastfeeding alternatives, such as formula feeding or induced lactation, just as any new mother would receive. The principle of justice ensures that these parents are given the same respect and opportunities to care for their child, even if the legal and biological relationships differ from traditional birth scenarios.

By actively involving the intended parents in these early stages, healthcare providers ensure that the child receives consistent, loving care from those who will ultimately raise them. This not only promotes the child's best interests but also honours the surrogate's wishes and facilitates a smooth transition for all parties involved. In many cases, the surrogate's consent to involve the intended parents in this care reflects their desire for the child to bond with their future caregivers, reinforcing the justice-based approach that prioritises the child's right to a stable and supportive environment.

The Child's Well-Being

The principle of justice in healthcare requires that all parties involved in surrogacy—particularly the child—are treated fairly and equitably. Ensuring the well-being of the child born through surrogacy is a fundamental responsibility of healthcare professionals. This encompasses psychological development, transparency about the child's origins, and the dynamics of the relationship between the child and the surrogate.

Psychological Development

Research indicates that children born through surrogacy generally exhibit positive psychological development, similar to those conceived naturally. A systematic review by Söderström-Anttila et al. (2015) concluded that there is no evidence to suggest that children born through surrogacy experience significant psychological difficulties compared to their peers (Söderström-Anttila et al., 2015). Healthcare professionals must ensure that, from a developmental perspective, children born via surrogacy receive the same attention and care as any child. This underscores the need for long-term support, including psychosocial interventions, if necessary, to promote a healthy developmental trajectory.

Disclosure of Surrogacy

An important aspect of the child's well-being is the transparency surrounding their conception. Open disclosure about the child's origins is widely considered beneficial for their psychological health. Igreja and Ricou (2019) emphasise that honesty regarding a child's conception through surrogacy fosters trust within the family and helps the child understand their unique identity (Igreja & Ricou, 2019). Healthcare providers play a critical role in advising intended parents on the importance of age-appropriate communication regarding surrogacy. They must advocate for transparency while respecting cultural and personal preferences. Failure to disclose the child's origins may result in confusion or distress later in life, which could affect the child's sense of self and relationships.

Relationship with the Surrogate

The nature of the relationship between the child and the surrogate can vary, often depending on the terms agreed upon by all parties involved. Some children maintain contact with their surrogates, while others do not, with the decision largely being shaped by the intended parents and surrogate. Imrie and Jadva (2014) reveal that surrogates often maintain positive relationships with the child and intended parents, with contact levels varying widely (Imrie & Jadva, 2014). In most cases, surrogates did not view the child as their own but were open to maintaining contact if desired.

The long-term impact of these relationships is an area of ongoing research, and healthcare professionals should provide guidance based on the most up-to-date findings. In regulated surrogacy arrangements, these relationships tend to be handled with more structure and support, leading to generally positive experiences for all involved (Jadva et al., 2012). However, in cross-border or unregulated surrogacy, the relationships are not well understood, and the legal frameworks may complicate contact between the child and the surrogate. Professionals must consider the child's best interests when advising on ongoing contact, ensuring that any relationship between the child and the surrogate is navigated with care, fairness, and sensitivity.

In summary the child's well-being is central to the ethics or ethical responsibilities of healthcare professionals in surrogacy. From ensuring positive psychological development to promoting transparency about the child's origins and guiding the relationship with the surrogate, healthcare providers must act with justice in mind. Their role extends beyond clinical care to encompass long-term support for the family, ensuring that the child's needs are met with fairness and integrity throughout their life.

The principle of justice in surrogacy requires a multifaceted approach to ensure fairness and equity across all aspects of the surrogacy process. This principle demands equal access to surrogacy services for all individuals, regardless of socioeconomic status, marital status, or other personal characteristics. In practice, however, commercial surrogacy often creates financial barriers that restrict access to those with substantial resources, thereby reinforcing inequalities in reproductive opportunities. By embedding justice into surrogacy practices and prioritising the child's emotional, legal, and psychological well-being, a more inclusive, fair, and equitable result may be achieved.

Section 7: Conclusion

This chapter has explored the intricate role of healthcare providers in the ethically complex world of surrogacy, particularly within the commercial framework. The absence of cohesive international regulations and the varying legal and ethical landscapes across the globe present unique challenges for healthcare professionals working in this field.

The discussion highlighted the paramount importance of adhering to the universal ethical principles—autonomy, beneficence, non-maleficence, and justice—as guiding lights for healthcare providers in surrogacy arrangements.

- Autonomy necessitates that healthcare providers champion the surrogate mother's right to self-determination and informed decision-making, ensuring their choices about their health and the birthing process are respected, even when potentially conflicting with the desires of intended parents or the stipulations of commercial contracts.
- Beneficence calls for proactive measures to promote the well-being of all parties involved, moving beyond simply avoiding harm to actively enhancing their physical, emotional, and psychological welfare.
- Non-maleficence underscores the duty to avoid causing harm, obligating healthcare providers to resist unnecessary medical interventions that might be driven by commercial interests rather than the health needs of the surrogate and the child.
- Justice demands fairness and equity in all aspects of surrogacy, ensuring that surrogates receive fair compensation and comprehensive medical care and are

protected from exploitation, while also considering the needs and rights of the intended parents and the child.

Informed consent, a cornerstone of ethical healthcare, emerges as a particularly complex issue in commercial surrogacy, often impacted by power imbalances, financial pressures, and the complexities of medical procedures. Healthcare providers must ensure that surrogate mothers are fully informed and empowered to make decisions about their bodies and medical care throughout the process. This includes using a clear and accessible language, verifying understanding, and addressing potential conflicts of interest that might compromise the surrogate's well-being.

This chapter emphasised the need for specialised training and professional guidelines to equip healthcare providers with the knowledge and skills necessary to navigate the multifaceted ethical dilemmas inherent in surrogacy.

By advocating for the development and implementation of robust ethical frameworks, healthcare professionals can play a crucial role in shaping a more just and compassionate surrogacy landscape that prioritises the dignity, rights, and well-being of all parties involved.

References

American College of Obstetricians Gynecologists (ACOG). (2016). Family building through gestational surrogacy. Committee Opinion No. 660. *Obstetrics and Gynecology*, *127*(3), e97–e103.

Anderson, E. S. (2020). Is women's labor a commodity? In S. Sherwin & B. Parish (Eds.), *Women, medicine, ethics and the law* (pp. 167–188). Routledge.

Armuand, G., Lampic, C., Skoog-Svanberg, A., Wånggren, K., & Sydsjö, G. (2018). Survey shows that Swedish healthcare professionals have a positive attitude towards surrogacy but the health of the child is a concern. *Acta Paediatrica*, *107*(1), 101–109.

Attawet, J. (2021). Mapping transnational commercial surrogacy arrangements in South and Southeast Asia. *The Medico-Legal Journal*, *89*(2), 128–132. https://doi.org/10.1177/0025817220985099

Attawet, J. (2022). The nexus between self-perception and behavioural responses of gestational surrogates' risk experiences. *Human Fertility (Cambridge, England)*, *25*(3), 562–568. https://doi.org/10.1080/14647273.2020.1870171

Attawet, J., Alsharaydeh, E., & Brady, M. (2024). Commercial surrogacy: Landscapes of empowerment or oppression explored through integrative review. *Health Care for Women International*, 1–19.

Attawet, J., Wang, A., & Sullivan, E. (2022). 'Womb for work' experiences of Thai women and gestational surrogacy practice in Thailand. *Human Fertility (Cambridge, England)*, *25*(5), 912–923. https://doi.org/10.1080/14647273.2021.1937716

Attawet, J., Wang, A. Y., Farquhar, C. M., Jordan, V., Li, Z., & Sullivan, E. A. (2022). Pregnancy and birth outcomes of single versus multiple embryo transfer in gestational surrogacy arrangements: A systematic review and meta-analysis. *Human Fertility (Cambridge, England)*, *25*(2), 217–227. https://doi.org/10.1080/14647273.2020.1785643

Bhatia, K., Martindale, E. A., Rustamov, O., & Nysenbaum, A. M. (2009). Review: Surrogate pregnancy: An essential guide for clinicians. *Obstetrician and Gynaecologist*, *11*, 49–54.

Blazier, J., & Janssens, R. (2020). Regulating the international surrogacy market: The ethics of commercial surrogacy in the Netherlands and India. *Medicine, Health Care and Philosophy*, *23*(4), 621–630. https://doi.org/10.1007/s11019-020-09976-x

Bodner, K., Wierrani, F., Grünberger, W., & Bodner-Adler, B. (2011). Influence of the mode of delivery on maternal and neonatal outcomes: A comparison between elective cesarean section and planned vaginal delivery in a low-risk obstetric population. *Archives of Gynecology and Obstetrics*, *283*, 1193–1198.

Brandão, P., & Garrido, N. (2022). Commercial surrogacy: An overview. *Revista brasileira de ginecologia e obstetricia: revista da Federacao Brasileira das Sociedades de Ginecologia e Obstetricia*, *44*(12), 1141–1158. https://doi.org/10.1055/s-0042-1759774

Cutting, R. (2018). Single embryo transfer for all. *Best Practice & Research Clinical Obstetrics & Gynaecology*, *53*, 30–37.

Feiglin J, Savulescu J. (July 2018). A New Ethical Model of Commercial Surrogacy Arrangements for Australia. *Journal of Law and Medicine* 25(4): 919–928. PMID: 29978675.

Fenton-Glynn, C. (2016). Outsourcing ethical dilemmas: Regulating international surrogacy arrangements. *Medical Law Review*, *24*(1), 59–75. https://doi.org/10.1093/medlaw/fwv044

Ferolino, A. P., Camposo, M. A. D., Estaño, K. C. L., & Tacbobo, J. M. R. (2020). Mothers for others: An interpretative phenomenological analysis of gestational surrogates' child relinquishment experiences. *Journal of Patient Experience*, *7*(6), 1336–1340.

Frankel, T. (2010). *Fiduciary law*. Oxford University Press.

Frati, P., La Russa, R., Santurro, A., Fineschi, B., Di Paolo, M., Scopetti, M., Turillazzi, E., & Fineschi, V. (2021). Bioethical issues and legal frameworks of surrogacy: A global perspective about the right to health and dignity. *European Journal of Obstetrics & Gynecology and Reproductive Biology*, *258*, 1–8.

Goli, M., Kohan, S., Oloonabadi, S. M. A., Farajzadegan, Z., & Heidari, Z. (2022). A reproductive health-care program for surrogate mothers: A mixed methods study. *Journal of Education and Health Promotion*, *11*, 250. https://doi.org/10.4103/jehp.jehp_437_21

Golombok, S., Blake, L., Casey, P., Roman, G., & Jadva, V. (2013). Children born through reproductive donation: A longitudinal study of psychological adjustment. *Journal of Child Psychology and Psychiatry and Allied Disciplines*, *54*(6), 653–660. https://doi.org/10.1111/jcpp.12015

González, N. I. (2020). Legal and ethical issues in cross-border gestational surrogacy. *Fertility and Sterility*, *113*(5), 916–919.

Gregory, K. D., Jackson, S., Korst, L., & Fridman, M. (2012). Cesarean versus vaginal delivery: Whose risks? Whose benefits? *American Journal of Perinatology*, *29*(01), 07–18.

Gruben, V. (2013). Women as patients, not spare parts: Examining the relationship between the physician and women egg providers. *Canadian Journal of Women and the Law*, *25*(2), 249–283.

Gupta, A., & Prasad, S. (2019). 'Outsourced pregnancy': Surrogate narratives from Hyderabad. *Contributions to Indian Sociology*, *53*(2), 299–327.

Gupta, J. A. (2012). Reproductive biocrossings: Indian egg donors and surrogates in the globalized fertility market. *IJFAB: International Journal of Feminist Approaches to Bioethics*, *5*(1), 25–51.

Igreja, A. R., & Ricou, M. (2019). Surrogacy: Challenges and ambiguities. *The New Bioethics*, *25*(1), 60–77.

Imrie, S., & Jadva, V. (2014). The long-term experiences of surrogates: Relationships and contact with surrogacy families in genetic and gestational surrogacy arrangements. *Reproductive BioMedicine Online*, *29*(4), 424–435. https://doi.org/10.1016/j.rbmo.2014.06.004

Jadva, V., Blake, L., Casey, P., & Golombok, S. (2012). Surrogacy families 10 years on: Relationship with the surrogate, decisions over disclosure and children's understanding of their surrogacy origins. *Human Reproduction*, *27*(10), 3008–3014.

Kamphuis, E. I., Bhattacharya, S., Van Der Veen, F., Mol, B. W., & Templeton, A. (2014). Are we overusing IVF? *BMJ*, *348*, g252. doi:10.1136/bmj.g252

Karandikar, S., Gezinski, L., & Huber, S. (2017). Exploring the physical and emotional stress of surrogate pregnancy among transnational Indian surrogates. *International Social Work*, *60*(6), 1433–1442. https://doi.org/10.1177/0020872817710549

Karandikar, S., Gezinski, L. B., Carter, J. R., & Kaloga, M. (2014). Economic necessity or noble cause? A qualitative study exploring motivations for gestational surrogacy in Gujarat, India. *Affilia: Journal of Women & Social Work*, *29*(2), 224–236. https://doi.org/10.1177/0886109913516455

Khalaf, Z. F., Shafiabadi, A., & Tarahomi, M. (2008). Psychological aspects of surrogate motherhood. *Journal of Reproduction & Infertility*, *9*(1), 43–49.

Kneebone, E., Beilby, K., & Hammarberg, K. (2022). Experiences of surrogates and intended parents of surrogacy arrangements: A systematic review. *Reproductive BioMedicine Online*, *45*(4), 815–830.

Lamba, N., Jadva, V., Kadam, K., & Golombok, S. (2018). The psychological well-being and prenatal bonding of gestational surrogates. *Human Reproduction*, *33*(4), 646–653.

Lepapa, N. (2021). *Hard labour: The surrogacy industry in Kenya – Part I*. The Elephant. Retrieved 16th Nov from https://www.theelephant.info/investigations/2021/05/28/hard-labour-the-surrogacy-industry-in-kenya-part-i/

Mackenzie, S. C., Wickins-Drazilova, D., & Wickins, J. (2020). The ethics of fertility treatment for same-sex male couples: Considerations for a modern fertility clinic. *European Journal of Obstetrics & Gynecology and Reproductive Biology*, *244*, 71–75.

Marinelli, S., Del Rio, A., Straccamore, M., Negro, F., & Basile, G. (2022). The armed conflict in Ukraine and the risks of inter-country surrogacy. The unsolved dilemma. *European Review for Medical and Pharmacological Sciences*, *26*(16), 5646–5650.

Mascarello, K. C., Horta, B. L., & Silveira, M. F. (2017). Maternal complications and cesarean section without indication: Systematic review and meta-analysis. *Revista de saude publica*, *51*, 105.

Munjal-Shankar, D. (2015). Autonomy, choices and consent in commercial surrogacy: Viewing through the Indian Lens. *Asian Bioethics Review*, *7*(4), 380–393.

Pande, A. (2010). Commercial surrogacy in India: Manufacturing a perfect mother-worker. *Signs: Journal of Women in Culture and Society*, *35*(4), 969–992.

Pande, A. (2014a). This birth and that: Surrogacy and stratified motherhood in India. *Philosophia*, *4*(1), 50–64.

Pande, A. (2014b). *Wombs in labor: Transnational commercial surrogacy in India*. Columbia University Press.

Practice Committee of the American Society for Reproductive Medicine and the Practice Committee for the Society for Assisted Reproductive Technologies. (2021). Guidance on the limits to the number of embryos to transfer: A committee opinion. *Fertility and Sterility*, *116*(3), 651–654.

Royal College of Midwives (RCM). (1997). *Surrogacy: Defining motherhood*. Royal College of Midwives.

Rozée, V., & Unisa, S. (2015). Surrogacy as a growing practice and a controversial reality in India: Exploring new issues for further researches. *Journal of Women's Health, Issues and Care 4*, 6(2), 3–7.

Rozée, V., Unisa, S., & de La Rochebrochard, E. (2020). The social paradoxes of commercial surrogacy in developing countries: India before the new law of 2018. *BMC Women's Health*, *20*(1), 234. https://doi.org/10.1186/s12905-020-01087-2

Samet, I. (2008). Guarding the Fiduciary's conscience—A justification of a stringent profit-stripping rule. *Oxford Journal of Legal Studies*, *28*(4), 763–781.

Saravanan, S. (2013). An ethnomethodological approach to examine exploitation in the context of capacity, trust and experience of commercial surrogacy in India. *Philosophy, Ethics, and Humanities in Medicine*, *8*(1), 10. https://doi.org/10.1186/1747-5341-8-10

Satz, D. (1992). Markets in women's reproductive labor. *Philosophy & Public Affairs*, *21*(2), 107–131.

Smith, M., Willmott, L., Trowse, P., & White, B. (2013). Back to the future: Prohibiting surrogacy for singles, same-sex and shorter-term heterosexual couples in Queensland. *Journal of Law and Medicine*, *20*(3), 638–654.

Söderström-Anttila, V., Wennerholm, U.-B., Loft, A., Pinborg, A., Aittomäki, K., Romundstad, L. B., & Bergh, C. (2015). Surrogacy: Outcomes for surrogate mothers, children and the resulting families—A systematic review. *Human Reproduction Update*, *22*(2), 260–276. https://doi.org/10.1093/humupd/dmv046

Taebi, M., Alavi, N. M., & Ahmadi, S. M. (2020). The experiences of surrogate mothers: A qualitative study. *Nursing and Midwifery Studies*, *9*(1), 51–59.

Tanderup, M., Reddy, S., Patel, T., & Nielsen, B. B. (2015a). Informed consent in medical decision-making in commercial gestational surrogacy: A mixed methods study in New Delhi, India. *Acta obstetricia et gynecologica Scandinavica*, *94*(5), 465–472. https://doi.org/10.1111/aogs.12576

Tanderup, M., Reddy, S., Patel, T., & Nielsen, B. B. (2015b). Reproductive ethics in commercial surrogacy: Decision-making in IVF clinics in New Delhi, India. *Journal of Bioethical Inquiry*, *12*(3), 491–501. https://doi.org/10.1007/s11673-015-9642-8

Tanderup, M., Pande, A., Schmidt, L., Nielsen, B. B., Humaidan, P., & Kroløkke, C. (2023). Impact of the war in Ukraine and the COVID-19 pandemic on transnational surrogacy–a qualitative study of Danish infertile couples' experiences of being in 'exile'. *Reproductive BioMedicine Online*, *47*(4), 103258.

Teman, E. (2010). *Birthing a mother: The surrogate body and the pregnant self.* University of California Press.

Trimmings, K., & Beaumont, P. (2011). International surrogacy arrangements: An urgent need for legal regulation at the international level. *Journal of Private International Law*, *7*(3), 627–647.

Triviño-Caballero, R. (2023). Caring for delivery: Healthcare professionals' ethical conflicts in surrogate pregnancy. *Hypatia*, *38*(3), 531–548.

Whittaker, A., Gerrits, T., & Weis, C. (2022). Emerging "repronubs" and "repropreneurs": Transnational surrogacy in Ghana, Kazakhstan, and Laos. *International Journal of Comparative Sociology*, *63*(5–6), 304–323.

Wilkinson, S. (2003). The exploitation argument against commercial surrogacy. *Bioethics*, *17*(2), 169–187.

Yee, S., Hemalal, S., & Librach, C. L. (2020). "Not my child to give away": A qualitative analysis of gestational surrogates' experiences. *Women & Birth*, *33*(3), e256–e265. https://doi.org/10.1016/j.wombi.2019.02.003

6 Reflections and Future Directions of Surrogacy Practice

Section 1: Reflections on the Surrogacy Journey

In recent years, surrogacy has emerged as an increasingly viable and, for many, a preferred pathway to family creation, propelled by evolving social, medical, and legal landscapes. The phenomenon of surrogacy is not just growing in incidence but also gaining acceptance, reflecting significant shifts in societal norms and technological advancements that now support a broader range of family structures. As more people face barriers to natural conception or navigate legal obstacles in adoption, surrogacy is filling a need for those determined to raise children with genetic ties. Understanding the forces behind this shift is crucial to appreciating why surrogacy is poised for continued growth in the years to come.

One of the primary drivers behind surrogacy's rise is the increasing acceptance of diverse family forms. In many societies, expanding recognition and acceptance of LGBTQ+ rights have opened doors for people to pursue parenthood in ways once unavailable. Surrogacy offers these couples a means to have children with biological connections, bypassing traditional obstacles associated with adoption, including restrictive legal requirements and limited eligibility in certain jurisdictions. Similarly, surrogacy provides a pathway for single individuals who may not meet conventional criteria for adoption but still wish to experience the joys and responsibilities of raising a child.

Additionally, rising rates of infertility—exacerbated by environmental factors, lifestyle changes, and underlying health issues—have contributed to surrogacy's increasing appeal. Many couples, after facing unsuccessful attempts at natural conception or in vitro fertilisation (IVF), turn to surrogacy as a last or preferred resort. As delayed childbearing becomes more common, especially in professional and highly urbanised populations, the likelihood of fertility complications also rises, making surrogacy an attractive option for individuals and couples facing age-related fertility challenges.

Moreover, while adoption has long been considered an alternative for those unable to conceive, it presents its own challenges. The legal and regulatory landscape surrounding adoption can be complex and arduous, requiring years of waiting, rigorous screening processes, and often intense scrutiny of prospective parents. Surrogacy, by contrast, though not without its own set of regulations and ethical

DOI: 10.4324/9781003511939-6

considerations, frequently offers a more controlled and predictable route for individuals and couples to have a child. In cases where adoption remains inaccessible due to restrictive policies, surrogacy presents an alternative means to family creation, circumventing the intricate processes that can make adoption lengthy and uncertain.

The role of technology has been pivotal as well. Advances in ART, particularly in IVF, have made surrogacy more successful and accessible. Genetic testing of embryos, personalised fertility treatments, and improved protocols in embryo transfer have increased success rates, making surrogacy a more feasible and hopeful option for prospective parents. Notably, such technological advances allow intended parents to have a direct role in the genetic makeup of their child, a factor that has significant emotional appeal for many.

Finally, the rise of surrogacy is also tied to the global expansion of medical tourism, with certain countries offering regulated, affordable surrogacy options as part of a larger fertility tourism industry. Although these arrangements are often subject to ethical scrutiny, the commercialisation of surrogacy has undeniably lowered financial and logistical barriers, making it more accessible for those willing to navigate the international landscape of reproductive medicine.

Taken together, these drivers of change signify a profound shift in the reasons people choose surrogacy, marking it not only as an alternative but also as an increasingly mainstream option for family-building. As the demand for surrogacy continues to grow, it is essential to consider these forces in shaping policies, ethical guidelines, and future directions that ensure safe and equitable practices for all parties involved.

As explored in previous chapters, surrogacy arrangements vary from traditional methods to more intricate gestational surrogacy. Beyond the distinction between these types, additional complexities arise from the different forms of surrogacy—altruistic and commercial. These variations profoundly impact the surrogacy journey for all parties involved, including surrogates, intended parents, healthcare providers, and the children born from these arrangements.

Increased Acceptance of Diverse Family Structures

In recent years, surrogacy has emerged as an increasingly viable and, for many, a preferred pathway to family creation. The increasing demand for surrogacy has been propelled by evolving social, medical, and legal landscapes. The phenomenon of surrogacy is not just growing in incidence but also gaining acceptance. This reflects a significant shift in societal norms and understanding of technological advancements that now support a broader range of family structures. As more people face barriers to natural conception or navigate legal obstacles in adoption, surrogacy is filling a need for those determined to raise children with genetic ties. Understanding the forces behind this shift is crucial to appreciating why surrogacy is poised for continued growth in the years to come.

One of the primary drivers behind surrogacy's rise is the increasing acceptance of diverse family forms. In many societies, expanding recognition and acceptance of LGBTQ+ rights have opened doors for same-sex couples, particularly male partners, to pursue parenthood in ways once unavailable (Brandão & Garrido, 2023; Ellenbogen et al., 2021). Surrogacy offers these couples a means to have children with biological connections, bypassing traditional obstacles associated with adoption, including restrictive legal requirements and limited eligibility in certain jurisdictions. Similarly, surrogacy provides a pathway for single individuals who may not meet conventional criteria for adoption but still wish to experience the joys and responsibilities of raising a child.

Many couples, after facing unsuccessful attempts at natural conception or IVF, turn to surrogacy as a last or preferred resort. As delayed childbearing becomes more common, especially in professional and highly urbanised populations, the likelihood of fertility complications also rises, making surrogacy an attractive option for individuals and couples facing age-related fertility challenges.

While adoption has long been considered an alternative for those unable to conceive, it presents its own challenges. The legal and regulatory landscape surrounding adoption can be complex and arduous, requiring years of waiting, rigorous screening processes, and often intense scrutiny of prospective parents. Surrogacy, by contrast, though not without its own set of regulations and ethical considerations, frequently offers a more controlled and predictable route for individuals and couples to have a child. In cases where adoption remains inaccessible due to restrictive policies, surrogacy presents an alternative means to family creation, circumventing the intricate processes that can make adoption lengthy and uncertain.

The role of technology has been pivotal as well. Advances in ART, particularly in IVF, have made surrogacy more accessible. Genetic testing of embryos, personalised fertility treatments, and improved protocols in embryo transfer have increased success rates, making surrogacy a more feasible and hopeful option for prospective parents. Notably, such technological advances allow intended parents to have a direct role in the genetic makeup of their child, a factor that has significant emotional appeal for many.

Finally, the rise of surrogacy is also tied to the global expansion of medical tourism, with certain countries offering regulated, affordable surrogacy options as part of a larger fertility tourism industry. Although these arrangements are often subject to ethical scrutiny, the commercialisation of surrogacy has undeniably lowered financial and logistical barriers, making it more accessible for those willing to navigate the international landscape of reproductive medicine.

Taken together, these drivers of change signify a profound shift in the reasons people choose surrogacy, marking it not only as an alternative but also as an increasingly mainstream option for family-building. As the demand for surrogacy continues to grow, it is essential to consider these forces in shaping policies, ethical guidelines, and future directions that ensure safe and equitable practices for all parties involved.

Global Trends in Attitudes towards Surrogacy

Attitudes towards surrogacy vary significantly worldwide, influenced by cultural, religious, and legal contexts. In many Western countries, acceptance of surrogacy is increasing, particularly when considered as an ART for infertility. Studies in Canada, the United Kingdom, and Australia demonstrate relatively high acceptance rates for surrogacy (Bruce-Hickman et al., 2009; Constantinidis & Cook, 2012). In contrast, countries such as Germany, Italy, and Sweden have generally shown less favourable attitudes towards surrogacy (Stöbel-Richter et al., 2009). Notably, Italy has enacted laws that completely ban surrogacy, both domestically and internationally, treating it as a criminal offence punishable by heavy fines and imprisonment (Marinelli et al., 2024; Zaami et al., 2022).

One significant finding is that acceptance of surrogacy often does not differ between infertile populations and the general public. Research in Turkey and Nigeria, where surrogacy is either legally restricted or lacks a clear regulatory framework, shows limited support among infertile populations, with approval rates as low as 15.1% and 24%, respectively (Rodríguez-Jaume et al., 2021). Religious and cultural factors play a role; for example, faith is often cited as a reason to prefer natural conception over assisted methods in Nigeria (Bello et al., 2014).

In countries with more progressive stances on reproductive health, such as Canada, intentions to use surrogacy as a last resort show higher acceptance rates, though the support fluctuates widely. In Canada, a smaller sample study found a 73% acceptance rate for surrogacy as an option if natural conception were not possible (Miall, 1989). In contrast, only 25% of respondents in the United States and Turkey indicated they would consider surrogacy in similar circumstances (Baykal et al., 2008; Lasker & Murray, 2001).

Global attitudes also show a preference for gestational surrogacy, where the surrogate has no genetic link to the child, over genetic surrogacy. In Japan, 20% of respondents preferred gestational surrogacy, and in Iran, 43.3% of women supported its use compared to 33.3% of men (Kian et al., 2014; Saito & Matsuo, 2009). In Western countries, the pattern is similar; for example, 82.1% of Greeks preferred gestational surrogacy over genetic surrogacy (Constantinidis & Cook, 2012).

Some studies investigate individuals' willingness to act as surrogates. In the United Kingdom, only 4.2% of women expressed willingness to be genetic surrogates, with a slightly higher percentage open to gestational arrangements (Poote & van den Akker, 2009). In Nigeria, where legal frameworks are less defined, 60.9% of infertile women stated a willingness to consider surrogacy, a surprisingly high figure given the cultural emphasis on natural pregnancy (Bello et al., 2014).

The topic of legalising surrogacy has also generated interest. While Germany maintains a legal prohibition, Iran has one of the highest support rates for legalisation, with 80% of respondents favouring regulation (Rahmani et al., 2011; Stöbel-Richter et al., 2009). In Spain, where surrogacy remains a contentious issue, 57.6% of respondents supported legalisation (Rodríguez-Jaume et al., 2021). In Australia, despite restrictions on commercial surrogacy, 55% of individuals residing in states where surrogacy is banned stated they would consider surrogacy if necessary (Everingham et al., 2014).

The acceptance of surrogacy for specific groups, such as same-sex couples or single parents, varies across regions. In Spain, 52.5% of respondents saw surrogacy as a valid way to assist same-sex couples (Rodríguez-Jaume et al., 2021).

However, motives for surrogacy related to convenience or lifestyle generally receive less support than medical reasons, such as infertility. Only 10.5% of Americans, for example, accepted surrogacy as an option for women fearing childbirth (Weiss, 1992), and similar sentiments appear in Greece and Canada, where over 80% of respondents disapproved of surrogacy for non-medical reasons (Chliaoutakis, 2002; Genuis et al., 1993).

Commercial surrogacy remains particularly divisive. In Australia, where it is prohibited in most jurisdictions, approximately 30% of the public still express approval under specific circumstances (Everingham et al., 2014; Kovacs et al., 2003). In contrast, attitudes in Iran are generally more permissive; only 5.9% of respondents considered compensation for surrogates to be "obscene," reflecting broader cultural and religious acceptance of commercial arrangements (Rahmani et al., 2011).

Globally, acceptance of surrogacy appears to be growing, particularly in Western countries. Most global surveys on surrogacy attitudes were conducted over ten years ago (Rodríguez-Jaume et al., 2021); more recent surveys would give us a better picture of the contemporary views, but trends tend to indicate increasingly favourable attitudes. However, attitudes continue to reflect diverse cultural and ethical beliefs, with preferences favouring medical motivations for surrogacy over social convenience and gestational arrangements over genetic connections.

Rising Infertility Rates

The global rise in infertility underscores complex demographic shifts with significant implications for family planning and the accessibility of fertility care (Fauser et al., 2024). Traditionally, family planning policies have focused on reducing unintended pregnancies and controlling population growth through contraception. This focus, driven partly by overpopulation concerns, has successfully lowered global fertility rates. However, many countries now face fertility rates well below replacement levels, with some regions projected to see population declines of up to 50% by 2100 if current trends persist (Fauser et al., 2024). These demographic trends signal a fundamental shift, necessitating a re-evaluation of how societies support family-building, as declining fertility poses economic and social challenges.

Given these trends, surrogacy and other ARTs may become increasingly critical in addressing fertility declines and supporting family-building. Family-building encompasses various pathways, including natural conception, ART, surrogacy, adoption, and fostering. These options offer vital alternatives for individuals facing infertility, a condition impacting millions worldwide, with associated psychological and social effects, including anxiety, depression, and social marginalisation (Fauser et al., 2024). As population demographics shift and birth rates decline, the role of surrogacy in complementing family-building efforts could grow considerably.

Despite advancements in ART—leading to as many as 10% of children born via fertility treatments in high-income countries—access to infertility care remains limited and financially burdensome, particularly in low- and middle-income countries (Chiware et al., 2021). This lack of access results in stark inequities in support for those seeking fertility care, with low-income individuals disproportionately affected. Some countries have responded by offering financial incentives or public funding for infertility treatments, but significant disparities in access remain, especially in the low- and middle-income countries.

Additionally, the decline in fertility has sparked discussions on reproductive rights and the ethical dimensions of family-building support. Although population growth reduction is still a priority in certain regions, framing infertility care solely in terms of population control undermines the personal and social importance of family-building. A social justice perspective suggests that all individuals, regardless of socioeconomic status or regional policies, should have equitable access to family-building opportunities, including surrogacy, ART, and other supportive care.

These concerning fertility trends highlight the need for broader family-building education and awareness, particularly for younger adults, to promote informed reproductive decisions and fertility awareness. Government support and public health strategies to expand access to fertility care are essential, particularly as surrogacy and related ARTs will likely play a more prominent role in addressing declining birth rates. Recognising family-building as a fundamental component of public health can ensure that surrogacy becomes an integral part of this conversation, providing an alternative pathway for those affected by infertility.

The decline in total fertility rate from 3.3 in 1990 to 2.3 in 2021 is a multifaceted issue influenced by social, economic, and environmental factors (Fauser et al., 2024). Factors such as shifts in family planning norms, later childbearing, and environmental contaminants contribute significantly to fertility reduction. Socioeconomic changes, gender equality advancements, and lifestyle choices also play crucial roles in this decline, and together, they suggest that ARTs—including surrogacy—may be necessary to counterbalance the demographic effects of decreased fertility. A replacement-level total fertility rate of about 2.1 children per woman is necessary to maintain stable populations (United Nations [UN], 2024). However, many countries face persistently low total fertility rate, challenging future demographic stability and economic growth.

Environmental and lifestyle factors further contribute to the fertility decline. Environmental contaminants, including endocrine-disrupting chemicals, impair reproductive health, with studies increasingly associating reduced fertility with exposure to pollutants like pesticides and industrial chemicals (Skakkebæk et al., 2022). Additionally, lifestyle factors like smoking, excessive alcohol consumption, and poor nutrition further exacerbate fertility decline by affecting gamete health (Gore et al., 2015).

In high-income countries, delayed childbirth due to educational and career commitments leads to increased infertility risk as natural fertility declines with age. Fertility is optimal until approximately age 31 but drops significantly by age 40 (Abma, 1997). In wealthier nations, where the age of first childbirth has risen by around one year per decade since 1970 (Fauser et al., 2024), delayed childbearing leads to fewer children, increased infertility treatment needs, and higher healthcare costs (Luke & Brown, 2007).

Countries with lower fertility rates are also experiencing shifts in population structure, creating both opportunities and challenges. While a temporary "demographic dividend" arises from a higher working-age population relative to dependents, persistently low total fertility rate eventually leads to an ageing population. To counteract this, some countries are implementing policies to support fertility, including increased access to ART and family-friendly work policies (De Geyter, 2019). However, in the low- and middle-income countries, access to ART is limited, reducing the potential impact of these policies on stabilising fertility rates (Chiware et al., 2021; Inhorn & Patrizio, 2015).

Given these trends, surrogacy and other ARTs are likely to become increasingly necessary as part of a comprehensive approach to fertility care. As fertility declines persist globally, surrogacy can serve as an essential resource for families, providing a viable pathway for those impacted by infertility and supporting broader demographic stability. Surrogacy should be part of strategic responses to fertility decline, offering a family-building option that reflects evolving societal and demographic needs.

Delayed Parenthood

The late 19th and early 20th centuries marked a significant change as women gained greater access to education and job opportunities. This development has coincided with advancements in healthcare and contraceptive methods. These factors have combined to significantly alter societal norms regarding childbearing. Women are increasingly delaying having children to focus on their education, career, and personal goals.

The concept of delayed childbearing is now widespread, no longer limited to the developed countries alone. Increasing numbers of women are opting to defer having children until later in life, often waiting until their 30s or even 40s. This shift challenges conventional ideas about the timing of parenthood. As societies modernise and become increasingly diverse and interconnected, the phenomenon of delayed childbearing has established itself as a global trend (Safdari-Dehcheshmeh et al., 2023; Zabak et al., 2023).

One of the primary reasons for this shift is the growing emphasis on education and career development. Both women and men increasingly prioritise higher education and professional achievements before starting a family, seeking to attain personal fulfilment and financial stability (Cooke et al., 2012). Navigating the demands of building a career and achieving their life goals has resulted in postponing parenthood.

Economic considerations further contribute to this trend. The rising costs associated with living, housing, and child-rearing can be daunting for many couples. Economic uncertainty and the desire to provide a better quality of life for future children often result in delays in family formation. As a result, individuals weigh their readiness for parenthood against the financial realities of raising a child in today's world (Zabak et al., 2023).

Cultural shifts also play a role in shaping attitudes towards parenthood. Traditional views regarding marriage and family formation have evolved significantly, allowing for greater flexibility in how individuals approach their personal lives.

It is increasingly common for people to prioritise personal goals and relationships over early family formation. Additionally, the societal acceptance of diverse family structures, including single parenthood and same-sex couples, fosters an environment where the timing of parenthood can be more fluid.

Advancements in reproductive technology are arguably the most revolutionary change in the landscape of parenthood. The development of ART, such as egg freezing and IVF, allows individuals to have children much later in life. These innovations provide greater control over fertility, enabling people to postpone parenthood until they feel ready, both personally and professionally. With these medical advancements, the risks associated with late parenthood, such as genetic conditions or fertility challenges, can be addressed but not be fully mitigated. It may also have contributed to a false sense of security that children can just as easily be had in later years when less fertile. Nevertheless, it allows prospective parents to comfortably extend their reproductive years.

Globally, these trends manifest in various ways, particularly in the increasing age of first-time parents. In many developed countries, the average age of first-time mothers has risen significantly, with women often having their first child in their 30s or even later (Zabak et al., 2023). Countries like Japan, Germany, and the United States have seen this trend, as individuals and couples navigate the demands of modern life. Concurrently, demographic shifts, including declining birth rates and an ageing population, create societal pressures that further delay family formation (Safdari-Dehcheshmeh et al., 2023; Zabak et al., 2023).

Urbanisation also plays a role, as individuals moving to cities often encounter housing shortages and increased living costs, prompting them to delay starting a family while they pursue education and career opportunities.

In this context, surrogacy emerges as a viable option for those grappling with the challenges of delayed parenthood. It provides a pathway for individuals and couples who may struggle with fertility issues, such as those who are older or those who identify as part of the LGBTQ+ community. Surrogacy allows them to fulfil their desire for parenthood, even if natural conception is not feasible. By utilising the advancements in reproductive technologies, surrogacy can enhance the likelihood of successful conception, making it particularly relevant for older prospective parents who may face fertility challenges.

Moreover, surrogacy offers individuals the opportunity to control the timing of their family planning. It allows them to have children when they feel personally and financially ready, aligning parenthood with their career and life aspirations. As societal acceptance of diverse family structures continues to grow, surrogacy supports the idea that family can take many forms and that there is no singular path to parenthood.

The global accessibility of surrogacy also plays a significant role in its appeal. As more individuals recognise surrogacy as a legitimate option, it becomes increasingly available to people from various backgrounds and circumstances. This is particularly true for those in countries where traditional pathways to parenthood may be limited due to societal or legal constraints. Global surrogacy arrangements can provide solutions for individuals seeking to navigate the complexities of modern life while pursuing their dreams of parenthood.

This trend of delayed parenthood reflects the evolving landscape of personal aspirations, economic realities, and cultural norms. Surrogacy stands out as a promising solution for many individuals and couples, offering them the chance to pursue parenthood on their terms. As society continues to embrace diverse family structures, surrogacy is likely to play an increasingly integral role in addressing the challenges associated with delayed parenthood, fostering a more inclusive understanding of what it means to build a family in the contemporary world.

With the trends in delayed childbearing it is imperative that policy frameworks are developed to address these emerging societal changes. As family dynamics evolve policies need to adapt and keep pace with these transformations. This includes the growing relevance of surrogacy as a family-building option for many individuals and couples. Policies must not only ensure the accessibility and safety of surrogacy arrangements but also clarify the ethical considerations and legal frameworks that govern them. By addressing the grey areas surrounding surrogacy, policymakers can help mitigate risks and protect the rights of all parties involved. Comprehensive reproductive healthcare services and work-life balance initiatives are increasingly important in supporting individuals who are navigating the complexities of delayed childbearing. The ability of policies to effectively respond to the changing needs of families will be key in enhancing the overall family well-being and fostering social cohesion, particularly as demand for surrogacy continues to grow in the future.

Adoption Complexity and Regulation

The legal and bureaucratic complexities of adoption can make it a lengthy and challenging process, with strict eligibility requirements that vary significantly by country. In contrast, surrogacy arrangements, although also regulated, sometimes offer a more straightforward route, especially for individuals or couples who may not meet the criteria for adoption in certain regions.

The complex regulatory environment governing intercountry adoption has deep historical roots, shaped by global events and evolving social attitudes. Intercountry adoption initially surged after conflicts such as the Korean War in the 1950s, as a response to the crisis of orphaned children in devastated countries. Over time, the practice continued to expand, particularly in countries of the Global North, as domestic adoptions declined due to improved access to contraception, changing societal attitudes, and legal options for family planning (Fong et al., 2016). The countries involved in intercountry adoptions have shifted in response to these social developments, with countries of origin evolving based on economic, political, and social changes (Selman, 2015).

Regulations on intercountry adoption have tightened significantly, particularly with the implementation of the Hague Convention on Protection of Children and Co-operation in Respect of Intercountry Adoption (HCIA). This convention, built on principles outlined in the United Nations Convention on the Rights of the Child (CRC), mandates that intercountry adoption should be pursued only after all other domestic care options have been exhausted. This "subsidiarity principle" aims to ensure that a child's care is prioritised within their own family or community whenever possible, reserving intercountry adoption as a last resort. This rigorous framework reflects a shift in how adoption is perceived—no longer merely a means to provide children with parents but also as a way to uphold children's rights and safeguard their best interests, even at the cost of creating additional bureaucratic layers (UNICEF, n.d.).

As intercountry adoption developed, concerns arose regarding its ethical implications. Social work scholars and practitioners highlighted the risks of exploitation, especially in cases where children from economically disadvantaged backgrounds were placed with families in wealthier nations (Freundlich & Phillips, 2000; Hollingsworth, 2003). This dynamic led to substantial criticism of the intercountry adoption process as one that potentially exploits poverty, creating an industry that often prioritises the desires of adoptive families over the well-being and rights of birth families. In response to such concerns, international treaties and domestic regulations have imposed stricter controls to prevent child trafficking and unethical practices. The CRC and HCIA, for example, include provisions that protect birth families by requiring informed and voluntary consent, as well as counselling to ensure that the relinquishment of a child is fully understood and uncoerced (Hague Conference on Private International Law [HCCH], 2008). Countries like Guatemala have instituted moratoriums on intercountry adoption in response to widespread abuse and child trafficking, highlighting the need for constant vigilance and stringent regulation (Monico, 2013).

In contrast to intercountry adoption, commercial global surrogacy has proliferated in a far less regulated environment. This growth reflects a demand for alternative family-building options, as the availability of adoptable children has decreased due to stricter adoption protocols and the prioritisation of domestic solutions. Surrogacy arrangements are often managed by private fertility clinics or legal intermediaries, with limited government oversight, especially in countries like the United States, where regulation can vary widely by state (Scherman et al., 2016). Without a framework comparable to the HCIA for adoption, commercial surrogacy exists in a global marketplace largely regulated by market forces rather than standardised international protocols or human rights conventions (Bromfield & Rotabi, 2014).

In countries where commercial surrogacy has taken root the unregulated nature of the industry has led to ethical and human rights concerns. Reports indicate that some surrogates, often recruited from economically marginalised backgrounds, experience inadequate informed consent procedures, where they may sign contracts they cannot read or fully understand (Nadimpally & Majumdar, 2017). Additionally, the practice of housing surrogates in dormitories for health monitoring has drawn comparisons to coercive environments where women's autonomy and movements are restricted (Rotabi & Gibbons, 2012). This lack of standardisation raises concerns about the potential for exploitation, as the primary regulatory mechanisms are often private agreements rather than legally enforced protections (Rotabi & Gibbons, 2012).

However, the regulatory void in surrogacy is not universally viewed as negative by those directly involved. Some research with Indian surrogates, for instance, indicates that these women often see surrogacy as a form of economic empowerment, despite its inherent risks. They have advocated for regulation that acknowledges surrogacy as labour, seeking legal frameworks that protect their rights as workers rather than as vulnerable parties to an exploitative transaction (Goswami et al., 2014; Karandikar et al., 2014). This perspective emphasises a key difference between surrogacy and adoption: while adoption frameworks emphasise the rights and welfare of the child, surrogacy also requires consideration of the surrogate's rights, particularly regarding labour protections and economic agency (Pande, 2014).

Ultimately, while both adoption and surrogacy involve complex ethical and regulatory issues, adoption is characterised by a more rigid international framework designed to protect vulnerable children and families from exploitation. Surrogacy, by contrast, largely lacks such protections, and its regulation, if any, is often fragmented and inconsistent. As commercial global surrogacy continues to grow, the need for an international regulatory framework to ensure the rights and well-being of all parties involved—particularly the surrogates and child—is becoming increasingly apparent. Developing such a framework may draw from the lessons learned in regulating intercountry adoption, adapting principles like informed consent, protection from coercion, and the preservation of individual rights to meet the unique challenges presented by surrogacy.

Diverse Experiences and Perspectives in Surrogacy

The surrogacy journey involves multiple stakeholders—surrogates, intended parents, healthcare providers, legal professionals, and, sometimes, surrogacy agencies. Each of these groups brings a unique perspective, driven by their roles, responsibilities, expectations, and experiences. For surrogates, the journey involves much more than just carrying a child; it requires navigating a complex landscape filled with physical, emotional, and often financial challenges (Taebi et al., 2020). Their experiences can vary widely, from feeling empowered by the process to feeling disempowered or even commodified, particularly in jurisdictions where surrogacy is highly commercialised (Attawet et al., 2024).

Intended parents, however, often experience a mix of hope, anxiety, and joy throughout the surrogacy journey (Hoechst & Sobottka, 2017; Kneebone et al., 2022). Their reflections are shaped by their motivations for choosing surrogacy—whether due to infertility, medical conditions, same-sex partnerships, or personal choices—alongside concerns about the ethical, legal, and emotional implications of the process. For many intended parents, surrogacy represents a deeply personal and emotional investment in their journey to parenthood. Their experiences can be heavily influenced by the degree of trust and transparency they establish with the surrogate and the healthcare professionals involved (Bhatia et al., 2009; Taebi et al., 2020).

Healthcare providers play a crucial role as custodians of ethical and safe medical practices in surrogacy arrangements. They must manage the differing perspectives and needs of surrogates and IPs, which can sometimes align but often conflict (Bhatia et al., 2009; Triviño-Caballero, 2023). Surrogates face unique health risks that require careful management by healthcare professionals, while IPs navigate emotional and legal complexities, particularly in regions where the rights of both parties are not clearly defined. This creates a dynamic environment where healthcare systems must continually adapt through evolving policies and protocols. However, significant gaps remain that need further attention. Healthcare providers are also tasked with balancing respect for the surrogate's autonomy with the desires of the IPs. Achieving this balance demands ongoing ethical reflection and a deep understanding of the sociocultural contexts in which surrogacy arrangements occur.

Positive and Negative Impacts on Healthcare Systems

The impact of surrogacy on healthcare systems is complex, presenting both positive advancements and significant challenges. On the positive side, surrogacy has driven innovation in reproductive medicine, leading to the development of specialised care protocols and supportive services for surrogates and IPs. Advancements in embryo transfer protocols, reproductive health screenings, and tailored psychological support for surrogates have emerged as critical components to ensure the safety and health of both surrogates and the babies they carry (Dar et al., 2015; Machtinger et al., 2017; Quinn & Huddleston, 2017). Surrogacy cases often push healthcare systems to adopt more sophisticated approaches to prenatal and postnatal care, setting higher standards for reproductive health practices overall. Additionally, the need for multidisciplinary collaboration among healthcare professionals—such as obstetricians, psychologists, and legal advisors—has strengthened integrated care models that benefit the broader healthcare system.

However, surrogacy also presents significant challenges that healthcare systems must navigate. Ethical dilemmas frequently arise, particularly when balancing standardised medical practices with patient-centred care. For example, while guidelines generally recommend a single embryo transfer for surrogates under 40 without prior pregnancy complications to minimise risks, some intended parents may pressure for multiple embryo transfers to increase the chances of a successful pregnancy, as they believe (Attawet, Wang, Farquhar, et al., 2022; White, 2017). This creates ethical conflicts for healthcare providers who must balance medical best practices with the expectations and desires of IPs.

Focusing on commercial surrogacy, the ethical landscape becomes more complex. There is a risk of exploitation where surrogates, particularly those from economically disadvantaged backgrounds, may face coercion or feel compelled to participate due to financial incentives (Walker & Van Zyl, 2017). This raises concerns about the commodification of women's bodies and reproductive capabilities. Moreover, the rights of the child born from surrogacy arrangements, such as their right to know their biological origins, often clash with contractual obligations that prioritise the preferences of intended parents. These issues highlight the need for robust guidelines and regulations that prioritise the rights and well-being of surrogates and children over the financial and contractual interests of intended parents.

The healthcare system's response to these complexities involves establishing stringent guidelines that promote ethical practices, safeguard surrogates from exploitation, and ensure comprehensive, evidence-based care for all parties involved. However, the ongoing debate about the extent of intended parents rights and autonomy within these arrangements complicates the creation of a universally cohesive healthcare policy. Addressing these positive and negative impacts requires a balanced approach that considers medical, ethical, and social dimensions, ultimately advancing a more just and supportive healthcare system in the context of surrogacy.

Finding Common Ground for the Well-Being of All Parties Involved

Finding common ground for the well-being of all parties involved in surrogacy—surrogates, intended parents, healthcare providers, and the children born from these arrangements—requires a nuanced and critically informed approach. The challenge lies in recognising both shared interests and conflicting priorities among stakeholders while fostering an environment that is ethical, transparent, and supportive.

Both surrogates and intended parents share a vested interest in a safe, ethically managed surrogacy process, but their perspectives and priorities may differ significantly. Surrogates often need fair compensation, autonomy over medical decisions, and guarantees that their health and well-being will be protected throughout the process. The need for autonomy is particularly crucial, as it involves decisions about their own bodies, including the number of embryos transferred, potential pregnancy termination, and overall birth care. Ensuring informed consent and respecting their choices are vital in preventing exploitation and ensuring ethical practice. Conversely, intended parents focus on a successful pregnancy outcome and the legal certainty of parentage. Based on these concepts, the differing priorities between surrogates and intended parents can lead to conflicts. This tension underscores the need for clear, ethical guidelines that effectively balance these competing interests, ensuring that surrogates' rights, autonomy, and safety are not compromised by the expectations or aspirations of intended parents. As surrogacy practices advance, there is also a growing emphasis on early involvement of IPs in the prenatal process to foster a stronger parent-child bond (Edwards et al., 2023; Sharan et al., 2001). However, this involvement must be carefully managed to respect the surrogate's autonomy and their rights over their body and medical decisions throughout the pregnancy.

The rights of the surrogates and the child at birth, as guided by current legal frameworks, should be critically reassessed to determine whether they adequately consider the rights of intended parents to their child at birth (Gelmann, 2010; Horsey et al., 2023). This complex interplay of rights—those of the surrogate, the child, and the intended parents—presents ongoing ethical dilemmas for healthcare professionals tasked with providing surrogacy care. These dilemmas often revolve around navigating the boundaries of surrogate autonomy while meeting intended parents expectations and ensuring the best interests of the child.

Healthcare providers, therefore, face significant challenges in balancing these ethical tensions. The lack of clear and consistent guidelines, policies, or protocols on how to manage these conflicts can lead to variability in practice and potential harm. The direction of future guidelines must be more explicit in addressing these points, providing healthcare professionals with a clear framework for best practices that optimises care for all parties and upholds the principle of "do no harm". By establishing comprehensive and ethically sound policies, healthcare systems can better support surrogacy arrangements that are fair, transparent, and centred on the well-being of the surrogates, intended parents, and child.

The involvement of legal experts, surrogacy agencies, and ethicists is crucial in establishing frameworks that address these ethical and legal complexities. Jurisdictional differences further complicate the establishment of universal surrogacy policies. In some regions, intended parents have extensive rights, while in others, the emphasis is more on the surrogate's autonomy and well-being. This variability necessitates flexible but robust policies that can adapt to local legal contexts while promoting core ethical principles, such as fairness, transparency, and non-exploitation. The absence of cohesive international guidelines on surrogacy results in significant variations in ethical standards, creating the potential for one party's interests to be prioritised over another. For example, a surrogate's rights may be compromised to accommodate the demands of intended parents, or the rights of children may be inadequately addressed. Therefore, it is essential to strike a balance that respects local laws while promoting a foundational standard of ethical practices that ensures fairness and equity for all parties involved.

A holistic approach to surrogacy must also incorporate comprehensive support systems that address not only medical but also psychological, social, and legal needs. Surrogates often face psychological burdens, such as coping with attachment, relinquishment, and societal stigmatisation. Meanwhile, intended parents may need support in navigating the complexities of legal parentage and developing realistic expectations regarding the surrogacy process. Tailored support services that include psychological counselling, legal advice, and postnatal care are essential to foster a positive and ethical surrogacy experience.

Section 2: Ongoing Medical Considerations

Surrogacy, though increasingly recognised as a viable family-building method, remains a subject of ongoing medical, ethical, and legal debate. These discussions are particularly concerned with the welfare of not just the surrogate and IPs but also the child born through surrogacy. Medical considerations are essential for safeguarding the health and well-being of all parties, and advancements in reproductive technologies, coupled with ethical complexities, continue to add layers of complexity to surrogacy practices. As such, medical issues and debates surrounding surrogacy remain active and continuously evolving.

Surrogate Autonomy versus Medical Decision-Making

One of the central debates in surrogacy revolves around the surrogate's autonomy in making medical decisions during pregnancy and delivery. While surrogates are the carriers of the pregnancy, intended parents have a vested interest in the health and well-being of the foetus. This can create tension, particularly in situations where medical interventions are required, such as a C-section or induction of labour (Attawet, Wang, & Sullivan, 2022; Hovav, 2020).

Healthcare professionals often find themselves in difficult ethical positions, as they must balance the surrogate's right to make decisions about her body with the interests of the intended parents and the foetus (Bhatia et al., 2009; Triviño-Caballero, 2023). In surrogacy arrangements, this dynamic is especially complex, as the usual patient-centred care model expands to include the expectations and desires of all parties. Navigating these competing interests can be challenging, especially when there is uncertainty about whose needs to prioritise—the surrogate, the intended parents, or the unborn child.

When these situations are mishandled or treated unequally, they can lead to emotional distress for everyone involved and strain the relationships between surrogates, intended parents, and healthcare professionals. If left unresolved, such conflicts may erode trust in the healthcare system, making future interactions more challenging and potentially resulting in long-term psychological impacts for all parties.

Health Risks and Long-Term Effects for Surrogates

The health risks associated with surrogacy have become a critical focus of ongoing medical debates, especially concerning surrogates who carry multiple pregnancies. While surrogacy offers a pathway to parenthood for intended parents, the long-term health consequences for surrogates are still being examined, with no consensus on how to best protect these women. Each pregnancy places immense physical strain on the body, and when compounded by the medical procedures necessary for surrogacy—such as hormonal treatments and embryo transfers—these risks can accumulate over time, leading to potentially irreversible health impacts (Gheauş, 2016; Simopoulou et al., 2018).

Like any pregnancy, surrogates are exposed to risks such as gestational diabetes, pre-eclampsia, and high blood pressure. However, when surrogates take on multiple pregnancies with insufficient recovery time, these risks are heightened (Selman et al., 2022). The body requires months, if not longer, to recover after pregnancy and childbirth, particularly in the case of surgeries like C-sections. Ongoing debates in the medical field question whether there should be stricter guidelines limiting how many times a woman can safely be a surrogate, with concerns about uterine damage, placenta accreta, and reproductive system degradation surfacing repeatedly (Gheauş, 2016).

Experts also argue about the cumulative risks of pregnancy-related complications. Conditions such as pre-eclampsia and gestational diabetes, which are already dangerous during pregnancy, can lead to chronic health issues like heart disease, hypertension, and Type 2 diabetes later in life (Yang & Wu, 2022). Repeated exposure to these conditions increases the chances that surrogates will face long-term health complications, yet the medical field still lacks consensus on how many pregnancies a surrogate should be allowed to undertake to minimise these risks.

The long-term effects on fertility are another focal point of the debate. Repeated pregnancies, especially those spaced too closely together, increase the likelihood of infertility, uterine rupture, and permanent reproductive system damage. Surrogates who undergo multiple pregnancies may not fully recover between each pregnancy, leaving their bodies vulnerable to heightened risks. Advocates for stricter health guidelines push for medical policies that protect surrogates from taking on more pregnancies than their bodies can safely handle.

Despite these concerns, there remains ongoing debate about the extent of a surrogate's autonomy in deciding how many pregnancies she can safely carry. Some argue that surrogates should have the right to make decisions about their own bodies and choose the number of pregnancies they wish to undertake, as long as they are fully informed of the associated risks. This perspective emphasises a surrogate's right to bodily autonomy and self-determination. However, others contend that the significant medical uncertainties and potential long-term health risks require stricter regulations to protect surrogates from taking on more than their bodies can handle. This argument highlights the need to safeguard surrogates' physical and mental health, particularly given the cumulative psychological and emotional toll that multiple pregnancies can impose

Medical Screening for Surrogates, Surrogates' Partners, and Intended Parents

Medical screening is critical in surrogacy arrangements, ensuring that surrogates are physically capable of carrying a pregnancy to term and minimising the risk of complications. Pre-existing medical conditions in surrogates can increase pregnancy-related risks, making thorough health assessments vital for the safety of both the surrogate and the foetus. However, as surrogacy practices evolve, ongoing discussions emphasise the importance of extending medical and psychosocial screenings beyond just the surrogate to include surrogates' partners and intended parents (Tsai et al., 2020). This holistic approach ensures the well-being of all parties involved and encourages a better understanding of their roles and rights in the surrogacy journey.

For instance, it is increasingly recognised that the surrogate's partner, if applicable, and the intended parents should also meet with mental health professionals to assess their emotional preparedness, support for the pregnancy, and any underlying psychological concerns. Furthermore, mental health evaluations help address the broader impact of surrogacy on each party's family and community. While bodies like the American Society for Reproductive Medicine (ASRM) provide guidance on these screenings, the timing, scope, and application of these evaluations are still being refined. There is a growing consensus that improving these guidelines and policies is essential to ensure that surrogacy arrangements are both comprehensive and supportive, benefiting everyone involved in the process.

Foetal Reduction and Selective Termination

Foetal reduction, which involves reducing the number of foetuses in a multiple pregnancy, and selective termination due to genetic abnormalities are highly sensitive and challenging aspects of surrogacy. In these situations, decision-making becomes particularly complex, as it extends beyond the usual autonomy of the pregnant woman. In surrogacy, the surrogate, though carrying the child, is not the intended parents, which raises important questions about who should have a say in critical decisions surrounding the pregnancy (Jones, 2018; Walker & Van Zyl, 2015).

In commercial surrogacy, it is often understood that intended parents may hold decision-making rights as part of their contractual agreement. However, in altruistic surrogacy, the surrogate generally retains the authority to make these decisions, although intended parents might choose not to proceed with the adoption if they disagree (Walker & Van Zyl, 2015). These scenarios create moral and emotional challenges for all parties—surrogates, intended parents, and healthcare providers—particularly when weighing what is in the best interest of the child. The complexity of these issues underscores the need for clear, well-structured policies that integrate surrogacy arrangements into the broader healthcare system, ensuring all parties are supported and guided through these difficult decisions.

Cross-Border Surrogacy and Medical Disparities

Cross-border surrogacy presents significant challenges in ensuring consistent medical care for surrogates and children. In countries with lower healthcare standards, surrogates may not receive the same level of prenatal and postnatal care as those in wealthier nations. These disparities raise ethical concerns about the exploitation of surrogates in economically disadvantaged regions, where they may be motivated by financial necessity to participate in surrogacy despite inadequate healthcare.

Debates surrounding cross-border surrogacy focus on whether international regulations should be implemented to ensure consistent medical standards for all surrogates, regardless of geographic location. Medical practitioners, legal experts, and human rights advocates continue to call for stricter oversight of cross-border surrogacy arrangements to protect the health and safety of surrogates and children.

Section 3: Ongoing Surrogacy Law Considerations

Surrogacy is regulated differently across the world, and its complexity is heightened when it involves commercial surrogacy. Countries have adopted diverse regulatory approaches, ranging from outright bans to permissive legal frameworks, resulting in a fragmented global landscape. Despite efforts to establish clear regulations or prohibit certain practices, new challenges continue to arise, including cross-border surrogacy disputes, the growth of surrogacy tourism, and persistent gaps in international legal frameworks. Legal and ethical issues surrounding surrogacy remain ongoing and unresolved, reflecting the evolving nature of this practice.

Fragmented and Evolving Legal Frameworks

One of the most prominent ongoing issues in surrogacy is the fragmented and evolving nature of legal frameworks across jurisdictions, which creates legal uncertainties for surrogates, intended parents, and children (Frati et al., 2021). These inconsistencies can significantly impact the recognition of parental rights, citizenship status of children, and the legal enforceability of surrogacy contracts. Surrogates and intended parents often find themselves navigating a maze of conflicting laws, with outcomes that vary depending on the legal system in place. A well-known example of this issue can be seen in cross-border surrogacy cases involving couples from countries where surrogacy is restricted or banned, such as France or Germany, who seek surrogacy services in countries with more permissive laws like Ukraine or Georgia. Upon returning home, these intended parents often face legal challenges as their home countries may not recognise the parentage established in the country of birth (Maydanyk & Moskalenko, 2020). This leaves children in legal limbo, sometimes without citizenship or legal recognition of the intended parents as their parents, resulting in lengthy court battles and unresolved legal statuses. One prominent case is the *Mennesson v. France* (2014) ruling by the European Court of Human Rights, where a French couple faced legal difficulties in obtaining parentage recognition for their surrogate-born children (Child Rights International Network [CRIN], 2019). Currently, although there have been some minor developments in recognising the rights of children born through international surrogacy, surrogacy as a practice remains strictly illegal in France. This legal stance has led many French couples to seek alternative solutions abroad, but it also continues to pose significant legal and ethical challenges upon their return to France, as they face obstacles in securing full legal recognition and rights as parents. This case exemplifies the complexities and consequences of navigating conflicting legal systems in the realm of surrogacy.

Inconsistent Legal Recognition of Parentage

For intended parents, the legal recognition of parentage is critical to establishing their rights as parents and ensuring they can make decisions about the child's welfare from birth. In jurisdictions like California, intended parents can secure pre-birth parentage orders, which grant them legal parentage before the child is born (Mulligan, 2024). This provides certainty and ensures that the intended parents can immediately assume parental responsibilities. Conversely, in countries like the United Kingdom and Australia, where pre-birth parentage orders are not recognised, intended parents must wait until after the birth to apply for a parental order (Horsey et al., 2023), creating a delay that can complicate the process and create legal risks if the surrogate changes her mind.

This delay can also lead to emotional and practical challenges, as the intended parents may be unable to make crucial decisions about the child's care in the immediate post-birth period. Additionally, the lack of pre-birth recognition can cause stress for surrogates, who may be left in a legal limbo, still considered the legal mother even when all parties agree that the intended parents should have full parental rights. These inconsistencies between jurisdictions highlight the need for more harmonised and transparent legal frameworks that safeguard the rights and interests of both intended parents and surrogates, ensuring a smoother transition for all parties involved in surrogacy arrangements. Without consistent legal recognition, the surrogacy process can become fraught with uncertainty and potential disputes, further complicating what is already a complex legal and emotional journey.

Cross-Border Surrogacy and International Legal Complexities

Cross-border surrogacy arrangements introduce significant complexities regarding legal parentage and citizenship. These issues can become particularly acute when children cannot return to their intended parents' home country after birth. The challenges of such arrangements were starkly illustrated during the COVID-19 pandemic when international travel restrictions left many IPs unable to travel to countries like Ukraine to collect their newborns. For instance, during the height of the pandemic, approximately 125 babies born to Ukrainian surrogates were stranded because intended parents from countries such as France, Germany, and Australia were barred from entering the country (Radio Free Europe Radio Liberty, 2024). This situation placed Ukrainian hospitals and surrogacy agencies in a precarious legal and ethical position, caring for newborns without the presence of their legal parents (Tanderup et al., 2023).

The war in Ukraine has further intensified these legal and ethical challenges. Many Ukrainian surrogates have found themselves in dangerous situations, trapped in conflict zones or forced to continue pregnancies under perilous conditions. Some surrogates have fled to safer regions or neighbouring countries where surrogacy laws differ, complicating their legal status as mothers, despite lacking a genetic connection to the child (König, 2023; Marinelli et al., 2022). This situation adds to the emotional and physical toll on surrogates, who may already be facing extreme hardships due to the war.

Intended parents have also faced unprecedented difficulties, unable to travel to Ukraine to witness the birth of their children or bring them home. This has led to babies being stranded in temporary shelters or unsafe environments like hotel basements or bunkers (Tanderup et al., 2023). These challenges mirror the earlier COVID-19 crisis, as intended parents navigate conflicting legal systems, struggle to establish parental rights, and deal with the emotional strain of being separated from their newborns.

Healthcare professionals in Ukraine have also been caught in the crossfire, as they continue to provide care to surrogates and newborns despite the ongoing conflict. Operating under unsafe conditions, these professionals face ethical dilemmas about who should make critical decisions for both the surrogate and the child. The legal status of intended parents under Ukrainian law, which recognises their rights from birth, often conflicts with laws in the parents' home countries, leaving healthcare providers uncertain about who holds the authority to make medical decisions.

The ongoing war has highlighted the vulnerability of children born through surrogacy, many of whom remain stranded without legal recognition or access to their intended parents. This scenario underscores the inadequacies in current international surrogacy regulations, exposing the urgent need for harmonised legal frameworks that protect the rights and welfare of all parties, especially the children, involved in cross-border surrogacy arrangements. The war in Ukraine, like the COVID-19 pandemic, has brought into focus the complexities and potential consequences of surrogacy arrangements when international cooperation and unified legal standards are lacking.

Section 4: Ongoing Ethical Debates

Ethical concerns around the potential exploitation of surrogates continue to fuel debates, with critics arguing that commercial surrogacy disproportionately targets economically vulnerable women (Attawet et al., 2024). Reports of surrogates receiving inadequate medical care or being pressured into conditions they did not fully understand persist, even in regulated settings. This exploitation risk is further highlighted in countries with newly established surrogacy industries, where the regulation is often underdeveloped or inadequately enforced (Attawet, 2021; Whittaker et al., 2022).

Despite ongoing efforts to mitigate these risks, the ethical debate remains unresolved, with ongoing research and advocacy focusing on the need for more robust informed consent processes, better healthcare provisions, and post-surrogacy support for surrogates. Advocacy groups and international organisations are actively calling for enhanced legal and ethical standards, demonstrating that the issue of exploitation is far from resolved.

Autonomy and Decision-Making Rights

In some jurisdictions, surrogates have limited decision-making rights during pregnancy, with the surrogacy contract dictating terms related to prenatal care, lifestyle choices, and medical interventions (Saravanan, 2013). For instance, in India, prior to the 2018 ban on surrogacy, agreements could include provisions requiring surrogates to undergo specific medical procedures or follow lifestyle restrictions aimed at prioritising the intended parents' needs and child's welfare over the surrogate's autonomy. This raises ethical concerns about the extent to which a surrogate's autonomy is respected and whether she retains the right to make decisions about her own body throughout the pregnancy.

Additionally, when foetal abnormalities arise, it becomes even more complex to determine who should have the authority to make decisions regarding abortion—the surrogate or the intended parents. In altruistic surrogacy, the surrogate generally retains the right to make such decisions, as they are carrying the pregnancy, while the IPs may choose not to adopt the child. However, in commercial surrogacy, the situation becomes more complicated. It is often assumed that as part of the contractual agreement, the intended parents gain the right to make decisions about the pregnancy, including abortion (Walker & Van Zyl, 2015). Surrogates may feel pressured to comply with the intended parents' wishes to avoid breaching the contract or facing legal consequences. These ethical dilemmas underscore the need for legal frameworks that protect the surrogate's autonomy and ensure her decision-making rights are respected throughout the pregnancy.

Informed Consent and Exploitation

Informed consent remains a significant ethical issue, as surrogates may not fully understand the physical, emotional, and legal implications of the surrogacy process.

This is particularly concerning in cases where economically vulnerable women are involved, raising risks of exploitation (Saravanan, 2013). Inadequate healthcare, unclear legal frameworks, and insufficient post-surrogacy support further exacerbate these concerns, especially in countries with underdeveloped surrogacy regulations. Although healthcare professionals are responsible for ensuring surrogates are fully informed, the involvement of surrogacy agencies and rigid contract terms can sometimes hinder their ability to provide unbiased guidance and support. Advocates call for stronger informed consent processes, ensuring that surrogates fully understand their rights, the risks involved, and their post-surrogacy options.

Intended Parents' Rights and Responsibilities

The rights of intended parents, especially in terms of legal recognition of parentage, vary widely by jurisdiction. In some countries, intended parents must wait until after birth to be legally recognised as parents, causing emotional and legal stress. Pre-birth orders, as seen in states like California, offer more certainty for intended parents but can also raise ethical concerns about undermining the surrogate's rights. Balancing intended parents' desire for early recognition with the surrogate's autonomy is an ongoing legal and ethical challenge.

Child Welfare and Rights

Children born through surrogacy face unique legal and social challenges, including issues of legal parentage, citizenship, and access to information about their biological origins. In cross-border surrogacy arrangements, children may be left stateless or without legal recognition in their intended parents' home countries, complicating their access to vital services like healthcare and education. Ensuring children's rights to identity and legal status remains a pressing issue, with ongoing calls for international legal reforms to protect their welfare (Rotabi et al., 2017).

The Hague Conference on Private International Law (HCCH) is actively addressing these challenges through its Parentage/Surrogacy Project, which aims to create a global legal framework for recognising parentage across borders (HCCH | Parentage / Surrogacy Project). This project is critical to ensuring that children born through surrogacy are granted legal parentage from birth, regardless of the country of their birth or where their intended parents reside. By establishing uniform legal standards, the HCCH seeks to protect the rights of children by preventing statelessness and ensuring that they have access to legal documentation (Hague Conference on Private International Law [HCCH], 2024).

Additionally, the HCCH emphasises the importance of protecting children's right to know their genetic and gestational origins. Access to this information is crucial for the child's identity and psychological well-being. In many cases, surrogacy arrangements, particularly those involving anonymous donations, can obscure a child's background, leaving them with limited information about their origins. The HCCH's work advocates for legal provisions that ensure children born through surrogacy can access this information, aligning with international child rights principles.

Countries like the United Kingdom are also considering national reforms to streamline the process of establishing parentage in surrogacy cases and improve access to information about the child's origins (O'Callaghan, 2024). These reforms, combined with the HCCH's efforts, aim to create a more cohesive legal framework that supports the welfare of children born through surrogacy, reducing the risk of legal and social complications and enhancing their long-term well-being.

Ethical Dilemmas Faced by Healthcare Professionals

Healthcare professionals often encounter ethical dilemmas in surrogacy arrangements, as they must balance the competing interests of surrogates and intended parents. Their primary obligation is to protect the surrogate's health and autonomy, yet the involvement of intended parents can create conflicts in decision-making and confidentiality. For instance, intended parents may request medical procedures or detailed updates on the surrogate's condition, which could compromise her privacy or pressurise her into decisions she may not fully agree with. Additionally, financial or contractual pressures from the intended parents can create a power imbalance, further complicating healthcare professionals' ability to prioritise the surrogate's best interests. Navigating these conflicts requires healthcare providers to carefully manage both the surrogate's rights and the expectations of intended parents while adhering to ethical and professional standards.

Section 5: The Future of Surrogacy and Healthcare Practice

The preceding chapters highlight the presence of established guidelines for pre-, during, and post-surrogacy arrangements. However, there is a notable lack of evidence-based practices or specific guidelines tailored for healthcare professionals in managing surrogacy birth care. Therefore, it is essential to develop comprehensive hospital policies that effectively address the management of surrogacy pregnancies and births.

Surrogacy pregnancy and birth healthcare requires a balancing of rights and interests between that of the surrogate, the intended parents, the child to be born, and the hospital and its staff. This is not dissimilar to any other pregnancy and birth, but surrogacy is complex and each case is different. Constant communication between the hospital and the parties is crucial to manage expectations and ensure the best possible outcomes.

Hospitals should have clear and accessible written policies for managing a surrogacy pregnancy and birth that set guidelines and allow for flexibility. Policies should be inclusive and staff should be trained to be inclusive and supportive of all forms of family creation.

The rights and best interests of the child are paramount and should be upheld by everyone involved. This includes recognising the right of the child to be part of a family and to be cared for by the intended parents, with the surrogate's consent. The surrogate's right to autonomy extends to the right not to care for the child they have birthed and to consent to the IPs caring for the child.

The United Kingdom offers a more structured approach to surrogacy birth care on a national level. The United Kingdom has developed a checklist for surrogacy birth plans, which includes detailed information that must be considered and agreed upon by all parties involved (Care in surrogacy: guidance for the care of surrogates and intended parents in surrogate births in England and Wales—GOV.UK (www.gov.uk)) (Department of Health & Social Care, 2024). This checklist covers several aspects:

- Names and Contact Details: information about the surrogate, IPs, and any partners, along with the community midwife supporting them.
- Birth-Planning Meeting: details on who attended the meeting, when it took place, and which healthcare professionals were involved in creating and agreeing on the plan.
- Surrogate Pregnancy Details: information on the surrogacy type (straight or host), expected delivery date, and any fertility treatments received.
- Antenatal Care: confirmation of routine antenatal care and details about who will attend scans and appointments with the surrogate.
- The Birth: preferences regarding the place of birth, birth partners, attendees in different birth scenarios (vaginal, planned caesarean, emergency caesarean), pain relief options, and decision-making if the surrogate cannot speak during birth.
- Handling of the Child at Birth: decisions about cord-cutting, skin-to-skin contact, and who will hold the baby thereafter.
- Post-Partum Care: plans for caring for the child post-birth, feeding methods (breast milk from the surrogate or IPs, donated milk, or formula), visiting rights, and discharge protocols.
- Postnatal Healthcare Needs: assessment and support for the physical, emotional, and mental health needs of both the surrogate and IPs, as well as the baby's needs.

While the United Kingdom offers a structured framework for managing surrogacy births at the national level, it still lacks conclusive evidence to guide clinicians on best practices. For example, there is no established consensus on the optimal timing or circumstances for involving intended parents during the birth process. Additionally, the lack of clear guidance on infant feeding—whether the surrogate or the intended mother should breastfeed—poses further challenges. The implications of these decisions on the child's well-being, as well as on the surrogate and intended parents, remain under-researched. Although some intended mothers may attempt induced lactation to breastfeed their surrogate-born child, evidence indicates that this process often results in only partial lactation, typically lasting about four weeks. In some cases, intended mothers may not succeed in lactation despite medical interventions. This variability complicates the ability of healthcare professionals to offer consistent and evidence-based advice on feeding options, highlighting the need for robust guidelines in this area.

Conversely, some countries may lack both a structured national framework and hospital-specific policies for managing surrogacy births. This absence of guidance creates significant challenges for healthcare professionals, who may struggle to determine whose rights and needs should be prioritised during care—whether those of the surrogate, IPs, or the child.

In response to these gaps, this book provides a set of recommendations for establishing surrogacy birth care policies. According to Sarah Jefford—a surrogacy lawyer with extensive experience in advocating for clients in complex surrogacy cases—drawing on her expertise to develop guidelines for healthcare systems that do not yet have clear policies in place. Below are Jefford's key recommendations for creating an effective surrogacy policy in the hospital setting.

Pregnancy Care: Healthcare providers should facilitate joint appointments for the surrogate and intended parents, with the surrogate's consent. The surrogate retains decision-making authority and privacy, but with her consent, medical information can be shared with the intended parents. Parentcraft and birth classes should be offered to the IPs.

Birth Planning: Healthcare providers should coordinate with both the surrogate and intended parents to ensure the surrogate's autonomy is respected. Plans for the birth, including the presence of intended parents, cord-cutting, and breastfeeding, should be discussed and agreed upon by all parties.

Feeding Baby: Feeding options for the baby, including induced lactation by IPs, breastfeeding by the surrogate, or formula feeding, should be decided collectively and supported by healthcare providers.

Postnatal Care: The surrogate's privacy is prioritised, and separate accommodations from the IPs and baby should be arranged if possible. The intended parents are generally responsible for the baby's care post-birth, while the surrogate is not obligated to provide such care.

Discharge from Hospital and Ongoing Care: The birth mother and baby may be discharged together or separately. The intended parents should receive home visits and child health nurse referrals, while the birth mother should receive postnatal care and follow-up with her general practitioner.

The absence of definitive research on these key aspects of surrogacy birth care underscores the urgent need for comprehensive studies to guide healthcare professionals and establish evidence-based guidelines. Without such guidelines, clinicians face significant challenges in making informed decisions that optimise outcomes for the surrogates, intended parents, and child. Future research should focus on addressing these gaps to ensure equitable and effective surrogacy practices that respect the rights and well-being of all parties involved.

International Concerns and Recommendations

Looking forwards around the legal landscape in which surrogacy operates, a number of significant concerns have been recognised at the international level. In the 2019 UN *Report of the Special Rapporteur on the sale and sexual exploitation of children, including child prostitution, child pornography, and other child sexual abuse material*, several recommendations around surrogacy were made (United Nations [UN], 2004). These recommendations began with the premise that included surrogacy within the realm of the UN CRC, as the potential exists for the exploitation of surrogates and the commodification of children born through these practices. Recommendations were comprehensive and far-reaching and covered both international recommendations and recommendations for the implementation of changes at the national level.

The recommendations included that, inter alia, at the national level states ratify the CRC and its three operational protocols and focus on the best interests of the child according to Article 3 paragraph one on the CRC. That states initiate legal reform for the establishment, recognition, and contestation of legal parentage the surrogate-born children, and to guarantee non-discrimination of surrogate born children, include ensuring healthcare coverage for surrogate-born children at the national level. It recommended that states work to preserve and maintain records around the genetic and gestational origin of surrogate-born children, ensure their rights to access that information exist, and allow mechanisms for surrogate-born children to access that information. These recommendations would work towards ensuring inclusivity for surrogate-born children having the same rights and support as afforded naturally born children.

Other recommendations included ensuring compliance of surrogacy arrangements with procedural and other minimum safeguard requirements to prevent legal uncertainty for surrogate-born children. They recommended that states develop policies to minimise the separation of surrogate-born children from IPs during the legal review process, not only for the surrogate child but also to reduce the burden on surrogates. In cases of abandonment, it recommended that a clear legal framework be put in place to ensure that IPs cannot avoid their parental responsibility. The report also made recommendations to ensure that policies prohibiting the sale, trafficking, abuse, and exploitation of children apply in the context of surrogacy and ensure that the commodification of children does not occur.

Several international recommendations were made, inter alia, including the following:

That the international community support comprehensive research and data collection on existing surrogacy practices that cover all stakeholders involved. That the international community include safeguards to be complied with to enable the recognition of legal parentage for surrogate-born children. Additionally, the Special Rapporteur reiterated that nothing in the recommendations should imply women who act as surrogates cannot make independent decisions about the autonomy of their own bodies. The recommended reforms show willingness of the UN in ensuring that surrogacy reform takes into account the best interest of children born of surrogacy and that the surrogates and the children born of these arrangements are supported within national legislation and also through international cooperation.

These legal reforms recommended by the UN Special Rapporteur would work towards creating a more egalitarian platform from which commercial and altruistic surrogacy can be undertaken. It will also protect the rights of the children born of surrogacy and make the recognition of parentage and gestational heritage and the legal recognition of their rights and nationality much less difficult.

Section 6: Conclusion

The complexities inherent in surrogacy practice require a nuanced and critically informed approach to healthcare policy and clinical practice. While surrogacy has driven significant advancements in reproductive healthcare and fostered multidisciplinary collaboration, the lack of structured, evidence-based guidelines for surrogacy birth care continues to present substantial challenges. This chapter advocates for the development of comprehensive hospital policies that equitably balance the rights and well-being of the surrogates, intended parents, and child. Establishing robust ethical frameworks is crucial to guiding healthcare providers in making decisions that respect surrogate autonomy while addressing the legitimate needs of IPs.

Future research and policy development must prioritise closing these critical gaps, ensuring that surrogacy practices are ethical, transparent, and equitable across different healthcare settings. By fostering greater collaboration among healthcare providers, legal experts, policymakers, and surrogacy advocates, the surrogacy care landscape can be transformed to better serve all parties involved. Such efforts will contribute to setting new standards for reproductive healthcare practices globally, promoting a more supportive and sustainable approach to surrogacy.

Call to Action for Stakeholders

The future of surrogacy practice hinges on the proactive actions taken by stakeholders across the spectrum today. Healthcare providers must commit to implementing best practices that ensure safe and ethical surrogacy care. Policymakers should focus on developing and harmonising regulations that safeguard the interests of all parties, particularly in the context of cross-border surrogacy arrangements. Surrogacy agencies and intermediaries must operate with transparency and accountability, providing comprehensive support to surrogates and intended parents throughout the surrogacy process. Finally, scholars and researchers should continue to expand the body of knowledge on surrogacy, delivering evidence-based insights that shape ethical, effective, and equitable surrogacy practices for the future.

References

Abma, J. C. (1997). *Fertility, family planning, and women's health: new data from the 1995 National Survey of Family Growth* (Vol. 19). Department of Health and Human Services Centers for Disease CLan.

Attawet, J. (2021). Mapping transnational commercial surrogacy arrangements in South and Southeast Asia. *Medico-Legal Journal*, *89*(2), 128–132. https://doi.org/10.1177/0025817220985099

Attawet, J., Alsharaydeh, E., & Brady, M. (2024). Commercial surrogacy: Landscapes of empowerment or oppression explored through integrative review. *Health Care for Women International*, (Jan 22), 1–19.

Attawet, J., Wang, A., & Sullivan, E. (2022). 'Womb for work' experiences of Thai women and gestational surrogacy practice in Thailand. *Human fertility (Cambridge, England)*, *25*(5), 912–923. https://doi.org/10.1080/14647273.2021.1937716

Attawet, J., Wang, A. Y., Farquhar, C. M., Jordan, V., Li, Z., & Sullivan, E. A. (2022). Pregnancy and birth outcomes of single versus multiple embryo transfer in gestational surrogacy arrangements: A systematic review and meta-analysis. *Human Fertility (Cambridge, England)*, *25*(2), 217–227. https://doi.org/10.1080/14647273.2020.1785643

Baykal, B., Korkmaz, C., Ceyhan, S. T., Goktolga, U., & Baser, I. (2008). Opinions of infertile Turkish women on gamete donation and gestational surrogacy. *Fertility and Sterility*, *89*(4), 817–822.

Bello, F. A., Akinajo, O. R., & Olayemi, O. (2014). In-vitro fertilization, gamete donation and surrogacy: Perceptions of women attending an infertility clinic in Ibadan, Nigeria. *African Journal of Reproductive Health*, *18*(2), 127–133.

Bhatia, K., Martindale, E. A., Rustamov, O., & Nysenbaum, A. M. (2009). Review: Surrogate pregnancy: An essential guide for clinicians. *Obstetrician and Gynaecologist*, *11*, 49–54.

Brandão, P., & Garrido, N. (2023). Commercial surrogacy: An overview. *Revista Brasileira de Ginecologia e Obstetrícia*, *44*, 1141–1158.

Bromfield, N. F., & Rotabi, K. S. (2014). Global surrogacy, exploitation, human rights and international private law: A pragmatic stance and policy recommendations. *Global Social Welfare*, *1*, 123–135.

Bruce-Hickman, K., Kirkland, L., & Ba-Obeid, T. (2009). The attitudes and knowledge of medical students towards surrogacy. *Journal of Obstetrics and Gynaecology*, *29*(3), 229–232.

Child Rights International Network (CRIN). (2019). *Mennesson v. France*. CRIN. Retrieved 25th Oct from https://archive.crin.org/en/library/legal-database/mennesson-v-france.html#:~:text=On%20the%20complainants%E2%80%99%20return%20to%20France,

Chiware, T. M., Vermeulen, N., Blondeel, K., Farquharson, R., Kiarie, J., Lundin, K., Matsaseng, T. C., Ombelet, W., & Toskin, I. (2021). IVF and other ART in low-and middle-i ncome countries: A systematic landscape analysis. *Human Reproduction Update*, *27*(2), 213–228.

Chliaoutakis, J. E. (2002). A relationship between traditionally motivated patterns and gamete donation and surrogacy in urban areas of Greece. *Human Reproduction*, *17*(8), 2187–2191.

Constantinidis, D., & Cook, R. (2012). Australian perspectives on surrogacy: The influence of cognitions, psychological and demographic characteristics. *Human Reproduction*, *27*(4), 1080–1087.

Cooke, A., Mills, T. A., & Lavender, T. (2012). Advanced maternal age: Delayed childbearing is rarely a conscious choice: A qualitative study of women's views and experiences. *International Journal of Nursing Studies*, *49*(1), 30–39.

Dar, S., Lazer, T., Swanson, S., Silverman, J., Wasser, C., Moskovtsev, S. I., Sojecki, A., & Librach, C. L. (2015). Assisted reproduction involving gestational surrogacy: An analysis of the medical, psychosocial and legal issues: Experience from a large surrogacy program. *Human Reproduction*, *30*(2), 345–352.

De Geyter, C. (2019). Assisted reproductive technology: Impact on society and need for surveillance. *Best Practice & Research Clinical Endocrinology & Metabolism*, *33*(1), 3–8. https://doi.org/https://doi.org/10.1016/j.beem.2019.01.004

Department of Health & Social Care. (2024). *Guidance Care in surrogacy: Guidance for the care of surrogates and intended parents in surrogate births in England and Wales*. GOV.UK. Retrieved 2 Sep from https://www.gov.uk/government/publications/having-a-child-through-surrogacy/care-in-surrogacy-guidance-for-the-care-of-surrogates-and-intended-parents-in-surrogate-births-in-england-and-wales#annex-b-checklist-of-information-to-be-included-in-surrogacy-birth-plan

Edwards, E., Jones, S., Kenwright, E., Hennessy, F., Horsey, K., Mahmoud, Z., & Marway, H. K. (2023). Care in surrogacy: Practice, ethics and regulations. *International Journal of Birth and Parenting Education, 13*. https://doi.org/https://ijbpe.com/journals/supplements

Ellenbogen, A., Feldberg, D., & Lokshin, V. (2021). Surrogacy: A worldwide demand. Implementation and ethical considerations. *Gynecological and Reproductive Endocrinology & Metabolism, 2*, 66–73.

Everingham, S. G., Stafford-Bell, M. A., & Hammarberg, K. (2014). Australians' use of surrogacy. *Medical Journal of Australia, 201*(5), 270–273.

Fauser, B. C., Adamson, G. D., Boivin, J., Chambers, G. M., de Geyter, C., Dyer, S., Inhorn, M. C., Schmidt, L., Serour, G. I., & Tarlatzis, B. (2024). Declining global fertility rates and the implications for family planning and family building: An IFFS consensus document based on a narrative review of the literature. *Human Reproduction Update, 30*(2), 153–173.

Fong, R., McRoy, R. G., & McGinnis, H. (2016). Overview of intercountry adoptions. In *Transracial and intercountry adoptions: Cultural guidance for professionals* (pp. 19–37). Columbia University Press.

Frati, P., La Russa, R., Santurro, A., Fineschi, B., Di Paolo, M., Scopetti, M., Turillazzi, E., & Fineschi, V. (2021). Bioethical issues and legal frameworks of surrogacy: A global perspective about the right to health and dignity. *European Journal of Obstetrics & Gynecology and Reproductive Biology, 258*, 1–8.

Freundlich, M., & Phillips, R. (2000). Ethical issues in adoption. *Adoption & Fostering, 24*(4), 7–17. https://doi.org/10.1177/030857590002400403.

Gelmann, E. (2010). I'm just the oven, it's totally their bun: The power and necessity of the federal government to regulate commercial gestational surrogacy arrangements and protect the legal rights of intended parents. *Women's Rights Law Reporter, 32*, 159.

Genuis, S. J., Chang, W.-C., & Genuis, S. K. (1993). Public attitudes in Edmonton toward assisted reproductive technology. *CMAJ: Canadian Medical Association Journal, 149*(2), 153.

Gheauş, A. (2016). The normative importance of pregnancy challenges surrogacy contracts. *AnALize: Revista de studii feminist, 6*(20), 20–31.

Gore, A. C., Chappell, V. A., Fenton, S. E., Flaws, J. A., Nadal, A., Prins, G. S., Toppari, J., & Zoeller, R. T. (2015). EDC-2: The Endocrine Society's second scientific statement on endocrine-disrupting chemicals. *Endocrine Reviews, 36*(6), E1–E150.

Goswami, L., Rotabi, K., & Bromfield, N. (2014). Force, fraud, coercion and exploitation: Abuses in intercountry adoption contrasted against what Indian women acting as surrogate mothers have to say about their experiences. International Forum on Intercountry Adoption and Global Surrogacy, The Hague, Netherlands.

Hague Conference on Private International Law (HCCH). (2008). *The implementation and operation of the 1993 Hague Intercountry Adoption Convention: Guide to good practice*. HCCH. Retrieved 25 Nov from https://www.hcch.net/en/publications-and-studies/details4/?pid=4388

Hague Conference on Private International Law (HCCH). (2024). *Parentage/surrogacy project*. HCCH. Retrieved 30 Oct from https://www.hcch.net/en/projects/legislative-projects/parentage-surrogacy

Hoechst, J. A., & Sobottka, S. C. (2017). Roadblocks to surrogacy. *Family Advocacy, 40*, 44.

Hollingsworth, L. D. (2003). International adoption among families in the United States: Considerations of social justice. *Social Work, 48*(2), 209–217.

Horsey, K., Arian-Schad, M., Macklon, N., & Ahuja, K. K. (2023). UK intended parents' characteristics, experiences, and views on surrogacy law reform. *International Journal of Law, Policy and the Family*, *37*(1), ebad004.
Hovav, A. (2020). Cutting out the surrogate: Caesarean sections in the Mexican surrogacy industry. *Social Science & Medicine*, *256*, 113063.
Inhorn, M. C., & Patrizio, P. (2015). Infertility around the globe: New thinking on gender, reproductive technologies and global movements in the 21st century. *Human Reproduction Update*, *21*(4), 411–426.
Jones, H. (2018). Contracts for children: Constitutional challenges to surrogacy contracts and selective reduction clauses. *Hastings Law Journal*, *70*, 595.
Karandikar, S., Gezinski, L. B., Carter, J. R., & Kaloga, M. (2014). Economic necessity or noble cause? A qualitative study exploring motivations for gestational surrogacy in Gujarat, India. *Affilia: Journal of Women & Social Work*, *29*(2), 224–236. https://doi.org/10.1177/0886109913516455
Kian, E. M., Riazi, H., & Bashirian, S. (2014). Attitudes of Iranian infertile couples toward surrogacy. *Journal of Human Reproductive Sciences*, *7*(1), 47–51.
Kneebone, E., Beilby, K., & Hammarberg, K. (2022). Experiences of surrogates and intended parents of surrogacy arrangements: A systematic review. *Reproductive BioMedicine Online*, *45*(4), 815–830. https://doi.org/10.1016/j.rbmo.2022.06.006
König, A. (2023). Reproductive entanglements in times of war: Transnational gestational surrogacy in Ukraine and beyond. *Medical Anthropology*, *42*(5), 479–492.
Kovacs, G. T., Morgan, G., Wood, E. C., Howlett, D., & Forbes, C. (2003). Community attitudes to assisted reproductive technology: A 20-year trend. *Medical Journal of Australia*, *179*(10), 536–538.
Lasker, J. N., & Murray, D. E. (2001). Attitudes toward technologies for conception: A 15-year follow-up. *Journal of Applied Social Psychology*, *31*(10), 2165–2183.
Luke, B., & Brown, M. B. (2007). Elevated risks of pregnancy complications and adverse outcomes with increasing maternal age. *Human Reproduction*, *22*(5), 1264–1272.
Machtinger, R., Duvdevani, N.-R., Lebovitz, O., Dor, J., Hourvitz, A., & Orvieto, R. (2017). Outcome of gestational surrogacy according to IVF protocol. *Journal of Assisted Reproduction and Genetics*, *34*, 445–449.
Marinelli, S., Del Rio, A., Straccamore, M., Negro, F., & Basile, G. (2022). The armed conflict in Ukraine and the risks of inter-country surrogacy. The unsolved dilemma. *European Review for Medical and Pharmacological Sciences*, *26*(16), 5646–5650.
Marinelli, S., Negro, F., Varone, M. C., De Paola, L., Napoletano, G., Lopez, A., Zaami, S., & Basile, G. (2024). The legally charged issue of cross-border surrogacy: Current regulatory challenges and future prospects. *European Journal of Obstetrics & Gynecology and Reproductive Biology*, *300*, 41–48. doi: 10.1016/j.ejogrb.2024.07.008.
Maydanyk, R. A., & Moskalenko, K. V. (2020). Towards creation of unified regulation on surrogacy in Europe: Recent trends and future perspectives. *Wiad Lek*, *73*, 2865–2870.
Miall, C. E. (1989). Reproductive technology vs. the stigma of involuntary childlessness. *Social Casework*, *70*(1), 43–50.
Monico, C. (2013). Implications of child abduction for human rights and child welfare systems: A constructivist inquiry of the lived experience of Guatemalan mothers publically reporting child abduction for intercountry adoption.
Mulligan, A. (2024). Surrogacy and the significance of gestation: Implications for law and policy. *Bioethics*, *38*(8), 674–683.
Nadimpally, S., & Majumdar, A. (2017). Recruiting to give birth: Agent-facilitators and the commercial surrogacy arrangement in India. In: M. Davies (Ed.), *Babies for sale:*

Transnational surrogacy, human rights and the politics of reproduction (pp. 65–81). London: Zed Books.

O'Callaghan, E. (2024). Surrogate born children's access to information about their origins. *International Journal of Law, Policy and the Family*, *38*(1), ebab009.

Pande, A. (2014). *Wombs in labor: Transnational commercial surrogacy in India*. Columbia University Press.

Poote, A. E., & van den Akker, O. B. (2009). British women's attitudes to surrogacy. *Human Reproduction*, *24*(1), 139–145.

Quinn, M., & Huddleston, H. (2017). Gestational surrogacy. In C. Simon & L. C. Giudicc (Eds.), *The endometrial factor* (pp. 228–233). CRC Press.

Radio Free Europe Radio Liberty. (2024). *Babies born to Ukrainian surrogates meet parents after pandemic restrictions ease*. Radio Free Europe Radio Liberty. Retrieved 25 Oct from https://www.marieclaire.com/health-fitness/a32433196/surrogacy-covid-19-ukraine/

Rahmani, A., Sattarzadeh, N., Gholizadeh, L., Sheikhalipour, Z., Allahbakhshian, A., & Hassankhani, H. (2011). Gestational surrogacy: Viewpoint of Iranian infertile women. *Journal of Human Reproductive Sciences*, *4*(3), 138–142.

Report of the Special Rapporteur on the sale and sexual exploitation of children, including child prostitution, child pornography, and other child sexual abuse material, UN GA Report A/74/162, July 15, 2019.

Rodríguez-Jaume, M. J., González-Río, M. J., & Jareño-Ruiz, D. (2021). Cross-border reproductive care: Opinions and attitudes of society towards surrogate pregnancy. *Current Sociology*, *69*(2), 266–285.

Rotabi, K. S., & Gibbons, J. L. (2012). Does the Hague Convention on Intercountry Adoption adequately protect orphaned and vulnerable children and their families? *Journal of Child and Family Studies*, *21*, 106–119.

Rotabi, K. S., Mapp, S., Cheney, K., Fong, R., & McRoy, R. (2017). Regulating commercial global surrogacy: The best interests of the child. *Journal of Human Rights and Social Work*, *2*(3), 64–73.

Safdari-Dehcheshmeh, F., Noroozi, M., Taleghani, F., & Memar, S. (2023). Factors influencing the delay in childbearing: A narrative review. *Iranian Journal of Nursing and Midwifery Research*, *28*(1), 10–19.

Saito, Y., & Matsuo, H. (2009). Survey of Japanese infertile couples' attitudes toward surrogacy. *Journal of Psychosomatic Obstetrics & Gynecology*, *30*(3), 156–161.

Saravanan, S. (2013). An ethnomethodological approach to examine exploitation in the context of capacity, trust and experience of commercial surrogacy in India. *Philosophy, Ethics, and Humanities in Medicine*, *8*(1), 10. https://doi.org/10.1186/1747-5341-8-10

Scherman, R., Misca, G., Rotabi, K., & Selman, P. (2016). Global commercial surrogacy and international adoption: Parallels and differences. *Adoption & Fostering*, *40*(1), 20–35.

Selman, P. (2015). Global trends in intercountry adoption: 2003–2013. Intercountry Adoption; Orphan rescue or Child trafficking?, Feb, 2013, Pepperdine University, Malibu, CA, US; Based on presentations at the aforementioned conference and at the 3rd International Meet on Adoption organized by Cara, New Delhi 19–20 February 2013.

Selman, R., Early, K., Battles, B., Seidenburg, M., Wendel, E., & Westerlund, S. (2022). Maximizing recovery in the postpartum period: A Timeline for rehabilitation from pregnancy through return to sport. *International Journal of Sports Physical Therapy*, *17*(6), 1170.

Sharan, H., Yahav, J., Peleg, D., Ben-Rafael, Z., & Merlob, P. (2001). Hospitalization for early bonding of the genetic mother after a surrogate pregnancy: Report of two cases. *Birth*, *28*(4), 270–273.

Simopoulou, M., Sfakianoudis, K., Tsioulou, P., Rapani, A., Anifandis, G., Pantou, A., Bolaris, S., Bakas, P., Deligeoroglou, E., & Pantos, K. (2018). Risks in surrogacy considering the embryo: From the preimplantation to the gestational and neonatal period. *BioMed Research International*, *2018*(1), 6287507.

Skakkebæk, N. E., Lindahl-Jacobsen, R., Levine, H., Andersson, A.-M., Jørgensen, N., Main, K. M., Lidegaard, Ø., Priskorn, L., Holmboe, S. A., & Bräuner, E. V. (2022). Environmental factors in declining human fertility. *Nature Reviews Endocrinology*, *18*(3), 139–157.

Stöbel-Richter, Y., Goldschmidt, S., Brähler, E., Weidner, K., & Beutel, M. (2009). Egg donation, surrogate mothering, and cloning: attitudes of men and women in Germany based on a representative survey. *Fertility and Sterility*, *92*(1), 124–130.

Taebi, M., Alavi, N. M., & Ahmadi, S. M. (2020). The experiences of surrogate mothers: A qualitative study. *Nursing and Midwifery Studies*, *9*(1), 51–59.

Tanderup, M., Pande, A., Schmidt, L., Nielsen, B. B., Humaidan, P., & Kroløkke, C. (2023). Impact of the war in Ukraine and the COVID-19 pandemic on transnational surrogacy–A qualitative study of Danish infertile couples' experiences of being in 'exile'. *Reproductive BioMedicine Online*, *47*(4), 103258.

Triviño-Caballero, R. (2023). Caring for delivery: Healthcare professionals' ethical conflicts in surrogate pregnancy. *Hypatia*, *38*(3), 531–548.

Tsai, S., Shaia, K., Woodward, J. T., Sun, M. Y., & Muasher, S. J. (2020). Surrogacy laws in the United States: What obstetrician-gynecologists need to know. *Obstetrics & Gynecology*, *135*(3), 717–722. https://doi.org/10.1097/AOG.0000000000003698

UNICEF. (n.d.). *The Convention on the Rights of the Child: The children's version*. Retrieved 25 Nov from https://www.unicef.org/child-rights-convention/convention-text-childrens-version

United Nations (UN). (2004). *Convention on the rights of the child (1989) Treaty no. 27531*. Retrieved from https://treaties.un.org/doc/Treaties/1990/09/19900902%2003-14%20AM/Ch_IV_11p.pdf

United Nations (UN). (2024). *World Population Prospects 2024*. Retrieved 25 Nov from https://population.un.org/wpp/

Walker, R., & Van Zyl, L. (2015). Surrogate motherhood and abortion for fetal abnormality. *Bioethics*, *29*(8), 529–535.

Walker, R., & Van Zyl, L. (2017). Beyond altruism: A case for compensated surrogate motherhood. In R. Shaw (Ed.), *Bioethics Beyond Altruism: Donating and Transforming Human Biological Materials* (pp. 165–185). Palgrave Macmillan. https://doi.org/10.1007/978-3-319-55532-4_7

Weiss, G. L. (1992). Public attitudes about surrogate motherhood. *Michigan Sociological Review*, *6*, 15–27. http://www.jstor.org/stable/40968959

White, P. M. (2017). "One for Sorrow, Two for Joy?": American embryo transfer guideline recommendations, practices, and outcomes for gestational surrogate patients. *Journal of Assisted Reproduction and Genetics*, *34*(4), 431–443. https://doi.org/10.1007/s10815-017-0885-7

Whittaker, A., Gerrits, T., & Weis, C. (2022). Emerging "repronubs" and "reproprеneurs": Transnational surrogacy in Ghana, Kazakhstan, and Laos. *International Journal of Comparative Sociology*, *63*(5–6), 304–323.

Yang, Y., & Wu, N. (2022). Gestational diabetes mellitus and preeclampsia: Correlation and influencing factors. *Frontiers in Cardiovascular Medicine*, *9*, 831297.

Zaami, S., Del Rio, A., Negro, F., Varone, M. C., Marinelli, S., & Montanari Vergallo, G. (2022). The March 2021 Italian constitutional court ruling on surrogacy: A prelude to common European legislation for the sake of reproductive health? *The European Journal of Contraception & Reproductive Health Care*, *27*(1), 61–66.

Zabak, S., Varma, A., Bansod, S., & Pohane, M. R. (2023). Exploring the complex landscape of delayed childbearing: Factors, history, and long-term implications. *Cureus*, *15*(9), e46291. doi: 10.7759/cureus.46291

7 Conclusion and Supplementary

Chapter 1: Introduction to Commercial Surrogacy

The introduction to commercial surrogacy has revealed the evolution of surrogacy practices from traditional to gestational surrogacy, the role of medical advancements, and the influence of legal, ethical, and market forces in shaping modern surrogacy. This chapter highlighted how geographic "repronubs" have become prominent hubs for commercial surrogacy due to favourable regulations and economic conditions. Additionally, it introduced the primary stakeholders, including surrogates, intended parents, medical professionals, and agencies, all of whom play essential roles in the process. The complexities highlighted in this chapter set the stage for a deeper exploration of the legal landscape, which defines the rights and obligations of all parties involved.

Chapter 2: Legal Framework and Challenges

The legal framework surrounding commercial surrogacy is diverse, with each jurisdiction offering different levels of protection for intended parents, surrogates, and children born from surrogacy arrangements. While some countries have well-defined laws, others operate in a legal grey area, creating significant risks for all parties involved. This chapter examined the pivotal role of pre-conception contracts, parental rights, and jurisdictional differences that can shape the experience and outcomes of commercial surrogacy. It underscored the legal hurdles faced by intended parents and surrogates, especially in cross-border surrogacy. This discussion paves the way for an examination of ethical considerations, which are often deeply intertwined with legal principles in surrogacy arrangements.

Chapter 3: Ethics in Commercial Surrogacy

The ethical considerations of commercial surrogacy are multifaceted, reflecting issues of fairness, power imbalances, and the rights of surrogates, intended parents, and the resulting children. This chapter explored how ethical concerns are heightened in cross-border surrogacy, where differences in wealth and legal protections create potential for exploitation. This chapter also highlighted ethical dilemmas

DOI: 10.4324/9781003511939-7

surrounding the commodification of the human body and the nature of informed consent for surrogates. Perspectives from surrogates, intended parents, and regulatory bodies were discussed, offering insights into the ethical tensions inherent in commercial surrogacy. These ethical considerations provide a foundation for understanding how health guidelines and policies are designed to protect the welfare of all involved.

Chapter 4: Surrogacy Practice Health Guidelines and Policies

Health guidelines and policy frameworks are critical in ensuring the safety, dignity, and rights of surrogates, intended parents, and children. This chapter outlined the need for comprehensive, evidence-based policies to address health risks, medical oversight, and the well-being of surrogates. Key considerations such as antenatal care, childbirth protocols, and post-partum support were emphasised, along with the role of healthcare providers in ensuring adherence to health guidelines. These health guidelines are essential for ensuring that surrogacy practices are safe and ethical, highlighting the crucial role of healthcare providers in upholding these standards.

Chapter 5: The Role of Healthcare Providers in Commercial Surrogacy

Healthcare providers play a fundamental role in the surrogacy process, offering medical, emotional, and ethical support to surrogates and intended parents. This chapter illustrated how healthcare professionals navigate medical complexities, ensure informed consent, and maintain ethical standards. It also highlighted the importance of interprofessional collaboration to ensure positive outcomes for all stakeholders. The insights gained in this chapter underscore the necessity of reflecting on the current state of surrogacy practices and exploring potential future improvements in the field.

Chapter 6: Reflections and Future Directions of Surrogacy Practice

The concluding chapter provided a reflective analysis of the current state and future trajectory of commercial surrogacy. It emphasised the need for more inclusive and evidence-based guidelines to support ethical practices, protect surrogates, and ensure the well-being of children born through surrogacy. The role of international cooperation in shaping global surrogacy policies was highlighted, along with calls for more robust health guidelines and greater legal clarity. Key areas for future research and policy development were proposed, focusing on safeguarding the rights of all parties and promoting equitable surrogacy practices worldwide. This reflective analysis underscores the continuous evolution of surrogacy practices and the ongoing need for multi-stakeholder engagement to ensure fair, ethical, and sustainable surrogacy arrangements.

Supplementary for Surrogacy Guidelines and Act in Australia

Link for Surrogacy Guidelines

The United Kingdom: hfea-draft-code-of-practice-9th-edition-consultation-version.pdf (https://www.hfea.gov.uk/media/2565/hfea-draft-code-of-practice-9th-edition-consultation-version.pdf), Care in surrogacy: guidance for the care of surrogates and intended parents in surrogate births in England and Wales—GOV.UK (www.gov.uk) (https://www.gov.uk/government/publications/having-a-child-through-surrogacy/care-in-surrogacy-guidance-for-the-care-of-surrogates-and-intended-parents-in-surrogate-births-in-england-and-wales)

US: Practice Guidance | American Society for Reproductive Medicine | ASRM (https://www.asrm.org/practice-guidance/)

Australia: Ethical guidelines on the use of assisted reproductive technology | NHMRC (https://www.nhmrc.gov.au/about-us/publications/art)

New Zealand: Stage One Consultation: Submissions Analysis—Posthumous Reproduction: A review of the current Guidelines for the Storage, Use, and Disposal of Sperm from a Deceased Man to take into account gametes and embryos (health.govt.nz) (https://acart.health.govt.nz/assets/Uploads/ACART/Publications/Advice-and-Guidelines-for-Gamete-and-Embryo-Donation-and-Surrogacy.pdf)

Australia/New Zealand: ANZICA-SURROGACY-GUIDELINES-OCTOBER-2022.pdf (fertilitysociety.com.au) (https://www.fertilitysociety.com.au/wp-content/uploads/ANZICA-SURROGACY-GUIDELINES-OCTOBER-2022.pdf)

South Africa: About SASREG—SASREG (https://sasreg.co.za/about-sasreg/)

Surrogacy Act in Australia

New South Wales: Review of Surrogacy Act 2010.pdf (nsw.gov.au) (https://www.parliament.nsw.gov.au/tp/files/73919/Review%20of%20Surrogacy%20Act%202010.pdf)

Queensland: Surrogacy Act 2010 (legislation.qld.gov.au) (https://www.legislation.qld.gov.au/view/pdf/2016-03-22/act-2010-002)

Victoria: Assisted reproduction (health.vic.gov.au) (https://www.health.vic.gov.au/patient-care/assisted-reproduction)

South Australia: Family Relationships Act 1975 (legislation.sa.gov.au) (https://www.legislation.sa.gov.au/__legislation/lz/c/a/family%20relationships%20act%201975/current/1975.115.auth.pdf)

Western Australia: Microsoft Word—SurrogacyAct2008_00-b0-08.docx (legislation.wa.gov.au) (https://www.legislation.wa.gov.au/legislation/prod/filestore.nsf/FileURL/mrdoc_14284.pdf/$FILE/Surrogacy%20Act%202008%20-%20%5B00-b0-08%5D.pdf?OpenElement)

Tasmania: View—Tasmanian Legislation Online (https://www.legislation.tas.gov.au/view/whole/html/inforce/current/act-2012-034#:~:text=(1)%20This%20Act%20is%20to,or%20her%20life%2C%20are%20paramount)

Northern Territory: Legislation Database (nt.gov.au) (https://legislation.nt.gov.au/en/Bills/Surrogacy-Bill-2022-S50?format=assented)

Australian Capital Territory: Parentage Act 2004 | Acts (https://www.legislation.act.gov.au/a/2004-1/)

Supplementary for Essential Tests and Recommendations

Designing essential tests and recommendations for **intended parents** and **surrogates** involves a multidisciplinary approach encompassing physical health, mental health, and ethical considerations. Below is a framework for testing categorised into **essential tests** and **recommendations** for both groups:

Intended Parents (IPs)

Tests	*Essential*	*Recommended*	*Details*
Physical health screening	✓		Comprehensive medical history and physical examination. Height, weight, and BMI
Fertility assessment	✓		**Males:** Semen analysis (sperm count, motility, morphology). **Females:** Ovarian reserve testing (Anti-Mullerian hormone (AMH) levels, follicle count).
Screening for infectious disease	✓		**Blood tests:** HIV, hepatitis B and C, syphilis. **STI screening:** Gonorrhoea, chlamydia.
Genetic testing		✓	– Carrier screening for hereditary genetic conditions. – Karyotyping to check for chromosomal abnormalities.
Blood group (ABO) and Rh factor compatibility	✓		Avoids complications with foetal Rh incompatibility.
-Female for pre-In vitro fertilization (IVF): Hb typing, TVS, Estradiol, LH, Prolactin, AMH, TSH, FT3, FT4			
Mental health and emotional readiness	✓		– Screening for mental health disorders. Examples not specific to surrogacy include: Patient Health Questionnaire (PHQ), Generalized Anxiety Disorder Scale (GAD-7), Kessler Psychological Distress Scale (K10/K6), General Health Questionnaire (GHQ). – Assessment of emotional readiness and resilience for surrogacy. Examples not specific to surrogacy include:) Psychological General Well-Being Index (PGWB), Connor-Davidson Resilience Scale (CD-RISC), Fertility Quality of Life (FertiQoL) Tool, Depression, Anxiety, and Stress Scale (DASS-21 or DASS-42), and Strengths and Difficulties Questionnaire (SDQ
Legal counselling		✓	Review surrogacy contracts to address parental rights, responsibilities, and compensation.
Educational programmes		✓	Inform about surrogacy processes, ART (e.g., IVF), and post-birth care.
Health and lifestyle		✓	Encourage a healthy lifestyle to support fertility (e.g., diet, exercise, avoiding alcohol and smoking).

Surrogates

Tests	*Essential*	*Recommended*	*Details*
Comprehensive medical history and gynaecological exam	✓		– Uterine evaluation (e.g., hysteroscopy, ultrasound) – Review of pregnancy and delivery history – Physical examination including weight and nutrition, exercise and lifestyle habits, – Medical history including current medications and supplements, menstruation, chronic health condition management, blood pressure check, pelvic exam, Pap tests, etc. – Height, weight, and BMI
Vaccination status check	✓		Recommended by CDC for anyone planning for pregnancy. Make sure vaccinated and up-to-date for: - Tdap (tetanus, diphtheria, and pertussis) – Hepatitis B – MMR (measles, mumps, and rubella) – Chickenpox – Influenza – Covid-19
Dental checkup		✓	During pregnancy, hormonal changes can lead to excessive gum inflammation, known as pregnancy gingivitis.
Infectious disease screening	✓		– HIV, hepatitis B & C, syphilis, rubella, cytomegalovirus – STI screening (e.g., gonorrhoea, chlamydia)
Blood tests	✓		Full blood count, blood sugar, thyroid function
Blood group (ABO) and Rh factor compatibility	✓		Avoids complications with foetal Rh incompatibility.
Antibody test (anti TG, anti TPO, PRL, TSH, FT3, FT4, ANA, anti-cardiolipin IgG, anti-cardiolipin IgM, Beta2IgG, Beta2IgM, Lupus, D-Dimer, NK cell, PT, INR, PTT)		✓	To protect the baby during pregnancy and after birth

Psychological evaluation	✓		Assessment of emotional readiness and motivation for surrogacy. Some general tools specifically designed for assessing emotional readiness and resilience include: Psychological General Well-Being Index (PGWB), Connor-Davidson Resilience Scale (CD-RISC), Fertility Quality of Life (FertiQoL) Tool, Depression, Anxiety, and Stress Scale (DASS-21 or DASS-42), and Strengths and Difficulties Questionnaire (SDQ)
Support system evaluation	✓		Ensures surrogate has emotional and logistical support.
Prenatal screening during pregnancy	✓		– Regular obstetric follow-ups – Routine infectious disease tests during pregnancy
Legal counselling		✓	– Ensures surrogate understands rights and responsibilities. – Clear understanding of relinquishing parental rights post-birth. – Should be independent legal advice.
Health recommendations		✓	– Adherence to prenatal care plans. – Abstaining from alcohol, smoking, and illicit drugs. – Balanced diet and moderate exercise consistent with pregnancy.
Educational programmes		✓	– Pregnancy management and self-care. – Handling emotional challenges during surrogacy. – Coping with post-birth separation and what to expect.
Insurance		✓	Ensure comprehensive coverage for prenatal care, delivery, and postnatal complications.

Links:

Pre-Pregnancy Testing Checklist (https://www.parents.com/getting-pregnant/pre-pregnancy-health/general/health-checks-to-have-before-becoming-parents/)

Preparing Your Body for +Pregnancy | IVF Australia (https://www.ivf.com.au/planning-for-pregnancy/how-to-get-pregnant/pre-pregnancy-health)

STI Screening in Pregnancy: CDC Recommendations—The ObG Project (https://www.obgproject.com/2016/10/16/std-screening-pregnancy-cdc-recommendations/)

Pregnancy | Pregnancy | CDC (https://www.cdc.gov/pregnancy/index.html)

Prenatal Antibody Screening: Purpose, Procedure, and Results (https://www.webmd.com/baby/antibody-testing)

Index

FSC
www.fsc.org
MIX
Papier | Fördert gute Waldnutzung
FSC® C083411

Kolibri 360 GmbH
Ferdinand-Jühlke-Straße 7
99095 Erfurt, Deutschland
produktsicherheit@kolibri360.de